IMPROVING SCHOOLS THROUGH ACTION RESEARCH

A Comprehensive Guide for Educators

CHER HENDRICKS

University of West Georgia

PEARSON
and

Boston   New York   San Francisco   Mexico City
Montreal   Toronto   London   Madrid   Munich   Paris
Hong Kong   Singapore   Tokyo   Cape Town   Sydney

For Randy, my first reader.

Senior Editor: Arnis Burvikovs
Series Editorial Assistant: Kelly Hopkins
Marketing Manager: Tara Whorf
Production Editor: Greg Erb
Editorial Production Service: Walsh & Associates, Inc.
Composition Buyer: Linda Cox
Manufacturing Buyer: Andrew Turso
Electronic Composition: Publishers' Design and Production Services, Inc.
Cover Administrator: Joel Gendron

For related titles and support materials, visit our online catalog at www.ablongman.com.

Library of Congress Cataloging-in-Publication Data

Hendricks, Cher.
    Improving schools through action research : a comprehensive guide for educators / Cher Hendricks.
        p.   cm.
    Includes bibliographical references and index.
    ISBN 0-205-38585-0
    1. Action research in education—Handbooks, manuals, etc.   I. Title.
LB1028.24.H46 2006
370'.7'2—dc22

                                                                        2005043109

Printed in the United States of America
10 9 8 7 6 5 4 3   09 08 07 06

CONTENTS

PREFACE

In 1999 I had my first experience with action research. As a quantitative researcher trained in inferential statistics methodology, I had for the past few years taught research design and statistics to educators working on master's, specialist, and doctoral degrees. In the fall of 1999, however, I learned I would be teaching a course in action research, and I must say I was not too happy about it. I had not learned about action research in my doctoral course work, and all I had heard about it was that it was not "real" research. To prepare for the course, I read a few of the action research texts that were available then, and I figured that all I needed to do was teach the empirical research process that I was familiar with and simply leave out the statistical analysis part. My goal was to plod my way through the teaching and hope that I would never again be asked to teach action research.

A few weeks into that first action research course, it became apparent that the teachers I was working with were becoming thoroughly invested in the process of investigating their practices. Further, as I reflected on the best ways to facilitate educators' action research studies, I realized that although the process of action research shared much with what I considered to be a traditional, empirical research framework, there was more to teaching and facilitating the process than merely teaching what I knew and leaving out the "statistics part." Instead, the process of action research involved careful analysis and understanding of the context of classrooms and schools—something that in all the studies I'd conducted before had to be completely controlled and manipulated. I saw, too, that through the collection and analysis of multiple data sources (including many types of qualitative data), validity and credibility of the studies could be even greater than that of many of the tightly controlled quantitative studies I had conducted or with which I had been involved.

As I discovered that I had much to learn about the process of action research, I began to read everything I could get my hands on that was related to the topic. My study of action research helped me understand how the process can and should work. I also discovered the ways in which action research empowers educators, allowing them to study their own practices and placing them in control of their professional development. In my own students I saw this empowerment begin to manifest itself. When the course was over, some students stayed in contact with me, relating stories of their ongoing action research studies. I was amazed to see that even beyond the requirements of the class, some educators continued to use the skills they had learned to improve their educational practices.

At the end of that first action research course, I found that I had a strong desire to teach more courses in action research. Whereas in past courses my role was to bring students into my world of academic research, in the action research course my role was to take myself into the world of practicing educators and show them ways to systematically investigate their educational practices. I began to feel much more comfortable in this new role—even more comfortable than I had been teaching research design and statistics—largely because I felt that educators were changed when they engaged in action research, and they were changed in very powerful and sustainable ways. I also began to see school improvement as a natural outcome when educators begin to study their practices. Many of the teachers and administrators I have worked with have positively impacted their schools and school districts, even though their initial action research studies may have focused on issues particular to one classroom or school. Frequently, these educators have been tapped by administrators in their schools or districts to share the results of their action research studies so that others can learn from their results as well as learn ways to study their practices.

My work facilitating educators' action research projects motivated me to write this text. Although many good textbooks have come on the market in the last few years, **I found that I needed one that went deeper into the processes of reflection, planning, data collection, and data analysis**, which I have attempted to accomplish in this text. **Also, I wanted to write a textbook that wasn't a cookbook about how to do each step of the process but instead suggested several ways to accomplish the different steps of the action research cycle**. This flexible approach represents my personal growth as an action researcher studying my own practice teaching/facilitating action research. When I began to teach action research, I taught it as I had taught quantitative research design, focusing on each linear step of the process and insisting that students complete each step following strict guidelines. My students, however, taught me that in action research there isn't just one way to engage in reflection nor is there one best method to increase validity in action research studies.

As I have worked with educators, I have realized that each individual has been shaped by his or her experiences as student and as educator. These experiences impact decisions made throughout the action research cycle. Thus, in the second chapter of this text the reader is asked to think about his or her core values as an educator as he or she engages in a reflective activity to identify a research area. At this point the reader is asked to make a decision, based on core educational values, regarding the type of reflection in which to engage. In subsequent chapters, the reader is asked to make other decisions—based on core values, the purpose of the study, and the audience (if applicable) that will see the results—that shape the study. It is hoped that the flexible nature of this text will allow for a wide variety of action research studies, from those that are strictly an educator's self-study to others that are collaborative and seek to shed light on issues of social justice.

Although there is flexibility in this text, there is a particular process of action research that is delineated, which is based on a cycle of reflecting, acting, and evaluating. Also, a focus of this text is that educators engaged in action research study an intervention chosen specifically to deal with the research problem identified through reflection. Thus, *acting* is considered in this text to be critical in the cycle of action research. The assumption is that educators act and then study their actions to determine whether they were effective for bringing out change. This position is related to the work of Lawrence Stenhouse, an important contributor to the action research tradition, who explained that teacher [educator] research should focus on the refinement of teachers' [educators'] art—their teaching—and not simply on personal evaluation or classroom observation.

In Chapter 1, which is an introductory chapter on research traditions in education, information and activities are provided to help readers understand the process of action research and the ways in which it can advance knowledge in education. Chapters 2 through 7 introduce various steps of the action research cycle including reflecting to identify a problem, reviewing the literature, initial planning of the study, choosing data collection strategies, final planning of the study, and strategies for analyzing data. Chapter 8 is a supplemental chapter for those who are interested in preparing a written report of their action research studies. Chapters 2 through 7 include chapter activities to help the reader through the various steps of the action research process. Many of these activities are tied to journaling (which helps the educator keep a record of action research activities) and/or to research paper activities (which show the educator how to use responses to the chapter activities to write various sections of a final research report).

I wish to thank my colleagues who served as reviewers for this textbook. Their comments and insights were invaluable and helped me revise this text: Robert Basofin, St. Xavier University/Skylight Professional Development; Mary C. Dalmau, University of Oregon; Bert A. Goldman, University of North Carolina at Greensboro; Priscilla Hartwig, St. Xavier University; Ileene Huffard, Freed-Hardeman University; Barbara Kawulich, University of West Georgia; Marco Muñoz, Jefferson County Public Schools; and Gary J. Skolits, University of Tennessee.

I hope that you will be impacted by action research as I have been and come to see it as a powerful way to study and improve your educational practice. I have now worked with many educators (teachers, principals, instructional lead teachers, media specialists, coaches, band directors, district level administrators) completing their first action research studies, and I have been privileged to watch them grow professionally and become empowered educators who feel completely in charge of the educational decisions they make. I have been impacted not only in watching others grow but also by realizing the ways I have grown. I, too, engage in action research as I study ways to improve my teaching and research facilitating. In fact, many revisions to the chapters in this text were a result of my own action research investigations. In learning about action research, I have been able to study my educational practice, and once you have learned the action research process, you, too, will have a very powerful tool that will enable you to study and improve your practice as an educator. You will feel more in charge of your professional growth. You will be able to tackle any problem that you encounter in a systematic way, and you will be able to justify your actions with data. You will also become proficient enough in conducting action research studies to teach your colleagues how to use the action research cycle. And I hope that you will, for our best chance of using research to improve schools is to put educators in charge of the process.

CHAPTER ONE

RESEARCH METHODS IN EDUCATION

CHAPTER GOALS

- Explain the ways various research methodologies—quantitative, qualitative, and action research—advance knowledge in education.
- Describe the origin, types, and processes of educational action research.
- Illustrate how action research can be used to effect school change and school improvement.
- Provide activities to demonstrate the ways in which quantitative, qualitative, and action research differ and to familiarize readers with published action research studies.

This chapter begins with a brief explanation of various methodologies that can be employed when conducting research studies in education. The uses of quantitative and qualitative methods of research are explained, and the ways in which practitioners, through action research, contribute to knowledge in education are described. The focus of this chapter is on action research and its origin, history, and processes. Activities are presented to illustrate the differences among research methodologies and to provide an opportunity to read published action research studies conducted by educational practitioners.

WAYS RESEARCH ADVANCES KNOWLEDGE ABOUT EDUCATION

Educational research is conducted to advance our understanding of a variety of issues and can focus on basic knowledge—such as the way the brain processes information—or on more applied concerns geared toward determining the effectiveness of certain actions (teaching or discipline strategies, for example). In education, research is used to develop theory, test hypotheses based on theory, study relationships among variables, describe educational phenomena, and determine whether actions result in desired outcomes, to name just a few of the many uses of educational research. In these varied pursuits, both quantitative and qualitative methodologies are employed to test hypotheses and answer research questions. In studies that focus on hypothesis testing and studying relationships among variables, researchers often use quantitative, statistical methods to analyze data. In studies in which developing theory or describing educational phenomena is the focus, qualitative methods are typically employed. In other studies, such as action research projects that concentrate on investigating whether actions result in desired outcomes, both qualitative and quantitative methodologies are often used.

Quantitative Research

To understand how quantitative research methods are used to advance knowledge in education, it is necessary to consider the traditional **epistemology** associated with quantitative research, which contends that reality is fixed and can be captured and understood (Denzin & Lincoln, 2000). The purpose of quantitative research is to test hypotheses and to generalize results of hypotheses tests beyond the individuals and settings that were part of the research study. In order to make such generalizations, quantitative researchers attempt to draw random samples of individuals to be studied, which then allows them to generalize results to the larger population from which the sample was drawn. For example, a quantitative researcher who randomly chooses 300 fourth-grade students from a large metropolitan school district to be in a study can generalize the results of that study to all fourth-grade students in that district. Another requirement for broad generalization is that the researcher control as many contextual variables in the setting as is possible. Thus, the researcher may utilize strategies such as using only predetermined valid and reliable measures to assess participants or scripting intervention methods so that all individuals in experimental groups receive precisely the same instruction. When contextual variables are adequately controlled and inferential statistical methods are used to test differences between groups (or relationships among variables), a researcher using quantitative methods can say with varying degrees of certainty whether differences or relationships found are chance differences or real differences. When differences or relationships are large enough, a researcher using quantitative methods can say with a certain amount of confidence that the differences or relationships are real. When differences are small, however, the researcher is unable to conclude whether the differences or relationships are real or are just due to a chance occurrence.

Qualitative Research

Whereas an assumption in quantitative epistemology is that reality is fixed, in qualitative research reality is something that can estimated but never fully captured (Denzin & Lincoln, 2000). Although researchers who use qualitative methods set out with different purposes as they conduct their studies, the general purpose in qualitative research is to understand and

---

Epistemology: A branch of philosophy concerned with the nature of knowledge and the relationship between the knower and the known.

interpret phenomena as they occur in natural settings. Researchers who use qualitative methods generally spend time in the field observing, talking to people, and analyzing artifacts and products of the setting under study. Researchers seek to make meaning from the information gathered from these multiple sources, but the purpose is simply to understand the setting, not to generalize findings beyond it. Thus, in a qualitative study, those who are studied are chosen purposively rather than randomly. Also, the context is examined, rather than controlled, and findings are presented in light of the "complex, interactive systems" of the lived-in world (Rossman & Rallis, 2003).

Action Research

The purpose of action research is for practitioners to investigate and improve their practices. The process is one of self-study; thus a teacher engaged in action research may, for example, study ways to increase student learning in his or her class, focusing on his or her intentions, methods, and desired outcomes as part of the investigation. As McNiff (2002) explains, the epistemology of action research is that knowledge is something that action researchers do—their living practice—rather than a fixed, static, or absolute entity. In action research, practitioners look systematically at ways to deal with issues they are close to, such as instructional practices, social issues of schooling, collaboration with colleagues, or supervision of staff. Rather than choose participants randomly or systematically, they work with the individuals (students, colleagues, teachers, staff, parents) around whom their everyday practices evolve. Context is not controlled but is studied so that the ways in which context influences outcomes can be understood. Data from variety of sources, including qualitative and quantitative measures, are collected and analyzed for the purpose of informing practice. Thus, all results feed back into the action research cycle so that the study is continuous, flexible, and constantly evolving.

Educational researchers use a variety of methods—both qualitative and quantitative—to investigate problems in education. The methods used are determined by the purpose of the study. If, for example, a researcher wishes to compare two different instructional methods for teaching students how to assess cause-and-effect relationships, and if the researcher wants to generalize results to a population represented by the sample in the study, using quantitative research methods would be a logical choice. If, however, a researcher wanted to understand how a teacher's communication with students affects their participation in the cause-and-effect learning activities, qualitative research methods would be best suited for the investigation. In some studies, researchers utilize both quantitative and qualitative methods as they investigate educational issues (see the study by Nath and Ross in Appendix A, which is used in Activity 1.1, for an example). Table 1.1 illustrates the ways in which quantitative, qualitative, and action research methods differ.

When practitioners—teachers, administrators, school counselors, media specialists—conduct action research studies in their settings, they often rely on qualitative data collection methods because they are interested in the contextual variables in their settings and the ways in which context influences the outcomes of their studies. Practitioners do frequently analyze quantitative measures, such as test scores, number of discipline referrals, or course averages, but these quantitative data are just one source of evidence that is analyzed with other qualitative sources of data such as observations and interviews. Further, although

TABLE 1.1   Differences among Quantitative, Qualitative, and Action Research

	QUANTITATIVE RESEARCH	QUALITATIVE RESEARCH	ACTION RESEARCH
Investigator/ Role	Higher education faculty/ personnel, graduate students. Investigator is an objective observer who studies others.	Higher education faculty/ personnel, anthropologists, graduate students. Investigator studies others through immersion in the research setting.	Teachers, administrators, school-support personnel. Students and/or higher education faculty are sometimes utilized as co-investigators. Investigator studies self and others.
Purpose	To test hypotheses related to educational theories.	To understand and interpret phenomena in natural settings; to generate hypotheses.	To identify and study a problem in the teacher's or administrator's school setting.
Audience	Higher education faculty/ personnel, graduate students.	Higher education faculty/ personnel, graduate students.	There is not always an intended audience, though there is great potential for educators to learn from each others' experiences through the sharing of action research outcomes.
Participants	A random sample chosen from a large population is desired.	A purposive sample is chosen.	Purposively chosen participants based on the intentions of the study. The researcher is also considered a participant.
Types of data collected	Objective, quantitative data such as test scores are often utilized. Data from surveys and questionnaires are also used.	Analysis of artifacts, observations, interviews.	Data from a variety of sources are desired. Observations, work samples or student artifacts, interviews, journal entries, and videotapes can be utilized.
Assumptions	With a random sample and control of contextual variables, broad generalizations can be made based on the outcome of the study.	Interpretations of data help to understand the phenomenon under study.	Results inform practice. Through action research, educators reflect and act, continually improving their practice.

quantitative measures are often part of the data collected in practitioner studies, inferential statistical methods are almost never used in data analysis because generalizing or inferring results beyond the study is not the goal, the sample is chosen purposively instead of randomly, and samples in practitioner studies are not usually large enough for statistical analysis to be useful.

Because qualitative and practitioner studies study context—rather than control it—and are less focused on generalizable knowledge than quantitative studies, there has been some debate about their usefulness for advancing knowledge about educational practices. However, because qualitative and practitioner researchers engage in studies that focus on the ways context impacts certain outcomes, it is reasonable to conclude that their results are applicable to settings with similar contexts. Further, applicability of results in qualitative and practitioner studies can be increased when detailed descriptions of the setting, participants, and context are provided. The number of action research studies that are being published in academic journals suggests that research by practitioners is a credible and valuable source of knowledge in education. As Dinkelman (2003) explains, "Although more traditional educational researchers debate the academic rigor of [teachers'] self-study . . . its rapid acceptance in the research literature has been nothing short of astonishing" (pp. 10–11).

Although higher education faculty and policy researchers have typically been the individuals responsible for adding to the educational knowledge base, much recent discussion on this topic has focused on including and valuing the practitioner's voice in research. In fact, the National Academy of Education (NAE, 1999) suggests that to increase the ability of research to contribute to educational improvement, support must be given "for projects in which professional researchers and professional educators share in the accountability for achieving success in improving educational practices and outcomes" (p. 9). The NAE explains that this collaborative type of research, which they call *integrated problem-solving research,* should focus on "practice and on engaging researchers and practitioners together in problem-solving and theoretical analysis" (p. 11). Although there remain a number of barriers to structuring the type of collaborative research endeavors suggested by the NAE and others (e.g., Buysse, Sparkman, & Wesley, 2003; National Research Council, 1999; Palinscar, Magnusson, Marano, Ford, & Brown, 1998), it is clear that many educational researchers desire for both practitioners and researchers to construct knowledge about education so that a clear connection can be made between what we know and what we do (Buysse et al., 2003).

All educational research—whether conducted by teachers, administrators, evaluators, university faculty, or others interested in studying educational issues—has the potential to enhance knowledge about teaching and learning. Dissemination of research findings, through sharing with colleagues, presenting at conferences, or publishing in teaching magazines or academic journals, adds to the knowledge base in education, and practitioners and university faculty alike are able to make real contributions to the knowledge base whether they use qualitative methods, quantitative methods, action research, or combination of methods to investigate educational concerns.

In Activity 1.1, two research articles on using cooperative learning are presented for comparison. The study by Michael DuBois (Appendix A, Article A.1), a middle school science teacher, is an example of an action research study in which qualitative methods were employed. The study by Nath and Ross (Appendix A, Article A.2), an educational consultant and a university professor, is an example of a study that used both qualitative and quantitative analyses to test hypotheses and answer research questions. The purpose of Activity 1.1 is to show how the various types of research contribute to the educational knowledge base. The sections of this chapter that are presented after Activity 1.1 describe the origin,

■ ■ ■ ■ ■ ■

ACTIVITY 1.1
COMPARISON OF ARTICLES ON COOPERATIVE LEARNING

To gain a better understanding of the ways in which quantitative, qualitative, and action research are used to generate knowledge in education, read and analyze two articles that use these different methods. These two articles are:

DuBois, M. (1995). Conceptual learning and creative problem solving using cooperative learning groups in middle school science classes. In S. Spiegel, A. Collins, & J. Lappert (Eds.), *Action research: Perspectives from teachers' classrooms.* Tallahassee, FL: Southeastern Regional Vision for Educators. Retrieved May 4, 2004, from ENC website: http://enc.org/professional/learn/research/journal/science/document.shtm?input=ENC-002432-2432_ch8

Nath, L. R., & Ross, S. M. (2001). The influence of a peer tutoring training model for implementing cooperative grouping with elementary students. *Educational Technology Research and Development, 49,* 41–56.

Once you have read both articles, which are available in Appendix A, answer the following questions:

1. What differences and similarities exist between the two articles in terms of the authors' reasons for conducting their respective studies?
2. Describe the ways in which participants were chosen in each study. What reasons did the authors give for the choice of participants?
3. Compare the types of data collected in each study. How were these data sources used to answer research questions and/or test hypotheses?
4. How were results reported in each article? Describe differences and similarities in reporting methods.
5. How do the authors of each study explain their intentions for future research based on their findings (see *Discussion*) sections?
6. In what ways does each article contribute to the educational knowledge base?

types, and processes of action research, which is followed by an explanation of the ways action research can be used for school improvement.

THE ORIGIN OF ACTION RESEARCH

In the 1930s, Kurt Lewin first described the theory of action research. His early research focused on workplace studies comparing methods for training factory workers. Lewin viewed action research as a spiraling process that included reflection and inquiry on the part of its stakeholders for the purposes of improving work environments and dealing with social problems (Burns, 1999). One the tenets of his theory was that democratic workplaces produce employees who take ownership of their work, which increases both morale and productivity. This idea became connected to Dewey and Count's progressive education movement, as Clem Adelman (1997) explains, because Lewin had created the methods that schools needed to become the driving force of democratic change within a community. Although it would be years before action research found its way to the classroom and to schools, Lewin is credited with the formalization of the theory and principles of action research.

While Lewin was developing his theory of action research, the Progressive Education Association was studying the ways in which **progressive education** was superior to traditional education in *The Eight Year Study*. Dewey challenged the emphasis placed on scientific methods in the study of education, asserting that practitioners should be directly involved in the process of research (Burns, 1999). However, as Schubert and Lopez-Schubert (1997) explain, there were a number of research flaws with The Eight Year Study, including a lack of true reflection in early studies (although Tyler, the evaluator for The Eight Year Study, did realize the importance of teacher reflection in school research) and mechanized research strategies that devalued the practical inquiry of teachers. These problems, exacerbated by the push at that time toward rigorous scientific studies in the field of education, prevented action research from taking hold (Burns, 1999). Schubert and Lopez-Schubert explain that the initial goals of action research have only recently begun to be realized, especially since the initiation of the teacher-as-research movement in United Kingdom in the 1970s and 1980s, inspired by Lawrence Stenhouse, who recognized teacher reflection as an important type of research.

In 1970, Stenhouse founded the Center for Applied Research in Education at the University of East Anglia in England with the objective of demystifying the practice of research and making it more useful and accessible to teachers. Cochran-Smith and Lytle (1993) explain that Stenhouse encouraged teachers to conduct their own research with the goal of improving their practices—an idea that was radical in its time because its impetus was Stenhouse's claim that researchers needed to justify themselves to practitioners rather than insist that practitioners justify themselves to researchers (Stenhouse, 1981). As Rudduck (1988) articulates:

> Stenhouse was critical . . . of inequality in relation to teachers and research. There were, in his view, two cultures—the culture of academic researchers, who are served by research, and the culture of practitioners, who are ruled by research or merely ignore it. He saw a need to analyze the structures that govern the production and distribution of research knowledge and that determine the right to engage in research acts. His aspiration was to bring educational research to the orbit of the practitioner's world. (pp. 35–36)

In Stenhouse's view, a basic flaw in the traditional thinking of academic researchers was that academic research devalued teacher judgment (Fishman & McCarthy, 2000). Stenhouse's idea was that the theory proposed by academic researchers was of little use unless teachers were able to test it. His position was that academic researchers and teachers had to work together for research to be meaningful and beneficial. Stenhouse (1981) asserted that:

Progressive Education: A child-centered approach to teaching and learning that focuses on the development of socially engaged intelligence. Progressive education seeks both to positively impact individual development and to foster social justice.

There is in the field of education little theory which could be relied upon by the teacher with-out testing it. Many of the findings of research are based on small-scale laboratory experi-ments which often do not replicate or cannot be successfully applied in classrooms. Many are actuarial and probabilistic, and, if they are to be used by the individual teacher, they de-mand situational verification . . .. The teacher has grounds for motivation to research. We re-searchers have reason to excite that motivation: without a research response from teachers our research cannot be utilized. (pp. 109–110)

Pushing for systematic, self-critical teacher research based on these ideas, Stenhouse initiated a large action research movement in the United Kingdom. Unlike earlier action re-search movements—which were unsuccessful largely due to the inability of the movement to get beyond a number of critics who supported scientific, empirical research studies—the phenomenon inspired by Stenhouse and his colleagues was successful and has endured. A number of action research proponents have impacted its growth in the last few decades. Many of these individuals are listed on the timeline in Figure 1.1, which reveals the devel-opment of the action research movement in the United States and abroad.

Today large action research networks exist in the United Kingdom, Australia, Canada, and the United States. Educational action research journals have been established, and many academic journals now publish action research studies. In addition, a variety of school district level action research networks have been created that encourage teachers to conduct action research and provide resources for teachers interested in conducting action research. Table 1.3 at the end of this chapter provides information on many of these action research sources as well as additional reading materials on the fascinating progression of the action research movement.

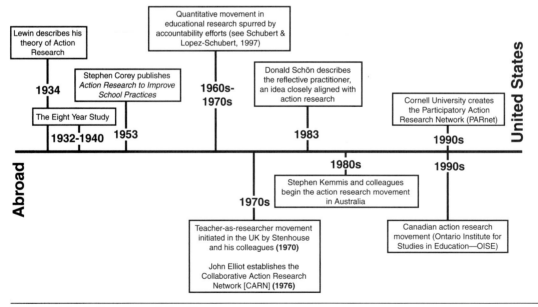

FIGURE 1.1   Action research timeline.

THE ACTION RESEARCH PROCESS

Stenhouse described action research as a systematic, self-critical inquiry. *Systematic* means that a certain structure, or set of steps, is utilized in the action research process. Action research theorists and practitioners follow a systematic set of procedures, though these procedures can vary slightly depending on individual preferences. For example, Kemmis and Wilkinson (1997) describe the action research process, which they term *participatory action research,* utilizing these steps: plan, act and observe, reflect, revise the plan, act and observe, reflect, and so on. Cole and Knowles (2000) describe similar steps that include developing a focus, gathering information, making sense of information through analysis and reflection, and acting based on findings. For Kemmis and Wilkinson and Cole and Knowles, the process of action research does not have an end. Rather, it is an unending reflective process that is graphically displayed in the shape of a spiral with each systematic step leading to the next step and continually beginning anew.

The action research process that will be described in this book follows the principle of systematic inquiry based on ongoing reflection. The process is a series of steps in which the action researcher reflects, acts, and evaluates. After evaluation, the process continues with reflection, action, and evaluation. Thus, the process shares the idea of spiraling, consistent with the notion that action research is an ongoing process that individuals use to constantly improve their practices. Figure 1.2 provides an example of how this process is utilized in action research.

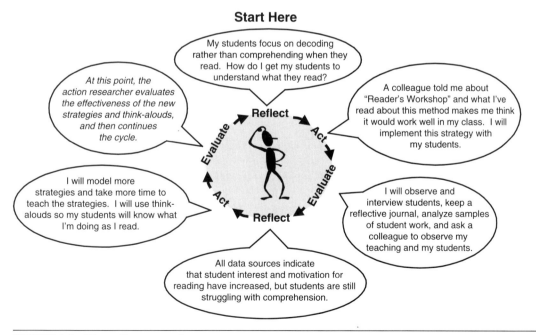

FIGURE 1.2   The action research process.

TYPES OF ACTION RESEARCH

Various types of action research have been identified and described, illustrating the different purposes, goals, and values of the different branches of study. Four types of action research—collaborative, critical, classroom, and participatory—are defined and described here. Understanding these terms helps educators become informed action researchers and allows them to think about the type of action research that most closely aligns with their own goals, purpose, and values.

> **COLLABORATIVE ACTION RESEARCH:** A system of action research in which multiple researchers from school and university settings work together to study educational problems. Collaboration among teachers and administrators may occur as well as collaboration among school personnel and university researchers. The goal of this type of research is to utilize the expertise of the collaborators and to foster sustained dialogue among educational stakeholders in different settings.

> **CRITICAL ACTION RESEARCH:** A form of action research utilized in educational settings that encourages wide collaboration among university researchers, school administrators, teachers, and those in the community. The goal of this type of research is to evaluate social issues so that results can be used for social change. Critical action research frequently focuses on educational disparities due to gender, ethnicity, and social class (see Kemmis & McTaggart, 2000; Kemmis & Wilkinson, 1997; Mcpherson, Aspland, Elliott, Proudford, Shaw, & Thurlow, 1998).

> **CLASSROOM ACTION RESEARCH:** A form of action research that is conducted by teachers in their classrooms with the purpose of improving practice. It values the interpretations that teachers make based on data collected with their students. Though it is frequently a solo endeavor, collaboration among classroom teachers can occur.

> **PARTICIPATORY ACTION RESEARCH:** A social, collaborative process of action research. The goal is to investigate reality so that it can be changed. This type of action research is considered to be emancipatory (the action researcher is able to explore practices within the limits of social structures), critical (the action researcher's goal is to challenge alienation, unproductive ways of working, and power struggles), and transformational (changing both theory and practice). The work of Kemmis and McTaggart (2000) provides in-depth information on participatory action research.

THE IMPORTANCE OF ACTION RESEARCH FOR IMPROVING SCHOOLS

Educational action research is a system of inquiry that teachers, administrators, and school support personnel can use to study, change, and improve their work with children and in schools. Through the action research process, educators are able to generate knowledge about their practice and share that knowledge with their colleagues, practices that Fullan (2002) suggests are key elements of producing lasting and sustainable change in schools.

Further, as Allen and Calhoun (1998) explain, the promise of action research is its capacity to help individuals, small groups, or even entire school faculties increase their understanding and improve their practice. In terms of using collaborative models of action research for school change, Allen and Calhoun state:

> For those seeking whole-school improvement—both in terms of student learning and in terms of the conditions of the professional workplace—action research places disciplined inquiry (i.e., research) in the context of focused efforts to improve the quality of the school and its performance (i.e., action). The integrity of the process for site-based school improvement lies in the union of the "researchers" and "action takers," for action research is conducted by those persons responsible for bringing about changes. Its ultimate aim is to have all faculty members and, eventually, students and parents involved in the research on student learning. (pp. 706–707)

Calhoun (2002), however, expresses the need for the development of systems to provide the time, support, and professional development activities necessary to encourage and sustain action research as a process of school improvement. With this support, action research becomes the guiding force behind professional development, allowing practitioners to study their own practices and be in charge of developing their professional work as educators.

There are a number of ways action research leads to school improvement. The educators with whom I have worked have expressed the ways in which action research improves schools and professionalizes the work of:

- **Teachers,** by allowing them to investigate ways to deal with issues related to student achievement, classroom management, students with special needs (such as the gifted, exceptional, or limited English proficient), and motivation.
- **Media specialists,** by giving them the opportunity to study ways to increase interest in reading, utilization of the media center, use of technology for student and teacher research, and teaming with teachers to develop and teach lessons.
- **Coaches,** because they can examine ways to increase skills in sport, evaluate the effectiveness of their coaching styles, increase persistence and perseverance, and include students with special needs in athletics.
- **Counselors,** by giving them the tools to study the usefulness of counseling programs (character education, bullying prevention, student advisement, career counseling), ways to identify students who need advocates, and ways to effectively communicate with teachers, students, and parents.
- **Principals,** who can encourage and evaluate action research by their teachers and who can conduct their own school improvement studies related to school climate, professional development, school-community relations, working with parents, curricular programs, student achievement, attendance, and discipline.
- **District administrators,** who can focus on issues such as the usefulness of professional development activities, student achievement, curriculum reform, training and induction of new school administrators, and teacher and administrator recruitment and attrition.

■ **Teachers of the arts, speech pathologists, support teachers,** who can investigate the ways they teach and interact with students, effective teaching strategies, motivation, achievement, and individual gains.

This list of the ways that school personnel can utilize action research is not meant to be exhaustive. These are just a few of the many ways action research can be used to improve classrooms and schools. Keep in mind that regardless of the various roles that exist in educational settings, the process of action research is the same—only the research problems are different. This means that teachers who learn to use action research to improve classrooms are able to use the same *process* of action research if they one day become a school or district administrator. Also, experienced action researchers are able to pass their knowledge—both of the process of action research *and* what was learned in the study—to colleagues, mentored individuals, and to supervisors.

By using action research to study problems such as those mentioned, educators can improve what occurs in classrooms and schools. Action researchers have the potential to impact students in a number of exciting ways, and they have the potential to learn a great deal about themselves in the process. There are several benefits of becoming an action researcher. The teachers, administrators, counselors, and media specialists whose action research studies I have facilitated describe a number of benefits of the process. They explain that conducting action research:

■ Professionalizes the work of educators because it puts them in charge of improving their practice and their professional development.
■ Encourages educators to work collaboratively.
■ Gives educators a voice in the field, allowing them to disseminate their findings so others can learn from their experiences.
■ Encourages educators to rethink the ways they evaluate their work and the work of students, increasing the likelihood that they will use multiple forms of measurement that are credible and useful and that can stand up to scrutiny.
■ Provides educators with rich sources of data that can be used to improve classrooms and can ultimately lead to school improvement.
■ Revitalizes educators' professional lives because it makes work exciting, fun, interesting, and rewarding.
■ Allows educators to develop the ability to articulate the choices they make and the methods they use, even if those methods are challenged.
■ Helps educators get to know students, both academically and personally, which increases mutual understanding and respect among teachers, parents, teachers, and administrators.

Many of these benefits are supported in the action research literature. Anderson, Herr, and Nihlen (1994), for example, assert that participating in action research can stimulate collegiality, empower educators, and give school personnel a voice in decision making in educational policy and change. Further, they suggest that engaging in action research allows educators to become creators of their own knowledge about teaching and learning rather than only consumers of others' research. Based on comments from teachers with whom she worked, Burns (1999) concluded that conducting research on their practice increased teachers' personal insight and self-awareness, helped them grow personally and professionally, gave them a method for coming up with solutions to institutional demands, and allowed them to have an opportunity to systematically reflect on the educational decisions they made. Calhoun (2002) states that educators who engage in action research are able to create instructional opportunities that are more effective and more intentional for student learning. She also states that action research is "a way of organizing collective work so that professional expertise is tended and extended, helping to build a strong professional learning community" (p. 23). Table 1.2 includes quotes about the benefits of action research from some of the educators with whom I have worked.

TABLE 1.2   Educators' Perspectives on the Benefits of Action Research

Conducting action research proved to be a very powerful experience for me. As a high school counselor, I was able to either confirm or deny assumptions I had about a specific counseling program within my department. In addition, the process of taking copious field notes allowed me the opportunity to determine how and why my conclusions happened. Thus, I not only gained concrete knowledge about an educational phenomenon, I also understood the intricate processes of it. I honestly believe I will always use action research as a tool to guide my practices in education.

—Daria, high school career counselor

Action research is valuable. It gave me insight into my own bias and how it impacts my interactions with students.

—Toni, high school teacher of gifted students

Conducting action research has positively affected me, my students and their parents, and our school. In my role as a physical education teacher, it is my responsibility to guide my students toward lifetime physical activity and good health. In a recent study I conducted, my students and their parents participated to determine if keeping a daily journal/log of exercise and eating habits would increase awareness of the importance of physical activity and a healthy diet. Because of the positive results generated by the study, I no longer have to tell students and parents how I "feel" about good health or what I "think" about its importance. There is now hard evidence in the form of results produced by parents and children working together toward a common goal of good health. Conducting action research studies such as this has informed and improved my practice by allowing me to work with stakeholders in my school in real time, in a real world setting.

—Scott, elementary physical education teacher

Action research allows me to be able to answer questions and work out problems that I have. I then have the data to back up why I want to do certain things in my classroom.

—Stacey, teacher in a multi-grade program

I have discovered a wonderful method of teaching ESL [English as a Second Language] students how to write. I have rediscovered how powerful working in a group can be. I will use action research again, especially when I run into a block or difficulty.

—Rebecca, elementary school counselor

BECOMING FAMILIAR WITH THE LANGUAGE AND PROCESS OF ACTION RESEARCH

The purpose of this text is to help educators carry out each step of the action research cycle as they engage in studies of their practice. Each of the remaining chapters describes a specific phase of the process based on the reflect–act–evaluate method: reflecting on practice to select an area to study, connecting theory to action through a review of related literature, planning and implementing the project, gathering information, making sense of collected information, and writing the final action research report. Before discussing the steps of the process in detail, though, it is important to familiarize yourself with the language of action research. A good way to get started is to read several action research studies, an activity that introduces the language, methods, and intricacies of action research. Reading action research studies is a good way to get an overall sense of what a project entails and the ways in which action research leads to school improvement and teacher empowerment. Also, reading studies conducted by others in the field of education helps generate research ideas for your own action research investigation.

The goal of Activity 1.2 is to provide you with the opportunity to read action research studies conducted by other educators. Studies can be found in many educational journals

■ ■ ■ ■ ■ ▬▬▬▬▬▬▬▬▬▬▬▬▬▬▬▬▬▬▬▬▬▬▬▬▬▬▬

ACTIVITY 1.2
READING ACTION RESEARCH STUDIES

Locate three action research studies to read and summarize. Choose articles that describe action research studies that were actually conducted rather than articles about action research. Good journals/websites include *Educational Action Research* [Triangle Journals], *The Journal of Scholarship of Teaching and Learning, The Reading Teacher, ARExpeditions, Networks: An Online Journal of Teacher Research, The Ontario Action Researcher,* The Action Research Lab at Highland Park High School, and the Eisenhower National Clearinghouse. Table 1.3 lists websites for these and other sites where action research studies can be located. After reading each study, write a response to each of these prompts:

1. Describe the reflections given at the beginning of the article that led the researcher to conduct the particular action research study (what problem was identified by the researcher and why was it important?).
2. Describe the actions that were taken by the researcher during the study (what did the researcher do to investigate the problem identified during the reflection process?).
3. Describe the evaluation techniques used by the researcher (what types of data were collected and how were they analyzed?).
4. Describe the researcher's reflections at the conclusion of the article (what did the action researcher learn and what did he or she intend to do next?).

After reading the three articles, explain the ways in which the authors' studies can impact school improvement and lead to teacher/educator empowerment.

and on a number of websites. Reading articles and summarizing them in terms of the reflective practices that initiated the studies, the actions taken by educators, and the methods used to evaluate actions will help to bring the action research cycle to life.

SUMMARY

This chapter revealed the ways in which various forms of research—quantitative, qualitative, and action research—can be used to advance knowledge about educational practices. The focus of the chapter, however, was on action research, a method practitioners can use to study and improve their practice. Introduced by Kurt Lewin as a process to investigate workplace issues and social problems, action research was slow to be accepted as a useful form of educational research but is now embraced as a valuable way to study classrooms and schools for school improvement. The spiraling reflect–act–evaluate process of action research was described, and four types of action research—collaborative, critical, classroom, and participatory—were introduced. A number of benefits of educational action research were presented including professionalizing the work of teachers, encouraging collaboration, and giving practitioners the opportunity to add to the educational knowledge base.

TABLE 1.3   Action Research Resources

Action Research Journals

Action Research International

    http://www.scu.edu.au/schools/gcm/ar/ari/arihome.html

AR*Expeditions*

    http://www.arexpeditions.montana.edu

Educational Action Research (Triangle Journals)

    http://www.triangle.co.uk/ear/

The Journal of Scholarship of Teaching and Learning

    http://www.iusb.edu/~josotl/

Networks: An On-line Journal for Teacher Research

    http://education.ucsc.edu/faculty/gwells/networks/

The Ontario Action Researcher

    http://www.nipissingu.ca/oar/

Action Research Articles on Special Education Issues

Moore, R A., & Brantingham, K L. (2003). Nathan: A case study in reader response and retrospective miscue analysis. *The Reading Teacher, 56,* 466–474.

(continued)

TABLE 1.3   Continued

Mortensen, S. (2002). Action research on cognitive rescaling. *Journal of Special Education Technology, 17,* 53–58.

Schoen, S. F., & Bullard, M. (2002). Action research during recess. *Teaching Exceptional Children, 35,* 36–39.

Schoen, S. F., & Schoen, A. A. (2003). Action research in the classroom: Assisting a linguistically different learner with special needs. *Teaching Exceptional Children, 35,* 16–21.

Action Research Articles on Early Childhood and Elementary Education Issues

Baumann, J. F., Hooten, H., & White, P. (1999). Teaching comprehension through literature: A teacher-research project to develop fifth graders' reading strategies and motivation. *The Reading Teacher, 53,* 38–51.

Bukowiecki, E. M., & McMacklin, M. C. (1999). Young children and narrative texts: A school-based inquiry project. *Reading Improvement, 36,* 157–166.

Espiritu, E., Meier, D. R., & Villazana-Price, N. (2002). A collaborative project on language and literacy learning: Promoting teacher research in early childhood education. *Young Children, 57,* 71–74.

Griffin, M. L. (2002). Why don't you use your finger? Paired reading in first grade. *The Reading Teacher, 55,* 766–774.

Knight, S. L., Wiseman, D. L., & Cooner, D. (2000). Using collaborative teacher research to determine the impact of professional development school activities on elementary students' math and writing outcomes. *Journal of Teacher Education, 51,* 26–38.

Reiner, K. (1998). Developing a kindergarten phonemic awareness program: An action research project. *The Reading Teacher, 52,* 70–73.

Schmidt, P. R., Gillen, S., Zollo, T. C., & Stone, R. (2002). Literacy learning and scientific inquiry: Children respond. *The Reading Teacher, 55,* 534–548.

Action Research Articles on Social Studies Issues

Bednarz, S. W. (2002). Using action research to implement the National Geography Standards: Teachers as researchers. *Journal of Geography, 101,* 103–111.

Dils, A. K. (2000). Using technology in a middle school social studies classroom. *International Journal of Social Education, 15,* 102–112.

Dixon, D. A. (2001). The three R's of school-university collaboration: Re-engaging classroom teachers by reframing social studies research. *Journal of Social Studies Research, 25,* 47–53.

Action Research Studies on Math and Science Issues

Briscoe, C., & Wells, E. (2002). Reforming primary science assessment practices: A case study of one teacher's professional development through action research. *Science Education, 86,* 417–435.

Goldston, M. J., & Shroyer, M. G. (2000). Teachers as researchers: Promoting effective science and mathematics teaching. *Teaching and Change, 7,* 327–346.

Keith, A. (2002). Action research brings results. *Science and Children, 39,* 32–35.

Murray-Ward, M., Huetinick, L., & Munshin, S. (1998). Developing mathematics teachers as researchers and leaders. *Teaching Education, 9,* 71–78.

Tinto, P. P., Shelly, B. A., & Zarach, N. J. (1994). Classroom research and classroom practice: Blurring the boundaries. *Mathematics Teacher, 87,* 644–648.

TABLE 1.3   Continued

Action Research Studies in Music and Art Education

Bresler, L. (1994). Zooming in on the qualitative paradigm in art education: Educational criticism, ethnography, and action research. *Visual Arts Research, 20,* 1–19.

Conway, C. M., & Borst, J. (2001). Action research in music education. *Update: Applications of Research in Music Education, 19,* 3–8.

Miller, B. A. (1996). Integrating elementary general music: A collaborative action research study. *Bulletin of the Council for Research in Music Education, 130,* 100–115.

Miller, B. A. (1999). Learning through composition in the elementary music classroom. *Bulletin of the Council for Research in Music Education, 142,* 87–88.

Rutkowski, J. (1996). Conducting research in the music classroom. *Music Educators Journal, 82,* 42–44.

Stankiewicz, M. A. (1997). Art teacher as researcher. *Art Education, 50,* 4–24.

Wiggins, J. H., & Bodoin, K. (1998). Painting a big soup: Teaching and learning in a second grade general music classroom. *Journal of Research in Music Education, 46,* 281–302.

Action Research Studies on Media Center Issues

Gordon, C. A. (1999). Students as authentic researchers: A new prescription for the high school research assignment. *School Library Media Research, 2.* [Available online at http://www.ala.org/aasl/SLMR/vol2/authentic.html]

Martin, J., & Tallman, J. (2001). The teacher-librarian as action researcher. *Teacher Librarian, 29,* 8–10.

Action Research Studies on Issues in Middle Grades Education

Brough, J. A., & Irvin, J. L. (2001). Parental involvement supports academic improvement among middle schoolers. *Middle School Journal, 32,* 52–61.

Lenenski, J., & McLaughlin, H. J. (1998). Wearing away the walls: Making a transition to student-initiated learning. *Journal of Research in Childhood Education, 12,* 231–243.

McLaughlin, H. J., Earle, K., & Hall, M. (1995). Hearing from our students: Team action research in a middle school. *Middle School Journal, 26,* 7–12.

McLaughlin, H. J., Watts, C., & Beard, M. (2000). Just because it's happening doesn't mean it's working: Using action research to improve practice in middle schools. *Phi Delta Kappan, 82,* 284–290.

Action Research Articles on Issues in School Counseling

Foster, L. H., Watson, T. S., & Meeks, C. (2002). Single-subject research design for school counselors: Becoming an applied researcher. *Professional School Counseling, 6,* 146–154.

McCall-Perez, Z. (2000). The counselor as advocate for English language learners: An action research approach. *Professional School Counseling, 4,* 13–22.

Whiston, S. C. (1996). Accountability through action research: Research methods for practitioners. *Journal of Counseling and Development, 74,* 616–623.

Action Research Studies in Physical Education

Barker-Ruchti, N. (2002). A study journey: A useful example of action research. *Journal of Physical Education New Zealand, 35,* 12–24.

(continued)

TABLE 1.3   Continued

Lock, R. S., Minarik, L. T., & Omata, J. (1999). Gender and the problem of diversity: Action research in physical education. *Quest, 51,* 393–407.

Studies on Using Action Research for School Change and Improvement

Calhoun, E. (2002). Action research for school improvement. *Educational Leadership, 59,* 18–24.

Crocco, M. S., Faithfull, B., & Schwartz, S. (2003). Inquiring minds want to know: Action research at a New York City professional development school. *Journal of Teacher Education, 54,* 19–30.

Gross, R. R. (2002). Research-driven school improvement. *Principal Leadership, 2,* 35–40.

Harris, B., & Drake, S. M. (1997). Implementing high school reform through school-wide action research teams: A three year case study. *Action in Teacher Education, 19,* 15–31.

Johnson, M., & Button, K. (1998). Action research paves the way for continuous school improvement. *Journal of Staff Development, 19,* 48–51.

Senese, J. C. (2002). Energize with action research. *Journal of Staff Development, 23,* 39–41.

Journals That Publish Action Research

Applied Language Learning

   (no current website)

Educational Studies in Mathematics

   http://kapis.www.wkap.nl/journalhome.htm/0013-1954

English Journal

   http://www.cc.ysu.edu/tej/

Journal of Physical Education, Recreation & Dance

   http://www.aahperd.org/aahperd/joperd_main.html

Journal of Research on Technology in Education

   http://www.iste.org/jrte/index.html

Leading and Learning with Technology

   http://www.iste.org/L&L/

Mathematical Teaching in the Middle School

   http://www.nctm.org/mtms/mtms.htm

The Quarterly (National Writing Project)

   http://www.writingproject.org/Publications/quarterly/

Teaching Children Mathematics

   http://www.nctm.org/tcm/

Teaching Exceptional Children

   http://www.cec.sped.org/bk/abtec.html

TABLE 1.3   Continued

Journal Issues

Educational Leadership, 59(6) (2002)

http://www.ascd.org/frameedlead.html

English Education, 32(2) (2000)

http://www.ncte.org/ee/

Language Arts, Volume 71(1) (1999)

http://www.ncte.org/elem/la/la0999.html

Phi Delta Kappan, 82 (2000)

http://www.pdkintl.org/kappan/kappan.htm

University, Regional, and School District Action Research Sites

Action Research at Bath University (UK)

http://www.bath.ac.uk/~edsajw/

Action Research at Queen's University (Canada)

http://educ.queensu.ca/~ar/

The Action Research Laboratory at Highland Park High School (Illinois)

http://www.d113.lake.k12.il.us/hphs/action/page1.htm

Action Research Network Ireland

http://www.iol.ie/~rayo/

Appalachian Educational Research

http://www.ael.org/rel/schlserv/tchrres.htm

Arizona Action Research Project

http://www.ade.state.az.us/resources/goals2000/default.asp

Brown University—Voices from the Field

http://www.lab.brown.edu/voices/archive.shtml

Collaborative Action Research Network [CARN] (UK)

http://www.uea.ac.uk/care/carn/

Eisenhower National Clearinghouse

http://www.enc.org/professional/research/journal/science/document.shtm?input=ENC-002432-2432

Literacy Inquiry Network (LINK) at University of Houston (USA)

http://www.coe.uh.edu/~lpatters/link/

(continued)

TABLE 1.3   Continued

Madison (WI) Metropolitan School District Classroom Action Research

http://www.madison.k12.wi.us/sod/car/carhomepage.html

National Council for Teachers of English (NCTE) Teachers as Researchers Page

http://www.ncte.org/rte/links4.html

National Science Teachers Association (NSTA) The Role of Research in Science Teaching

http://www.nsta.org/159&id=30

Participatory Action Research Network [PARnet] (USA)

http://www.parnet.org/

Purdue University Calumet Elementary Science Support Projects

http://essc.calumet.purdue.edu/projects

Additional Reading Materials

Atweh, B., Kemmis, S., & Weeks, P. (Eds.). (1998). *Action research in practice. Partnerships for social justice in education.* London: Routledge.

Carson, T. R., & Sumara, D. (Eds.). (1997). *Action research as a living practice.* New York: Peter Lang Publishers.

Corey, S. M. (1953). *Action research to improve school practices.* New York: Teachers College Press.

Elliot, J. (1978). What is action research in schools? *Journal of Curriculum Studies, 10,* 355–357.

Elliot, J. (1991). *Action research for educational change.* Philadelphia: Milton Keynes/Open University Press.

Kemmis, S. (1993). Action research and social movement: A challenge for policy research. *Education Policy Analysis Archives, 1.* [Available online at http://epaa.asu.edu/epaa/v1n1.html]

Schön, D. (1987). *Educating the reflective practitioner.* London: Jossey-Bass.

CHAPTER TWO

GENERATING RESEARCH IDEAS THROUGH REFLECTION

CHAPTER GOALS

- Explain the ways reflection can be used to generate ideas for action research.
- Describe the history and definitions of reflection in educational practice.
- Illustrate different types of reflection including reflection-in-, -on-, and -for- practice, autobiographical, collaborative, and communal reflection, internally and externally directed reflection, and reflexive inquiry.
- Suggest ways to use the different types of reflection throughout the action research process.
- Provide reflection activities that reveal ways to align action research studies with personal goals and values.

The goals, benefits, and the reflect–act–evaluate process of action research were presented in Chapter 1. This chapter focuses on reflection, both an initial step and an ongoing process of action research. In this chapter, the history of reflection in education is described, types of reflection are defined, and the act of reflection—at the beginning and throughout the process of action research—is discussed. Presented first are three examples of the reflective process that illustrate various types of reflection and how reflection is used to generate ideas for action research studies.

These reflection examples illustrate different ways educators reflect on practice. In Example 1, the focus of the reflection was on an issue of social justice, and it extended beyond Danetta as she asked her colleagues to reflect on the disparity she believed she had identified and then sought a more intensive and shared study of the issue. In Example 2, Jack's reflection was focused inward and was autobiographical in nature. The direction of his reflective inquiry centered on his experiences as a student and how those experiences influence his teaching goals. Susan's reflection in Example 3 is similar to Danetta's because she, too, is interested in reflecting with others in her school to tackle a problem that extends

REFLECTION EXAMPLE 1

Danetta, an elementary school guidance counselor, considers how to best serve a small group of students with recurring behavior problems. She reviews the students' files and then observes them in and out of class both formally and informally over several weeks, which leads her to question whether these students, who are all Hispanic, are being disciplined differently than the African American students who make up a large majority of the student body. At a faculty meeting, Danetta shares her concerns with teachers, administrators, and school support personnel, describing her analyses of student files and observational notes. This educational community discusses the concerns and decides that members will reflect on and critically analyze their practices, continue their conversation on the issue, and meet later to consider whether action needs to be taken.

REFLECTION EXAMPLE 2

Jack, a middle school reading teacher, becomes frustrated with his students' apathy toward reading. As a child, Jack had little opportunity to read outside of school and was, in fact, a slow reader throughout elementary school. In sixth grade, his teacher, Ms. Gonzales, sparked his interest in reading, first by working with him every day after school on his reading skills, and then by supplying him with books such as *I Am the Cheese* and *The Chocolate War* by Robert Cormier. From sixth grade through high school, Jack devoured books, which helped him succeed in school and earn a scholarship to college. The first college graduate in his family, Jack attributes his success to reading. In college, he decided to become a middle school language arts teacher so that he, like Ms. Gonzales, could help students develop a love of reading. Now in his second year of teaching, Jack questions his ability to foster a love of reading in his students. In his first year of teaching, he existed strictly on survival mode, making sure he covered the required material and kept his kids in line. Now, more confident in his classroom management skills but disillusioned by a mandated curriculum that focuses on the mechanics of language arts rather than on reading and writing, Jack wants to find a way to cover the required material, get his kids excited about reading and writing, and open their worlds through literature.

REFLECTION EXAMPLE 3

Susan, a fourth-year high school principal in a small, rural school, is concerned with the lack of community she senses in the educators at her school. In the last few years, many teachers have retired, and their jobs have been filled with young teachers just out of college. The result is a teaching pool that is made up of about half who are older, experienced teachers and half who are younger teachers just a few years older than the senior class. Though Susan had hoped that the more experienced teachers would step in to mentor the new teachers, this has not happened. In actuality, the experienced teachers tend to eat lunch together, talk with each other between classes, and sit together at faculty meetings, whereas the younger teachers socialize after school hours but stay in their classrooms working independently during school hours. Susan plans to bring all the teachers together to discuss ways to build a sense of community among the teachers and administrators at the school. She will also ask the new teachers to discuss their mentoring needs with each other, and she will ask the experienced teachers to come up with ways to help the new teachers be successful.

beyond a single classroom. Susan, like Danetta, wants to involve faculty in a process of collaborative reflection, although the goal of that reflection in Susan's case is related to shared decision making rather than to social justice.

In the three reflection examples, the educators reflected on their practice as they considered their values and goals and focused on desired outcomes. Reflections such as those presented in the examples are a starting point for generating research ideas. For example, Danetta's reflection leads to the study of the ways in which educational disparity based on race can be examined and rectified. Jack's reflection can direct him to study methods that can help students connect with literature. Susan's reflection targets how to build a sense of community among teachers at her school through mentoring and collaboration.

REFLECTION: ITS HISTORY AND DEFINITIONS

Most educators have been exposed to the idea of reflection, perhaps even so much so that the term elicits little personal meaning. The term *reflective practitioner* is extensively used in education literature, and as Norlander-Case, Reagan, and Case (1999) explain, most teacher education programs are committed to the idea of preparing reflective practitioners. Although the idea of reflection is pervasive in education, there remains some debate about how reflection is defined. Bullough and Gitlin (2001) suggest that too often the push for teachers to become reflective practitioners who study their practice results in ". . . only empty slogans [that] boil down to nothing more than a plea to 'think hard' about what they are doing and why they are doing it" (p. 13). Reflection involves more than simply thinking about practice, though, and in order to understand the process of reflection and its role in action research, it is important to consider the history of reflection in education.

John Dewey described the act of reflection in *How We Think* (1910, 1933). Dewey (1933) explained that reflective thinking is a process directed at seeking a conclusion through inquiry. This definition of reflection goes beyond the notion that reflection is merely thinking about a problem. Instead, thinking about a problem is a first step of reflection. Norlander-Case, Reagan, and Case (1999) stress the problem-solving nature of Dewey's definition of reflection, asserting that for Dewey true reflection could only occur when an individual is confronted with a problem, recognizes it, and then attempts to resolve the problem rationally.

In their synthesis of research on reflection, Sparks-Langer and Colton (1991) explain that although Dewey referred to reflection in his writings in the early 1900s, few educators embraced the concept until Donald Schön's work on reflective practices was published in the 1980s. Schön's early work was based on his studies of reflective practices of individuals in fields other than education. Later, he expanded his work to include the reflective practices of teachers, and in this work Schön proposed that teachers learn in large part as they reflect on their everyday practices (Sparks-Langer & Colton, 1999).

TYPES OF REFLECTION

In this section, various types of reflection are described. Presented first is a discussion of reflecting-on-, -in-, and -for-action, acts of reflection that center on when the reflection takes place. Next, reflection is discussed in terms of the purpose of the reflection, focusing on Rearick and Feldman's (1999) autobiographical, collaborative, and communal reflection, which is then compared to Stevenson's (1995) description of internally and externally directed reflection that occurs in either a public or private context. Finally, reflexive inquiry, a type of reflection that focuses on an individual's understanding of how experiences and values impact actions, is discussed.

Schön (1987) describes two types of reflection in which individuals engage: **reflection-on-action** and **reflection-in-action**. Reflection-on-action occurs as individuals reflect on actions and thoughts after they have taken place. Reflection-in-action takes place as the action occurs. Killion and Todnem (1991) expand Schön's model of reflection to include the concept of **reflection-for-action**, which they define as reflection that occurs as a result of reflecting in and on action. Reflection-for-action, the authors explain, is a way of guiding future action based on past thoughts and actions.

To clarify these three types of reflection, consider this extension of Jack's reflection that was presented at the beginning of the chapter: Reflecting-in-action, Jack observes students who are fidgeting and inattentive during a literature discussion. As the discussion progresses, it becomes apparent that students have not read the story that was assigned for homework the night before. Jack begins to question his students about why they haven't read the assignment, and some students express their boredom with reading. As more students become involved in the conversation, a few students say they don't like to read at all, and others say that the stories in their literature textbook aren't interesting. At the end of the day, Jack reflects-on-action, considering what his students said about reading, his informal observations of their behavior and attitude during most reading lessons, and his own feelings about the importance getting kids excited about reading. Reflecting-for-action, Jack decides to start the next day's lesson with a student-led discussion about the best books or stories they have read. He believes that if he can find out what interests his students, he will then be able to structure reading lessons around the kinds of books and stories that are most appealing to them.

Whereas Schön (1987) and Killion and Todnem (1991) discuss reflection in terms of when it takes place, Rearick and Feldman (1999) describe three types of reflection used in action research studies that are based on the purpose of the reflection. The first type, **autobiographical reflection**, has at its focus the researcher's study of his stories, beliefs, and values and how they may affect the actions he takes. Jack's reflection in Example 2 at the beginning of this chapter is an example of autobiographical reflection. The focus of Jack's reflection was on his own experience as a student, which impacted his beliefs and values as an educator. **Collaborative reflection**, the second type of reflection, involves the practitioner's looking to others to enhance understanding. When engaging in collaborative reflection, the action researcher must analyze and interpret the ideas and perspectives of

---

Reflection-on-Action: Thinking about thoughts and actions after they have taken place.

Reflection-in-Action: Thinking about thoughts and actions as they occur.

Reflection-for-Action: Thinking about thoughts and actions to plan for future action.

Autobiographical Reflection: A practitioner's reflection that involves thinking about the ways in which history, beliefs, and values affect action.

Collaborative Reflection: Reflection shared with others for the purpose of enhancing self-understanding by understanding the perspectives of others.

others, which can result in the development of a critical community of individuals who collaborate and reflect to solve problems. Reflection Example 3, Susan's reflection on ways to build a sense of community among teachers in her school, illustrates how collaborative reflection can be used in action research. The third type of reflection, **communal reflection**, goes a step beyond collaborative reflection, focusing on social justice, freedom, and democracy. Communal reflection allows practitioners to engage in discourse and debate on philosophical and moral issues and is grounded in the notion that "the action researcher engaging in communal reflection sees the emptiness of his or her actions separate from public action" (Rearick & Feldman, p. 336). Danetta's reflection in Example 1 demonstrates the ways in which communal reflection can be used to tackle an issue of social justice—the disparity in discipline procedures for racially diverse groups.

The types of reflection described by Rearick and Feldman (1999) indicate a hierarchy of reflective practices. Autobiographical reflection, a solitary type of reflection, occurs when a practitioner considers his or her values and experiences in light of the actions he or she takes. If the practitioner discusses with others these actions and the reasons for taking them and then solicits feedback from colleagues, the turn is taken toward collaborative reflection. If the researcher further attempts to situate his or her actions within the context, history, or culture of his or her setting through discussions related to the moral and philosophical bases of his or her actions, then the result would be communal reflection.

In describing the structural and cultural conditions necessary for supporting practitioner research, Stevenson (1995) explains differences in internally and externally directed reflection. The ways in which these types of reflection are carried out, explains Stevenson, is determined by whether the reflection occurs in a public or private context. **Internally directed reflection** that takes place in a private context, meaning that it takes place either as a solely individual action or as an internal dialogue, is closely aligned with Rearick and Feldman's (1999) autobiographical reflection. Reflection in this case occurs in the thoughts or actions of an individual—a self-examination similar to Jack's—and is related to the individual's personal, career, and educational histories. When the practitioner's internally directed reflection takes place in a public context, which means that the practitioner communicates his or her internal reflection with others through dialogue and sharing of other individuals' internal reflections, the reflection process is analogous to collaborative reflection. **Externally directed reflection**, which Stevenson explains is reflection that focuses on the values and norms of an educator's community, is similar to Rearick and Feldman's communal reflection, particularly when the externally directed reflection takes place in a public context where all voices are allowed and expected to contribute to "developing organizational forms that enable faculty to engage in the collaborative pursuit of 'best practices'" (Stevenson, p. 206). The way in which these types of reflection are related is illustrated in Figure 2.1.

Communal Reflection: Collaborative reflection that is undertaken for the purpose of engaging in the study of issues related to social justice.

Internally Directed Reflection: Reflection that takes place as an individual action or an internal dialogue.

Externally Directed Reflection: Reflection that takes place in a public context in which multiple voices are expected to contribute to studies of best practices.

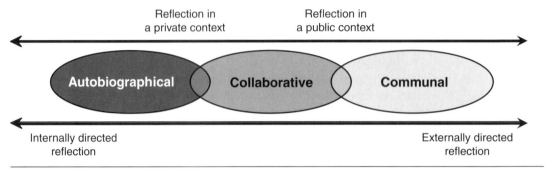

FIGURE 2.1   **Types of reflection.**

Some educators and theorists have expanded the act of reflection to include its *reflexive* nature. Cole and Knowles (2000) explain that through **reflexive inquiry**, educators connect their personal lives with their professional careers. In describing differences between reflective and reflexive processes, Cole and Knowles state:

> Reflective inquiry is an ongoing process of examining and refining practice, variously focused on the personal, pedagogical, curricular, intellectual, societal, and/or ethical contexts of professional work. . . . Reflexive inquiry . . . is reflective inquiry situated within the context of personal histories in order to . . . understand personal (including early) influences on professional practice. (p. 2)

Based on this definition, reflexive practice can provide educators with a framework for knowing where they have come from in order to understand where they are going and the decisions they make as educators. Reflexive inquiry is related to Rearick and Feldman's (1999) autobiographical reflection because it places present thoughts and actions in the context of past thoughts, action, and history. Placing reflexive inquiry in the context of the pressures teachers face—due to the accountability and standards movements, for example—Bullough and Gitlin (2001) suggest that when teachers understand themselves and the contexts in which they teach they are better able to answer the question, "Can I be who I am in the classroom?" (p. 44).

The types of reflection presented here—reflecting-in-, -on-, and -for-action, autobiographical, collaborative, and communal reflection, internally and externally directed reflection, and reflexive inquiry—overlap, illustrating the dynamic and somewhat complex nature of reflective inquiry. These various ways to think about reflection, however, can allow an action researcher to choose reflective methods that are most closely aligned with his or her goals, beliefs, and values. A practitioner who desires to understand the ways his or her past experiences as a student and educator influence her current practices would likely choose reflexive, autobiographical, internally directed methods of reflection. An educator whose goal is to identify and correct educational disparities due to gender, race, or

---

Reflexive Inquiry: Considering past experiences and actions in order to understand how they impact present and future actions and thoughts.

■ ■ ■ ■ ■ ▬▬▬▬▬▬▬▬▬▬▬▬▬▬▬▬▬▬▬▬▬▬

ACTIVITY 2.1

LINKING TYPES OF REFLECTION TO THE WORK OF EDUCATORS

As you respond to the questions and prompts in this activity, consider the various types of reflection, how you currently reflect on practice, and the ways in which different forms of reflection can be used in studies of educational practice.

1. Describe times, as an educator, that you reflected in, on, and for action.
2. Consider the various types of reflection presented in the previous section of Chapter 2, and then respond to the following prompts:
   a. At present, do you think you would feel most comfortable engaging in autobiographical, collaborative, or communal reflection? Explain the reason for your answer.
   b. In your current reflective inquiry as a practitioner, is your reflection internally or externally directed? Explain the reasons why this is so.
   c. What do you consider to be your core values as an educator? Engage in reflexive, autobiographical reflection and then describe the experiences you have had as a student and educator that have shaped your core values.

social class would focus on communal, externally directed reflection (*How can we as an educational community reflect together to deal with disparity?*), though the process of the reflection could include internally directed autobiographical and reflexive inquiry (*What about my history and my values make this an area that is important to me?*).

In Activity 2.1 questions and prompts are presented to encourage examination of the various types of reflection. The purpose of the activity is twofold. First, the questions and prompts provide opportunities to think about the ways you reflect as a practitioner. Second, the activity is meant to stimulate thoughtful consideration of new ways to reflect on practice and to think about reflection in light of your educational goals and values.

REFLECTION IN ACTION RESEARCH

When reflecting in action research, there are several considerations to be made. First, reflection must be critical, which requires going beyond merely thinking about experience. Action that follows experience is a key element in reflection. Thus, for a principal to be truly reflective she must go beyond thinking about the problem of teacher attrition in her school; she must consider actions to deal with the attrition problem. Second, reflection is a meaningful and important part of a practitioner's professional development. Reflection allows the educator to consider issues and problems relevant to his own practice and then act in ways to study or resolve those issues, guiding his own development as a professional educator. Third, self-understanding, whether through autobiographical reflection or internally directed reflection, is an important part of the reflective process because it allows an educator to focus on the ways in which her experiences and values affect her actions.

The process of action research begins with systematic, critical reflection. Reflection helps to identify a problem to investigate, and by considering how the different types of reflection can be used to study practice, practitioners can choose ways to reflect that are most closely aligned with personal values, beliefs, and goals of their action research studies. It is important to note, however, that reflection does not end once a research problem is identified. Reflection is the first step in choosing an area to study, but reflection is also an ongoing activity that is engaged in throughout the study. The reflections that are made each day during an action research study become one of the most useful types of data collected during the project. Recording reflections is also a powerful way to document ongoing professional development.

REFLECTING TO IDENTIFY A RESEARCH FOCUS

As you begin reflecting on your practice and the issues you face as an educator to identify an area for your action research study, remember to frame your reflections in terms of the *actions* that you can take to proactively study the issue and the *outcomes* that you would like to occur. When educators are first beginning reflective activities, they sometimes focus on big issues such as "Is there a difference in the way we treat Hispanic and African American students with discipline problems?" "Why don't students like to read?" and "Why does our school lack a sense of community among teachers?" The problem with focusing on big issues is that they are not outcome and action oriented. That's not to say that the issues listed cannot be studied at all. In fact, each of the previous questions, which are broad topics based on Danetta's, Jack's, and Susan's reflection examples from the beginning of the chapter, can easily be focused into a good action research study:

- Danetta asked teachers in her school to make observations to determine whether Hispanic and African American students were being disciplined differently. If observations do indicate a disparity, action can be taken: Teachers can collaborate to determine how to enforce consistent discipline procedures. Once a method is established, action is taken, and the teachers can evaluate the effectiveness of the action. The desired outcome is equitable treatment of all students in the school.
- Jack has identified the outcomes he desires: to cover required material, get kids excited about reading and writing, and to open students' worlds through literature. In order to determine whether those outcomes can be met, he must seek actions that he can undertake (for example, starting a Reader's and Writer's Workshop in his class).
- In her reflection example, Susan has identified a desired outcome (building a sense of community among teachers) and actions to take to reach that outcome (bringing together new teachers to discuss mentoring needs, having experienced teachers collaborate to determine ways to mentor new teachers, starting a mentoring program).

In these examples, broad, general research questions have been narrowed to focus on specific actions and outcomes. As you begin thinking about an area that you wish to study, remember to concentrate your reflections in an area or areas where you can make a change (action-focused) and then examine the effects of this change (outcome-focused).

Provided here is an example of a middle school principal's reflection of a problem he has faced as an administrator. Roy offers a well-articulated reflection, focusing on a specific issue that is important to him, the actions he is considering taking to study this issue, and the outcomes he hopes to see. Notice, too, elements of Roy's story—autobiographical information that includes his history, beliefs, and values—that show the reflexive nature of his thinking.

As a new administrator several years back I was amazed at the lack of good teaching skills I observed in some teachers. These were experienced teachers who had a difficult time with classroom management, time on task, communication with parents, and content knowledge in their subject areas. As a teacher, I had assumed that all teachers were experts at what they did. As I have matured as an administrator and an educator, I recognized that I made judgments about the skills of teachers based upon my own experience as a teacher. As I further reflected on this problem, I realized that many teachers never go to graduate school. Many teachers are satisfied with having an undergraduate teaching degree and have no desire to further their education. While I realize that the decision to further one's education is a personal one, I am concerned about the benefits lost when teachers do not seek to further their knowledge.

As a principal, I want to raise the standard of teacher knowledge at my school. My problem is how to raise the standard. This is important to me because in this age of accountability, I am the one held accountable for the results of my school. But even more important to me is the issue of my personal accountability. I am an educator because it is my calling. I do this because I want to help children. I am committed to providing the students with whom I am charged a quality education. In order to provide this quality education for students, we must have quality teachers. Teachers must further their education either formally or informally to provide students with quality.

My area of focus is to research the use of teacher study groups at my school. In the study groups, teachers will read literature on topics related to the development of good teaching practices and strategies. The study groups will meet to discuss this literature, much in the same way that individuals discuss books in book clubs. The prospect of creating study groups creates its own set of problems. When will teachers have the time to participate in groups? Who will set up the groups? What topics will teachers study? Where will the resources be found for teachers to use in the study groups? What will be the impact on students as a result of teachers participating in study groups? The study group concept and these related questions will be the focus of my school-based action research study.

As you engage in reflective activities to determine a research focus, consider your personal history, beliefs, and values as well as those perplexing, intriguing, and difficult issues that you face daily as an educator. As research topics are identified, utilize the processes of reflecting in, on, and for action, which will help to clarify your understanding and beliefs about the topic as well as actions that might be taken and outcomes that are desired. In addition, think about whether it is important to engage in autobiographical, collaborative, communal, internally directed or externally directed reflection, reflexive inquiry, or a combination of reflective activities. Figure 2.2 includes notes I jotted after engaging in a passionate debate with doctoral students about scripted reading instruction, an instructional method used widely in public elementary schools in Georgia that involves

FIGURE 2.2   Reflective notes from scripted instruction conversation.

3/10/03 I had an interesting conversation with several doctoral students tonight about scripted instruction. During our conversation I became aware that several of the students, who are teachers and administrators, think that there is a lot of value in scripted instruction, especially in schools with low achievement. As I think about this now, I realize that my argument to them (that scripted instruction is counter to treating teachers as professionals) may have fallen on deaf ears. I am passionate about empowering teachers, but I'm not in the trenches facing an accountability movement.

3/17/03 We had another discussion on scripted instruction today, but in the last week, as I considered that I, too, used scripted instruction years ago as a special education teacher, I have really had to try to come to terms with two competing values: First, in my experience, scripted instruction works. But forcing teachers to use scripted instruction takes away their autonomy and may prevent them from engaging in the teaching activities they think are most effective. I guess as we continued the conversation tonight, we were in fact engaged in a sort of collaborative reflection. Each person shared his/her perspective on the issue, though I felt like a real outsider. There was consensus among the teachers and administrators that scripted instruction does increase test scores and does help the majority of new teachers who struggle in teaching reading when left to their own devices. When I brought up the issue of teacher autonomy, I was the only person in the conversation passionate about it. Everyone else agreed that autonomy is important, but they felt that student achievement is more important. This took us to another conversation on the preparation of teachers and their ability to take control of studying their effectiveness. We had no resolution, but I definitely have a better understanding of the reasons schools are embracing scripted instruction. I think, too, that the others may be thinking about how scripted instruction takes away teaching autonomy. I don't think that values have changed, but for my part I have to admit that my values get messy in light of the realities educators face. There are issues here of social justice, which I hadn't considered before—the right of students to learn to read and the right of teachers to be treated as professionals. I suppose real communal reflection is a long way off, but I can't help feeling that social justice is where my argument is based, even though I have to keep in mind that my own history includes teaching with scripted instruction, and teaching very successfully. My core value as an educator is that I do whatever it takes to help students succeed. In my past, I used scripted instruction to do that. Now that my work focuses on facilitating educators' study of their practice through action research—and now that I have seen how incredibly powerful it is for empowering teachers—I must try to find a way to reconcile—or at least hold onto—these two competing values.

teachers' following completely scripted lesson plans to teach reading. This example shows the ways I have reflected on my own practice and on my work with educators. As I engage in reflection, I find that I often reflect inwardly, considering first my educational values and beliefs. As I continue to reflect, which takes place over the course of several days, as is indicated in the figure, I tend to think about ways my experiences as a teacher, and often even as a student, may be impacting the directions I choose to follow. Though I don't always look for ways to reflect autobiographically, collaboratively, and communally, in this particular reflection, elements of each were important.

The reflection displayed in Figure 2.2 has not yet led me to my own action research study on the issues described, but as I continue engaging in discourse about scripted instruction and empowerment, I am considering conducting a study with elementary school principals and their first-year teachers that would involve having the new teachers engage in self-study (action research) of their reading instruction. In my reflections thus far, I am unsure of the outcomes I desire—Do I want to work with first-year teachers to help them create their own effective reading instruction? Do I want to help them learn to use action research to study ways to tailor and adapt the mandatory scripted instruction so that there can be a teaching focus that goes beyond getting students ready for the achievement test? Do I want to work with principals to create action-research based professional development activities for new teachers that focus on reading instruction?—and therefore I am unable to determine what actions might be taken. But, in this initial stage of reflection, I continue to collaborate with the teachers and administrators with whom I work, and I also engage my university colleagues in discussions on scripted instruction, teaching autonomy, and teacher empowerment. These discussions, which involve elements of all the types of reflection described in this chapter, will eventually lead to my own action research study.

REFLECTIVE JOURNALS

One tool that I often use when reflecting is a reflective journal. Other methods are useful as well, including having conversations with others (particularly for collaborative and communal reflection) and recording those conversations. A reflective journal is a place to store information that comes from private, internal thoughts and from conversations with others. In recording reflections and actions, educators are able, as Christine O'Hanlon (1997) explains, to create an archived resource of professional development. O'Hanlon expresses the power of journal writing in fostering the development of sustained critical thought. Cole and Knowles (2000) refer to journaling as a way to "pause, reflect, reenergize" (p. 49), which they view as a necessary activity in the sometimes frenetic world of teaching.

One way to begin the action research process is to start keeping a journal. A journal can be kept in a looseleaf notebook, a diary, a composition book, or as an electronic journal on a computer. Journal writing can be used at the beginning of a study as a research focus is identified and as attempts are made at engaging in the different types of reflective activities. In addition, writing in a journal throughout an action research study is a good way to record observations, ideas, challenges, successes, and failures, and it provides a way to keep track of how different types of reflection are used throughout the course of the project. Several suggested journaling techniques are offered for consideration here:

- Write information as soon as you can. It isn't always possible to stop what you are doing and write in your journal, but as soon as you get a break, write a few notes to help jog your memory later when you have more time to think, reflect, and write.
- Hobson (2001) suggests jotting quick notes on lesson plans, sticky notes, or in a notebook. Even writing a word or two can help you remember important occurrences, thoughts, or concerns.
- Set aside time each day to review the notes you have jotted down that day. As you review the notes, expand them in detail in your journal.

- Remember that context is critical in action research. Include contextual information in your journal entries. For example, don't just write, "Several teachers approached me angry about the new attendance policy for the school." Instead, provide context information such as, "The teachers who were angry seem to frequently come to my office with complaints about my management as principal of this school. In an incident last week and in today's incident, I get the feeling that these teachers are quick to react to management that they feel is 'top down.' Mrs. J., who is typically the leader in these confrontations, stated today, 'We are tired of being micromanaged with these policies that we have no voice in making.' However, teachers have had a say during faculty meetings about creating and enforcing school policies. Mrs. J., though, has missed three of the last five meetings."

- Include in your journal entries actions you might consider taking and outcomes you wish to occur. The principal in the previous example could include *actions* and *outcomes* this way, "*I need to better communicate with this group of teachers, especially Mrs. J. And perhaps I need to conference with Mrs. J. privately, explaining my management style and goals for this school and eliciting from her the management style she uses as a teacher, the management style she desires from a principal, and her goals for the school* [actions]. *I want this school to have a positive climate for teachers and students, and I want teachers to feel valued as decision-makers* [outcomes]."

- Review your journal as often as you can. Don't simply add to your journal without referring to events you have already recorded. Reviewing your journal occasionally will allow you to see themes and patterns that may be important. In order to see developmental patterns, make generalizations, and formulate hypotheses from reflections, Hobson (2001) suggests writing dates and times on each entry to keep track of chronology of events.

- When engaged in collaborative or communal reflection, audiotape the discussion. The audiotape becomes a record of the group reflection, and if it is transcribed (put into printed form), the written record can be used to document the activity.

- Use technology in collaborative reflection activities. Online bulletin boards, chat room discussions, and communication via email and/or listservs provide a number of ways to encourage collaborative reflection among educators. Using technology provides all members of the community an opportunity to participate in the discussion, and written records can be generated from each of the sources listed here. A benefit of using technology in this way is that people who are reluctant to talk during face-to-face discussions are often much more comfortable contributing their ideas and opinions electronically.

The last part of this chapter focused on using reflection to identify a research focus. The importance of critical reflection that is action and outcome oriented was described, and methods for documenting reflection, both at the beginning of and throughout the study, were presented. Activity 2.2 presents prompts that will help you identify a research focus through reflecting on practice.

NOTE: The symbol ✍ is used in Activity 2.2 to indicate that this is a journal activity. Throughout the remainder of the text, when the symbol appears in a chapter activity, it signifies that journaling will be part of the activity. The symbol ▤ is used to alert you to the fact that the activity can be expanded to become part of a research paper. If you are writing a research paper for a course, presentation, publication, or as a professional growth activity, follow the directions next to the research paper icon. This symbol will be used throughout the remaining chapters of the textbook.

■ ■ ■ ■ ■ ▬▬▬▬▬▬▬▬▬▬▬▬▬▬▬▬▬▬▬▬▬▬▬▬▬▬▬▬▬▬▬▬▬

ACTIVITY 2.2
REFLECTING TO IDENTIFY A RESEARCH FOCUS

Choose a way to document your reflections. Journaling provides a written record of reflection and is perhaps the simplest method of documenting reflection. Other methods involve audiotaping or videotaping reflections. If you choose to audiotape or videotape, it may be necessary to add written documentation transcribed from the tapes. Once you have chosen a method to document your reflections (written, electronic, taped journal), respond to the following prompts:

1. There are a number of potential action research studies that could be conducted on your practice, and several broad topics are presented here:

student achievement	behavior/discipline	school climate
mentoring	teacher attrition	attendance
counseling programs	inclusion	team teaching
collaboration	needs of at-risk students	dropout prevention
motivation	extracurricular participation	media services
technology	professional development	✈ parental involvement

   Think about which of these topics are issues in your work as an educator. Provide a documented reflection on the two topics (either from this list or on other topics of your own choosing) that you are most interested in or about which you feel the most passionate.

2. Add to your documented reflection the outcomes you desire regarding these two topics and the actions you might take in pursuit of those outcomes.

3. Choose one of the topics as your area of research focus. Expand your reflection to include the types of reflection (reflecting in, on, and for action, autobiographical, collaborative, or communal reflection, internally directed or externally directed reflection, reflexive inquiry) most closely aligned with the goals of your study and with your core values as an educator (refer to your responses from Activity 2.1).

▤ **Research Paper Activity:** Use your documented reflection to write a brief introductory paragraph on your area of research focus. Write the reflection in first person. Include in the focus the desired outcome and the actions you are considering taking. Write a brief description of your educational role (teacher, principal, administrator) and your setting (grade level, subject area, etc.). Include relevant information about the reflective process(es) you used to identify the focus, and illustrate the ways these processes reflect your core educational values. Use a heading such as *Reflection* or *Research Focus* for this paragraph.

SUMMARY

The purpose of this chapter was to explain the ways in which reflective inquiry is used in the process of action research. The history of reflection in education was presented, and different types of reflective inquiry and the ways they can be used in action research studies were described. In addition, methods were presented for documenting reflective inquiry. A goal of this chapter was to illustrate the power of reflective processes not only in the action research cycle but also in the everyday practices of educational practitioners. Now that an area of research focus has been identified, the next step is to learn more about it through reviewing related literature. Reviewing the literature, a process of connecting theory to practice, is the focus of Chapter 3.

CHAPTER THREE

CONNECTING THEORY AND ACTION

Reviewing the Literature

CHAPTER GOALS:

- Explain the professional, intellectual activity of reviewing literature in order to connect theory and action.
- Describe methods of searching for literature to review.
- Illustrate ways to choose, evaluate, and synthesize published research and to use it to inform practice.
- Suggest ways to organize and write the literature review.
- Provide writing activities that take practitioners through various steps of the literature review writing process.

The activities in Chapter 2 involved reflecting on practice to identify an area of research focus. With the topic (focus) identified, it is now time to learn more about it so that activities, interventions, or innovations (actions) can be planned that can help achieve the desired outcomes. Reviewing literature is important for a variety of reasons. First, reviewing literature on the topic under investigation provides an opportunity to learn what is already known about the topic. Second, in reviewing related literature one can learn about other researchers' (both practitioners' and university researchers') successes and failures using various interventions, which can help identify useful practices that can be incorporated into the study plan. It should be noted that the focus of this chapter is on writing a review of literature, which is a necessary part of writing an action research paper or report. If the creation of a paper is not the goal of your study, you may wish to use the strategies in this chapter simply to locate and synthesize research findings so that the study you plan is connected to best practices found and described in the literature.

REVIEWING LITERATURE AS A PROFESSIONAL, INTELLECTUAL ACTIVITY

Reviewing the literature is an important step in conducting educational research regardless of whether quantitative, qualitative, or action research methodologies are employed. In quantitative research, a literature review must be conducted after research questions have been identified but before hypotheses have been generated. The reason for this is that hypotheses must be theory-driven, and theory is not known or completely understood until literature pertinent to that theory has been thoroughly studied. Because the goals of qualitative and action research are different from the goal of quantitative research, the purpose of literature review is also somewhat different. In qualitative research, which has as its goal understanding and theory-building, reviewing the literature may occur at the beginning or end of the study as the researcher attempts to link what was learned in the qualitative investigation with what is known from the literature.

In educational action research, the literature review is completed prior to beginning the study but after initial research questions are identified, which helps in the planning and implementation of actions and interventions taken. A practitioner who spends time reading studies relevant to his or her own investigation is able to clarify the goals of the study and to discover new strategies that seem to have great potential in the investigation. Insight can be gained regarding ways to collect and evaluate data for the project. At the least, new information is learned that increases knowledge and understanding of the topic being studied. Becoming informed allows the practitioner to connect existing best practices to the actions he or she chooses to take.

The study and review of published research to inform practice is an important and valued activity in many professions. Medical researchers, scientists, and other professionals familiarize themselves with the knowledge in their fields before conducting research. Trial lawyers review case law prior to going to trial. Being well-informed means that these professionals are less likely to make mistakes in their studies (or trials), and they are more likely to engage in work that is important and valuable. Though often not seen as a valuable professional activity for educators, reviewing educational research is an important and necessary activity for practitioners' professional development. Consider the argument made by Fecho (1992), a secondary English teacher and action researcher, who explains that if teachers do not read educational theory and participate in ongoing classroom research, they diminish their potential to be seen as professionals and intellectuals. The point here is that teachers have a responsibility both to engage in reading educational research and to carry out research in their own classrooms, an idea supported by Calhoun (2002). Through the combination of these activities, theory and action are connected and teachers create what Fechco calls a "distinctive interpretive community" of professionals with a collective voice that can be heard and can effect change (p. 266).

The National Board of Professional Teaching Standards (NBPTS) also clearly indicate that teachers should engage in research on their own practice, and they include the expectation that teachers study professional literature and base their practitioner studies on findings from research. For example, the Early Childhood/Generalist Standards state:

> [Accomplished teachers] may also conduct research in their classrooms or collaborate with other professionals to examine their practice critically. For example, they may conduct systematic classroom-based inquiry to solve problems or answer questions related to their teaching practice. They select from theories, emerging practices, current debates, and promising research findings those that could improve their practice. In doing so, they explore topics in which they may have limited expertise and experiment with alternative resources, approaches, and instructional strategies to improve their teaching. Accomplished teachers consider the prevailing research findings about young children, learning, and intelligence while acknowledging the limitations of this evidence. They are able to distinguish trends from real breakthroughs and hype from knowledge. They are conscious that not all ideas about how practice should change are good. They stay current with and evaluate professional and other literature and curricular materials affecting families and schooling in their community. (NBPTS, 2001, p. 60)

The NBPTS standards for other subjects and grade levels include similar language, indicating the value of reviewing literature and learning from published research to inform educational practices.

So how exactly does reviewing the literature help a practitioner engaged in action research? To answer that question, consider this example: Jack, our middle school reading teacher from Chapter 2, wants to study the effectiveness of using reading clubs to increase students' engagement with literature. Reviewing literature about reading clubs can help Jack identify their potential benefits. Literature on reading clubs might also provide information about activities that make them successful and unsuccessful. If, for example, other studies have found that reading clubs with more than eight participants are difficult to manage, it would be sensible for Jack to plan for the club to have fewer than eight students or to create several clubs with eight or fewer members in each. Reviewing published research may also help in identifying ways to observe and measure student engagement.

SOURCES OF TOPIC-SPECIFIC LITERATURE

Various sources, such as books, journal articles, and conference papers, may be used as resources when reviewing literature. In some cases, educational books are especially useful in the process of reviewing the literature. For example, Jack, the teacher who is interested in starting a reading club, might find Harvey Daniels' (2002) book *Literature Circles: Voice and Choice in Book Clubs and Reading Groups* or Day, Spiegel, McLellan, and Brown's (2002) book *Moving Forward with Literature Circles* to be good resources for learning how to structure an effective reading club. In addition, though, Jack would also want to read research related to the implementation of book clubs. Journal articles (and possibly papers presented at professional conferences) on book clubs could be reviewed to determine what other researchers and educators have found in their studies about using book clubs in classrooms. Thus, whereas Daniels' book on literature circles would inform Jack about strategies for forming a reading club, journal articles would inform him of others' results when they implemented reading clubs in their settings.

Sources of literature vary in terms of ways they are useful in the process of action research. Usefulness can depend greatly on the type of literature chosen to review. For example, in searching for literature on reading clubs, Jack is likely to find books on reading clubs as well as articles in the form of reviews of literature, opinion pieces, teaching suggestions, and research studies. These different types of literature vary in their usefulness for informing Jack's own study on reading clubs. Books that explain ways to set up reading clubs can be very helpful, particularly if the book's author(s) have based their suggestions on extended experience with implementing reading clubs. Reviews of literature, which largely contain information about other researchers' findings on reading clubs, could also be helpful to Jack because literature reviews contain a number of references, and references of those studies that closely resemble what Jack hopes to accomplish can be located and reviewed. Finding a well-written, complete, recent literature review on reading clubs could save Jack a lot of time reviewing the literature because it would provide a review of (and a list of) much of the reading club literature.

Opinion pieces and teaching suggestions are generally less helpful when reviewing literature because they are typically written based on experience and instinct and contain little or no data to support the authors' contentions or suggestions. Research studies, however, can be very helpful for informing educators' action research studies. Unlike opinion pieces and teaching suggestion articles, research studies are based on the authors' actual structured studies of particular topics. Research studies include data to support results, and they can provide various forms of helpful information regarding ways to implement reading clubs, ways to measure outcomes, and ways to analyze sources of data. One note of caution, however: Some research studies, particularly quantitative studies that involve use of inferential statistics to analyze data, can be difficult to understand. One strategy I use when reviewing studies such as these is to read the article several times and make notes or highlight the basics, including: What was the research question or hypothesis? What was the intervention? What types of data were collected? What were the results? What conclusion did the author(s) make about the intervention? The most difficult part for me is sifting through the results, especially when complicated inferential statistical methods have been employed. However, even in a sea of numbers and statistical jargon, an author will almost always plainly state the results. For example, here is part of the *Results* section of an article by Blum, Lipsett, and Yocum (2002) entitled *Literature Circles: A Tool for Self-Determination in One Middle School Inclusive Classroom:*

> The students' responses to the two surveys demonstrated that the students did have an understanding of the difficulties they faced as readers. Based on the classroom teacher's understanding of the students, it is believed that the self-assessments were accurate. The first analysis of variance (ANOVA) compared the means of the survey responses, and significant differences were found between the two groups. The members of the target group recognized that their reading skills were not as good as those of the remainder of the class, $F = 6.513$, $p = .024$. These students reported that they had difficulty understanding what they read, $F = 21.344$, $p < .001$; remembering what they read, $F = 19.045$, $p = .001$; and explaining what they read, $F = 7.519$, $p = .017$. . . . After a semester of practice, the second survey showed a dramatic change in comparisons of group means. The second ANOVA showed that the significance in three of the four areas had disappeared: self-assessment, $F = 2.773$, $p = .120$; remembering what they read, $F = 2.920$, $p = .111$; and explaining what they read,

F = 1.019, p = .331. In the area of understanding what they read, the target group still perceived a significant difference between themselves and the remainder of the class, F = 5.735, p = .032. However, this difference was not as dramatic as in the initial survey. (pp. 104–105)

Although some of the information—such as use of ANOVA and inclusion of F values and p-values—may be unclear, the other information provided is fairly simple to understand. At the beginning of the study, the target students felt their reading skills were lower than other students' skills, and they said they had difficulty understanding, remembering, and explaining what they read. After a semester of practice [in the reading circle], the target students were more confident in their reading skills, remembering what they read, and explaining what they read. However, they still believed they were not as capable as their peers in understanding what they read.

Some published research studies may contain so much technical statistical information that they are not very useful for informing practitioner research. In working with practitioner researchers, the decision is often made to forego review of extremely technical articles because understanding them requires the specialized knowledge and skills of individuals who have been trained in quantitative analysis. A good rule to use when determining whether to include a technical article is to ask, "Does this study contain the kind of information that can help inform my practice as an educator?" If the answer is yes but you lack the prerequisite knowledge to understand the article without assistance, ask a person skilled in quantitative analysis (such as the school district assessment coordinator, a colleague who has taken statistics courses, or a university faculty member) to help you make sense of the article.

SEARCHING FOR LITERATURE TO REVIEW

There are a number of ways to find topic-related literature to review, and many resources are available online, which increases the availability of sources. It is *not* recommended, however, to find information by conducting a search using an Internet search engine. Searching this way may result in a number of websites that include information on the research topic, but the quality of the information is unknown. Also, much information found this way will not be the type of information that is useful when reviewing literature. A better way to search for articles on issues in educational research is to use a computerized database such as *ERIC, ProQuest,* and/or *EBSCOhost.* These three databases can be accessed from any computer with Internet access. However, accessing ProQuest and EBSCOhost through a university library will yield a greater number of free, full-text online articles because college and university libraries typically subscribe to a number of full-text journals. If you access an online database without going through a library, there is a greater chance that you will have to pay to read and/or receive journal articles.

Another way to access journal articles is through journal websites. *Networks: An Online Journal for Teacher Research* currently publishes three issues per year, and all articles are available full text through the journal's website, which can be accessed at http://education.ucsc.edu/faculty/gwells/networks/. *Early Childhood Research and Practice* (http://www.ecrp.uiuc.edu/) is another journal that makes full-text articles available at its website Table 3.1, which can be found at the end of this chapter, provides a list of educational journals that can be accessed via the web. While some of these journals make available all articles free to the public, others may provide only tables of contents, abstracts, or a limited number of free articles per issue.

Yet another way to find resources on a research topic is to check with the school or school system media specialist to determine which journals are available in the school media center. Media specialists in P–12 schools often subscribe to a number of journals for teachers' and administrators' use, and these journals can be reviewed for relevant articles. Though it is a bit more time consuming than using a computer database, browsing through hard copy journals can often result in locating relevant articles that can inform the educator's action research study. However, to save time, ERIC can be utilized to search for articles in the particular journals available in the media center. This process will be described in more detail in the next section of this chapter.

When using online databases, searches are conducted using keyword descriptors. Keywords or descriptors are terms related to the topic of interest. Jack, our example teacher, could start with the keyword *reading club* as he begins his database search. Searching using this term will result in a list of articles in which this keyword is found. Searching ERIC using the keyword *reading club* resulted in over 100 matches. Searching other databases is a similar process of looking for matches based on keywords or descriptors. Because each database is slightly different, the three subsequent subsections of this chapter provide guidance in searching the ERIC, ProQuest, and EBSCOhost databases.

ERIC

The ERIC homepage can be accessed online at http://www.eric.ed.gov/. Instructions for using ERIC are available by clicking on the *Help* tab in the top righthand corner of the page. Figure 3.1 displays the ERIC homepage. You can begin a basic keyword search from the homepage by entering keyword descriptors of interest in the box that says *Search the Database.*

Entering the keyword descriptor *reading clubs* will search the database for all articles and papers that include the phrase. When I searched the database for *reading clubs,* 547 results were returned (see Figure 3.2). Results can be further narrowed by clicking on the tab that says *Narrow My Results.* Clicking that tab provides the opportunity to narrow the search by adding other keyword descriptors and/or ERIC thesaurus descriptors to the search and limiting results by publication date and publication type. Figure 3.3 displays results when results were limited adding the keyword *middle school* and setting the publication date range to 1999–2003.

Clicking on the article title of the matching document opens a new screen with more detailed information about the document, including an abstract and information on how to obtain the document. The EJ or ED number three columns the right of the article title is called the ERIC accession number and is used to identify each document. Thus, each ERIC document has its own unique EJ or ED accession number. An accession number that begins with EJ is an ERIC journal article, which means that it has appeared in a published journal. An accession number that begins with ED is an ERIC document, which means it could be a teaching guide, conference paper, opinion article, project description, or technical report.

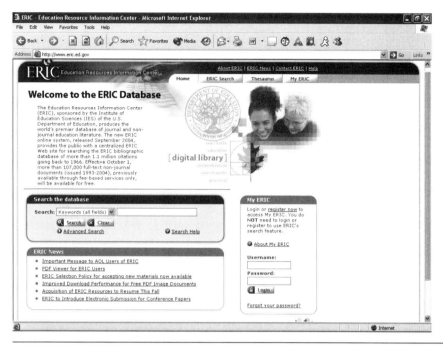

FIGURE 3.1   ERIC homepage.

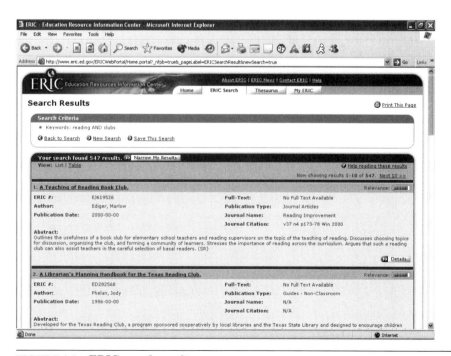

FIGURE 3.2   ERIC search results page.

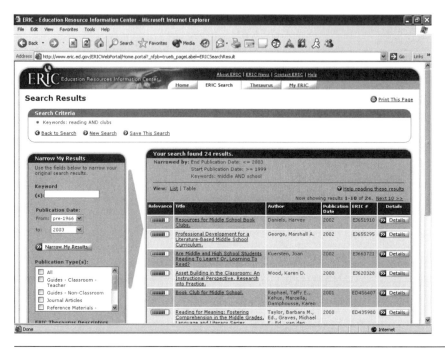

FIGURE 3.3   Limiting results in the ERIC database.

More often, research study articles will have EJ accession numbers. Although research studies sometimes have ED accession numbers, particularly those that are conference papers, be advised that a research article with an ED number has not necessarily been scrutinized through peer review, a method by which articles are evaluated by experts in the field before they are published.

Earlier it was mentioned that it is possible to use ERIC to search for articles in particular journals. This can be done by using the *Advanced Search* feature, which is available on the ERIC homepage under *Search the Database.* After clicking on *Advanced Search,* enter keyword descriptors, place the name of the journal in one of the search term boxes, and change the search field to *Journal Name.* Figure 3.4 illustrates a search of the keyword descriptor *literature circles* in the journal *The Reading Teacher.* This strategy can be helpful for an educator who has access to certain journals either personally or through a school library or media center and wishes to determine whether any topic-specific articles are available in those journals. This strategy makes unnecessary manual searches through stacks of journal issues.

ERIC searches can be expanded and narrowed by utilizing various search tools. As explained previously, results can be limited by adding additional search terms, limiting publication dates and publication types, and searching for articles in particular journals. ERIC searches can be expanded by using the online *Thesaurus* feature. Clicking on *Thesaurus* on the ERIC homepage provides access to the various terms related to keywords, which can expand a search by increasing related search terms. Detailed information on how to use the *Thesaurus* feature is included in the *Help* section on the ERIC homepage.

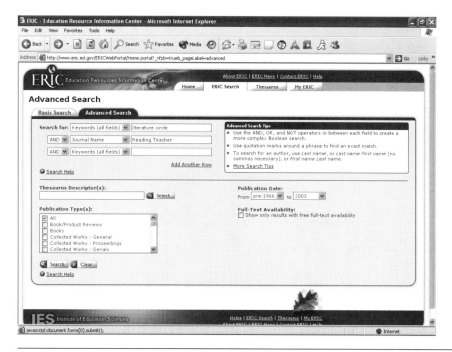

FIGURE 3.4   Searching ERIC for articles in particular journals.

ProQuest

ProQuest is an online database that provides access to full-text journal articles. When Pro-Quest is used to search the ERIC database, many of the matches are available for immediate viewing as either an HTML file or PDF file. Many university libraries and some public libraries subscribe to ProQuest, and it is necessary to go through a library website to use the database. University students can typically access the ProQuest database from home by going through their university library's website. The process of searching ProQuest is very similar to searching the ERIC database. Keyword descriptors are used and various fields can be searched to find matching articles. Figure 3.5 displays the ProQuest site as it was accessed through my university library's website.

Entering the keyword descriptors *literature circles* and *middle school* and then checking the boxes *Show Results with Full Text Availability Only* and *Show Articles from Peer Reviewed Publications Only* resulted in four matching articles (see Figure 3.6). Next to each article title are icons that indicate its available format. The summary icon (📇) indicates that the abstract is available for the article. Thus, clicking on this icon will bring up a screen that contains only the abstract of the article. The page icon (📄) indicates that the text of the article is available in HTML format. The page plus graphics icon (📄) indicates that the text and graphics of the article are available in HTML. Finally, the page image icon (📷) indicates that the article is available in PDF format, which means that it can only be read using Adobe Acrobat Reader. This reader can be downloaded free from the Adobe website (http://www.adobe.com/products/acrobat/).

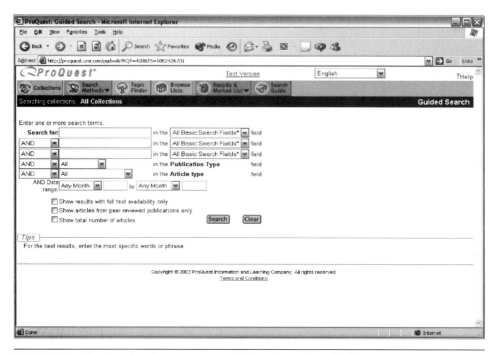

FIGURE 3.5   ProQuest main page accessed through a university library.

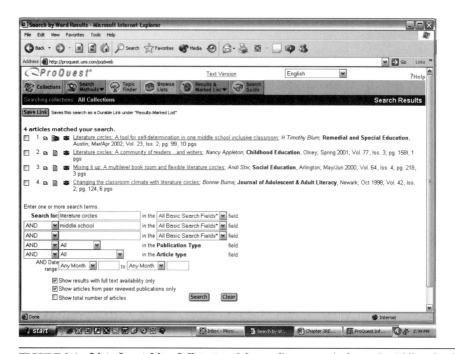

FIGURE 3.6   List of matching full-text articles on *literature circles* and *middle school*.

There are several ways to expand and limit searches using ProQuest. Just as in using the ERIC database, keyword descriptors can be added to limit matches or removed to expand matches. Limiting searches can also be accomplished by selecting certain fields to be searched (as was described when searching the ERIC database), limiting searches to full-text only documents, limiting searches to documents that were peer-reviewed (those that were reviewed and then recommended for publication by scholars from the author's field), and limiting searches to documents published during a certain year or range of years. ProQuest's *Topic Finder*, which can be accessed from the ProQuest homepage by clicking on the tab labeled *Topic Finder,* can be used to find articles on various educational topics. Clicking on the tab labeled *Search Guide* will bring up a help screen that provides detailed information on ways to search for articles using the ProQuest database.

EBSCOhost

The EBSCOhost database is similar to ProQuest in that the only way to access full-text articles through it is to access the database through a university or public library that subscribes to its services. EBSCOhost is different from ProQuest because full-text ERIC documents (rather than only ERIC journal articles) are available through EBSCOhost. Searching EBSCOhost is similar to searching using ProQuest. Keyword descriptors are entered to begin the search, and searches can be limited and expanded in the same way that ProQuest searches can be limited and expanded. Figure 3.7 displays the EBSCOhost main page accessed through my university library's website.

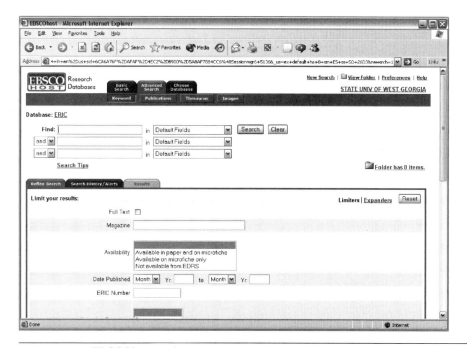

FIGURE 3.7   EBSCOhost main page accessed through a university library.

Entering two search terms, *reading clubs* and *middle school,* and limiting the search to only full-text documents resulted in two matching documents, illustrated in Figure 3.8. As indicated, one match is a journal article found in *Middle School Journal* and the other is an ERIC document that is available full-text in HTML format. The benefit of using EBSCOhost is that many full-text ERIC documents, which are not available through ProQuest, are available through the EBSCOhost. In addition, many full-text journal articles are also available through EBSCOhost in both HTML and PDF formats. Clicking on the document title will open up a summary screen that provides the abstract of the article as well as the full text of the article, if available. In addition, icons near the top of the screen can be clicked on to change the viewing format (HTML or PDF), if different formats are available.

Documents Not Available Full-Text

Searching only for articles that are available with full text can significantly limit the number of matches found, and it can result in missing relevant articles that could greatly enhance the quality and usefulness of the literature review for informing educational practices. Journal articles that are not available full-text may be available in hard copy form in a university or public library where they can be copied at minimal cost. Higher education students can also use their library's interlibrary loan system to order journal articles (as well as books) that are not available in their local library from other libraries. At many in-

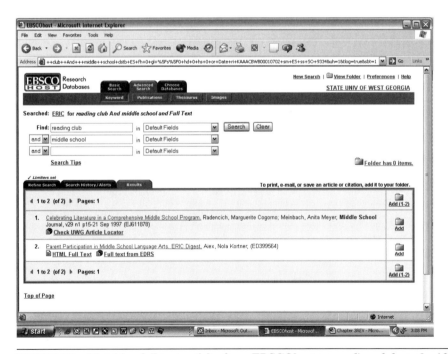

FIGURE 3.8   Matching full text articles from EBSCOhost on *reading clubs* and *middle school.*

stitutions, interlibrary loan is a free service, and often articles and books are delivered within a week of the request. Some interlibrary loan systems also use technology to speed up delivery time of articles. My library, for example, often receives articles from other libraries that have been scanned and delivered electronically. The point here is to make sure not to discount articles that are unavailable electronically. Accessing full-text articles is quick and relatively simple, but limiting a literature review to only articles that can be accessed immediately is counter to what thoughtful practitioners do. Instead, search for those books and articles that are relevant, are of high quality, and that seem to best be able to inform the educational practices that will be investigated.

CHOOSING, EVALUATING, AND SYNTHESIZING REVIEWED LITERATURE FOR ACTION RESEARCH STUDIES

The process of reviewing literature involves choosing relevant literature that can help to inform the action research study, evaluating the literature in terms of what it means and how information can be used, and synthesizing information so that major points or themes from the literature are used to guide the action research study. Reviewing literature is not a process of listing related articles or summarizing individual articles or books in separate paragraphs (which is actually an annotated bibliography). Instead, the process is one of finding themes in the literature that can be used to inform the action research study and organizing the themes in a logical, coherent way.

Choosing Literature

The previous section of this chapter provided guidelines for finding literature to review. However, after sources are located, the next step is to determine whether they are useful for guiding the action research study. The process of choosing literature takes time and patience. First, once sources are located, they should be quickly skimmed to determine whether they contain relevant information that can help serve as a link between the research problem described in the reflection and the actions that will be implemented and studied (refer to Activity 2.2 from the previous chapter). Consider Jack's research problem, which is to determine whether reading clubs can be used to increase students' engagement with literature. In his initial search for literature to review, he locates two books and nine research articles. Figure 3.9 graphically illustrates the nine chosen articles Jack located after searching ProQuest using the keyword descriptor *reading clubs.*

The original list of matching documents contained forty-four sources, but Jack skimmed the titles of each article and reduced the list to the nine most relevant titles. The box to the right of the figure contains coded notes Jack has made on each article as he skimmed over them. The codes are: LR—literature review; IG—instructional guidelines; RES—research article; REF—reference list provided; CS—case study; EV—evaluation methods provided. Thus, the first article, by Kong and Fitch, is a research article that contains a literature review, instructional guidelines, evaluation methods, and a reference list. Article 3 is a classroom case study that includes a literature review, instructional guidelines, and references. Article 4, though the title sounds promising, is a report on the establishment

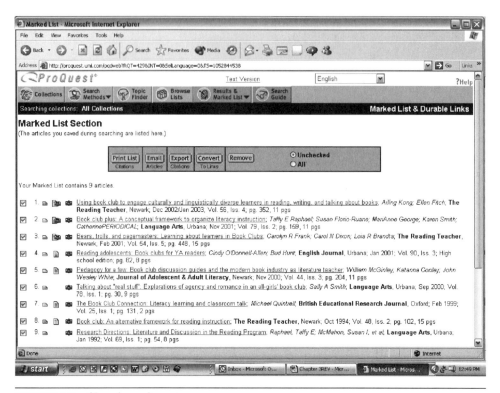

FIGURE 3.9   Choosing relevant sources.

of an inquiry-based partnership between college students and elementary and middle school students who are members of book clubs. Article 7 turned out to be a book review.

After this closer look at the articles, the next step is to carefully read each article to further determine the relevancy of each. In Jack's case, the first article is the only true research study in the list—which means it contains sections on identification of the problem, a review of relevant literature, a description of the methods used, results of analysis of collected data, and conclusions based on those results—though there are several case study articles that focus on results in particular classrooms. The first article focuses on a group of students who are culturally and linguistically diverse, which is a bit different from the setting in which Jack teaches. However, the article does discuss increasing student engagement, helpful strategies for evaluating student learning are provided, and the students in the study are just a few years younger than Jack's students. In addition, there are several references in the article's citation list that have interesting titles that Jack will locate. Based on the ways the article is useful and relevant, Jack would likely keep this article for now. Articles 5 and 6, however, do not seem particularly useful for helping guide Jack's study. Article 5 focuses on the weaknesses associated with book club discussion guides and their potentially negative impact on readers' analytical processes. Article 6 focuses on reading clubs for adolescent girls, and although the age group is similar to the age group Jack works with, the article focuses on talk among adolescent girls involved in a book club. Article 6 does, however, contain references that may be interesting and useful to Jack.

The process of choosing sources for the literature is one of constant decision making. What should be kept? What should be disregarded? How can a search be expanded if, in choosing articles, too few sources remain? In Jack's case, his search has thus far resulted in finding two books—Daniels (2002) and Day et al. (2002)—and just a handful of articles that are only peripherally related to the direction of his action research study. This, however, is a normal part of the literature review process. Searches must be limited and expanded depending on whether too few or too many sources are found. The next thing for Jack to do is complete another search using different search terms. Articles on literature circles may be helpful, and Jack might also want to expand his search using the keyword descriptor *increasing reading engagement.* When more matching sources are found, each article should be skimmed and the most relevant sources should be kept. Then a more in-depth reading of each article should occur to determine whether to keep the source or throw it out. In addition, reference lists in the articles should be scanned to determine if relevant titles are included. If potential sources are found this way, the articles or books must be obtained and read to determine whether they are good literature review sources.

Evaluating Literature

In choosing sources for the literature review, an initial evaluation is made regarding the relevancy of the source for informing the action research study. However, once sources are chosen, they must be further evaluated to determine the ways in which the reviewed information can be used to guide the action research process. Questions to ask in evaluating the literature include:

- *Relevancy:* Does the source provide information that can help inform my action research study? For example, does it provide information about ways to structure the intervention or innovation I am interested in trying? Does it provide conclusions made by other researchers on the intervention I want to implement? What can I learn from the source that can help me in the planning of my action research study?
- *Credibility:* Does the source seem credible? If the source is not a research study, are the claims and/or suggestions made by the author based on his or her extensive experience? If the source is a research study, are the results of the study supported by data and do the research methods seem sound?
- *Similarity:* Is information in the source based on the study of a setting that is similar to mine? Is it based on the study of participants (teachers, students, etc.) who are similar to the participants who will be in my study?

Synthesizing Literature

Once sources have been chosen based on their relevancy, credibility, and similarity to the action research study being planned, the next step is to synthesize information. Synthesizing involves connecting information into a coherent, integrated whole, and this process cannot occur until all relevant sources have been thoroughly read. In reading sources, common themes or topics typically emerge, and it is around these topics that a synthesized literature review is written. One common mistake in writing a literature review is to organize the review by sources, which results in a review that is simply a list of the information from each source. Instead of organizing by sources, the review should be organized by topic.

In Jack's case, several topics may emerge as he reads his sources, such as ways to structure reading clubs, the reading/writing connection, ways that students talk about books in reading clubs, the history of literature circles and book clubs, and the positive impact of reading clubs. Identifying these as topics means that several different sources have included information in each of these areas. As topics are identified, a determination must be made regarding the relevancy of each topic for informing the action research study being planned. For example, in Jack's case, he wishes to implement a reading club to get his students excited about literature. As Jack considers the topics he has located from his sources, he may decide that three seem most relevant. Because he has little experience with reading clubs, it is important to him to read all he can on how best to structure one. Thus, one topic he will review is the structuring of reading clubs. Also, because he wants to learn all he can about the positive ways reading clubs impact students (and to see if the literature supports his belief that reading clubs can get students excited about reading), he will review this topic, too. A third topic he is interested in is the reading/writing connection, because his students are even more apathetic about writing than they are about reading. For the purpose of this particular study, Jack chooses not to include information on the history of book clubs and literature circles or on the ways in which students talk about books in reading clubs because these topics do not, at this stage of his study, provide the kind of relevant information he needs to plan his own reading club.

The process of identifying topics and then choosing topics that are most pertinent is part of synthesizing information. Once related topics are chosen, they are organized and expanded into subtopics, and then a cohesive, synthesized literature review is written. This process is explained in more depth in the following section of the chapter.

ORGANIZING AND WRITING THE LITERATURE REVIEW

A simple yet effective way of organizing the literature is to make an outline using the topics and subtopics that have been identified from the sources. In the previous example, Jack narrowed his literature review topics to three subjects: the structure of reading clubs, the positive effects of reading clubs, and the reading/writing connection. Next, he must determine how best to present the information—he must choose a logical sequence for the information. As he considers the structure, Jack begins an outline, organizing the topics in the way that seems to make most sense. Next, he looks back to the literature to determine the subtopics associated with each main topic. For example, in reading his sources, Jack determines that there are several positive effects of reading clubs—improving reading comprehension, encouraging collaborative learning, increasing motivation and desire to read, providing opportunities for discussion, allowing students or groups of students to work at their own reading levels—and that these effects can be classified as *positive student effects* (improved reading comprehension and motivation) and *positive instructional effects* (encouraging collaborative learning, providing opportunities for discussion, and allowing students to work at their own reading levels). A structure starts to develop that can be graphically displayed in a standard outline format, which is shown in Figure 3.10.

Notice in Figure 3.10 that sources have been listed next to *improved comprehension* and *improved motivation.* In creating an outline, sources that support topics and subtopics

---

FIGURE 3.10   Beginning literature review outline.
Literature Review Outline for Reading Club Study

I.   Positive effects of reading clubs
    1. Positive student effects
        a. Improved comprehension (Daniels, 2002; Day, Spiegel, McLellan, & Brown, 2002; Raphael & McMahon, 1994; Kong & Fitch, 2003)
        b. Increased motivation (Daniels, 2002; Day, Spiegel, McLellan, & Brown, 2002; O'Donnell-Allen & Hunt, 2001; Raphael, Florio-Ruane, & George, 2001)
    2. Positive instructional effects
        a. Encourages collaborative learning
        b. Provides opportunities for discussion
        c. Allows students to work at their own reading levels

II.   Structure of reading clubs
    1. Selection of books
        a. Teacher selected
        b. Student selected
        c. Same/different books for each group
    2. Group structure and activities
        a. Group member roles/teacher role
        b. Scheduling meetings
        c. Fostering discussion and promoting participation
    3. Evaluation
        a. Teacher observation
        b. Student journals
        c. Self-evaluations by students
        d. Book logs
        e. Conferencing with teacher

III. Reading/writing connection
    1. Benefits
        a. Encouraging deep thinking
        b. Personal connection with the literature
        c. Connections across texts
    2. Informal writing
        a. Notes in books
        b. Journal entries
        c. Responses to prompts
        d. Letter writing to reading club members
    3. Formal writing
        a. Written book projects
        b. Letter writing to teacher
        c. Book reviews

---

can be listed on the outline, which makes it easier to use the outline to write the literature review.

In this example, Jack chose to·structure the main topics beginning with the benefits of reading clubs and then moving to structuring reading clubs and finally the reading/writing connection. Though the main topics could have been ordered differently, Jack felt that beginning with structuring reading clubs and then following with the benefits of reading clubs would result in a review that wasn't cohesive. Structuring the review that way would result in sloppy organization that would basically present the information as *Here's how to create a reading club—here's why reading clubs are good—here's how to connect reading and writing in reading clubs.* In his view, starting with the benefits of reading groups, which include subtopics covered in the subsequent main topics (for example, fostering collaboration is listed as a benefit under main topic one and then a description of how to encourage collaboration is further discussed under main topic two) helped to focus the review and provided a way to make connections among the various topics and subtopics. In this way, the information is presented as *Here are the benefits of reading clubs based on the research—here are ways to structure effective reading clubs—here is how to foster a reading/writing connection in a reading club.*

Whereas some individuals find outlining to be a simple way to prepare the structure of a literature review, others may find a prewriting strategy such as clustering (sometimes called idea mapping) to be more effective. In clustering, topics and their relationships are displayed graphically. Figure 3.11 illustrates how clustering could be used to design an idea map that displays reading club topics and the way in which these topics are related.

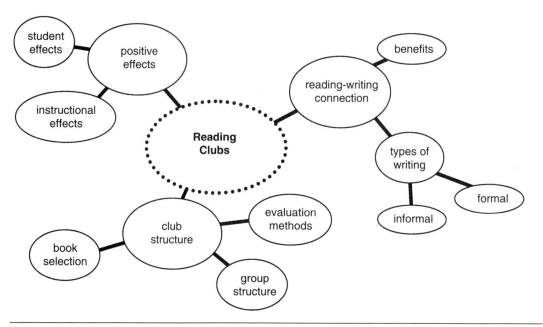

FIGURE 3.11   Reading club idea map.

In creating an idea map, the main topic is written first (reading clubs), and then subtopics are clustered around that topic based on the ways the subtopics are related to the main topic and to each other. An idea map like the one in Figure 3.11 can be developed prior to an outline, or it can be developed instead of an outline. If an idea map is used in place of an outline, sources should be connected to subtopics on the graphical illustration just as they were linked to topics in the written outline in Figure 3.10.

Once the outline or idea map has been completed and sources have been linked to topics and subtopics, the next step is to write the literature review. Writing the review requires synthesis of information under each topic and/or subtopic. This means that information from each source must be connected in a way that makes sense and that flows. Also, sources must be referenced in a scholarly format (typically APA in educational studies, though MLA is sometimes used) throughout the literature review. In Figure 3.12, a paragraph from Jack's literature review is included. Notice that the paragraph conveys information on one subtopic—the positive effect of increased reading comprehension—and that three different studies that relate to this subtopic are reviewed and cited. Notice, too, that the ways in which the studies are related or connected is made clear through transitional sentences or phrasing. For example, the fourth sentence begins "Other smaller studies also show the positive effects . . ." This phrasing lets the reader know that the previously described study by Daniels was a larger scale study and that other smaller studies reveal similar findings regarding increased reading comprehension.

Figure 3.12 is not meant to be a template for writing paragraphs in the literature review. Instead, it is one example of how information on reading clubs' impact on reading comprehension can be presented. A number of other ways would also suffice. Jack could have begun the paragraph with an overview of the various reading comprehension strate-

FIGURE 3.12   Example paragraph from literature review on reading clubs.

One of the positive effects of students working in reading clubs is improvement in reading comprehension. Daniels (2002) reports results from a study in Chicago in which teachers were trained to implement literature circles and reading-writing workshops in their classes. In grades 3, 6, and 8, students in these classes outperformed citywide gains in reading comprehension. Other smaller studies also show the positive effects of reading clubs on reading comprehension. Kong and Fitch (2002/2003), for example, studied the effects of a book club on students in a culturally and linguistically diverse, combined fourth- and fifth-grade classroom. Over the course of the academic year, students in the book club read eleven books that they both responded to in writing and discussed in various group settings. Comparisons of their comprehension strategies at the beginning of the year (before becoming part of the book club) and then at the end of the school year revealed gains in making predictions, verifying information, previewing, self-questioning, summarizing information, and drawing from background knowledge. A study by Raphael and McMahon (1994) resulted in similar outcomes. In their study of fourth- and fifth-grade students who were part of a book club for one to two years, the researchers noted gains in students' skills in synthesizing information, locating and discussing central themes, and taking on various perspectives when discussing literature.

■ ■ ■ ■ ■ ■

ACTIVITY 3.1
REVIEWING THE LITERATURE

Follow the steps for searching for literature to review, choosing sources, determining topics and subtopics, and organizing and writing the literature review:

1. Use online databases such as the library catalog (to search for books) and ERIC, Pro-Quest, and/or EBSCOhost (to search for articles, conference papers, etc.) to search for sources related to the research topic identified in Activity 2.3. Use keyword descriptors in your search. Acquire books, articles, and other sources found in your search.
2. Skim sources and keep those that are most relevant to your study. Next, carefully read each source and determine the relevancy of each. Keep the most relevant sources.
3. If necessary, expand the search to acquire more sources. Search using new keyword descriptors and acquire sources from the reference lists of the articles, books, and other previously acquired literature.
4. Read all sources and keep those that are the most relevant, credible, and similar to the study you are planning. Once sources are chosen, carefully reread each, making notes on the topics discussed in each reference.
5. Generate a list of topics that emerged from the literature. Create an organized, structured outline of these topics and add subtopics. Next to each subtopic, list sources in which the subtopic is discussed.

Research Paper Activity: Use your outline to write a draft literature review. Be sure to follow APA guidelines (see Chapter 8). Synthesize information so that information is provided on each topic/subtopic. Be sure that multiple references/sources are described for each topic or subtopic. Use transitional sentences or phrases in your writing to connect ideas. Use a heading for the literature review such as *Literature Review, Review of Literature, Connection to Best Practices,* or another appropriate heading. Place the literature review after the reflection written in Activity 2.2.

gies that have been shown to increase as a result of reading clubs, and then he could have followed that introduction with information from each specific source. One aspect of synthesis is determining ways to present information so that it is both organized effectively and connected to other relevant and related information.

Writing a review of the literature is a challenging task, even for individuals who have written a number of reviews for previous research studies. The task can be made much more simple, however, by carefully choosing relevant literature, spending time reading each source carefully and thoughtfully, thinking about ways sources are connected, establishing topics and subtopics, and organizing topics into a structured outline. Sharing the work with a collaborator can also help, and collaborating in the process allows for discussion and refinement of topics and subtopics as well as ways to organize and present information. There are also a number of internet sites on writing literature reviews that may be helpful, and two are provided here:

- University of Alabama-Huntsville: http://www.uah.edu/library/guides/litrev.html
- University of Wisconsin-Madison: http://www.wisc.edu/writing/Handbook/ReviewofLiterature.html

SUMMARY

The purpose of this chapter was to explain the steps of conducting a literature review, which is a necessary step in action research that allows educators to connect what is known from research (theory and best practices) with what will be done in the practitioner's particular study. Information was provided on the steps of reviewing the literature, which include searching library catalogs and online databases for sources related to the topic under study, evaluating and choosing literature, defining topics and subtopics from the literature through synthesizing information from all sources, organizing information, and writing the review. The focus of the next chapter is on using the information learned through the review of literature to plan an intervention that will be implemented in the action research study.

TABLE 3.1   Educational Journal Descriptions, Internet Addresses, and Online Availability

JOURNAL TITLE	TYPES OF INFORMATION PROVIDED	WEB ADDRESS	FULL-TEXT ONLINE
American Educational Research Journal	In-depth reviews of literature on topics in education.	http://www.aera.net/pubs/aerj	No. TC only.
The American Journal of Education	Research, theory, synthesis articles, policy, and practice.	http://www.journals.uchicago.edu/AJE	No. TC only.
American School Board Journal	Newspaper-type articles on various topics in education.	http://www.asbj.com/	Yes.
Bilingual Research Journal	Issues and research on bilingual education.	http://brj.asu.edu/	Yes.
Contemporary Educational Psychology	Academic research articles related to cognitive processes of learning.	http://www.elsevier.com/wps/find/journal_browse.cws_home	Yes.
Contemporary Issues in Early Childhood	Articles about research, reviews of literature.	http://www.triangle.co.uk/	Yes.
Current Issues in Education	Articles related to research, practice, and policy in education.	http://cie.asu.edu/	Yes.

(continued)

TABLE 3.1 Continued

Early Childhood Research and Practice	Research on the development and care of young children.	http://www.ecrp.uiuc.edu/	Yes.
Early Childhood Research Quarterly	Research on educating children through age 8.	http://www.elsevier.com/wps/find/ journal_browse.cws_home	No. TC & AB only.
Educational Action Research	Various forms of action research in education.	http://www.triangle.co.uk/	Yes.
Educational Evaluation and Policy Analysis	Academic articles related to evaluating educational policy.	http://www.aera.net/pubs/eepa/index.htm	Yes.
Educational Leadership	Articles on P–12 curriculum, instruction, administration, and leadership.	http://www.ascd.org/cms/index.cfm? TheViewID=347	Selected FT. TC given.
Educational Researcher	Reviews on topics related to broad educational theories.	http://www.aera.net/pubs/er	Yes.
Educational Technology & Society	Research and commentary on the uses of technology in education.	http://ifets.ieee.org/periodical/	Yes.
Educational Theory	Discussions of theoretical problems in education.	http://www.ed.uiuc.edu/eps/ Educational-Theory/index.html	Archived only.
Education Week	Newspaper format.	http://www.edweek.org	Yes.
The Electronic Journal of Science Education	Research and literature reviews related to science education.	http://www.unr.edu/homepage/jcannon/ ejse.html	Yes.
The Elementary School Journal	Research on problems in the classroom.	http://www.journals.uchicago.edu/ESJ/	TC only.
English Journal	Teaching ideas for middle and high school English teachers.	http://www.ncte.org/pubs/journals/ej	Selected FT. TC given.
Exceptional Children	Academic research on teaching exceptional children.	http://www.cec.sped.org/bk/ec-jour.html	No. Current TC only.
International Journal of Education in the Arts	Research in the areas of art theory, music, visual arts, drama, dance, and literature.	http://ijea.asu.edu/	Yes.
Issues in Educational Research	Australian journal of research on teaching issues.	http://education.curtin.edu.au/iier/iier .html	Yes.

TABLE 3.1 Continued

Journal of Adolescence	Articles on teaching, research, guidance, and counseling of teenagers.	http://www.elsevier.com/wps/find/journal_browse.cws_home	Yes.
Journal of Cases in Educational Leadership	Research on the preparation of educational leaders.	http://www.ucea.org/cases/	Yes.
Journal of Curriculum & Supervision	Articles related to curriculum and supervision policies and related issues having to do with teaching, learning, and leadership	http://www.ascd.org/cms/index.cfm?TheViewID=365	TC only.
Journal of Learning Disabilities	Research on the education of individuals with learning disabilities.	http://www.sagepub.com/journal.aspx?pid=251	No. TC only.
Journal for Research in Mathematics Education	NCTM journal that includes research, literature reviews, and theoretical analyses.	http://my.nctm.org/eresources/journal_home.asp?journal_id=1	No. AB only.
The Journal of Scholarship of Teaching & Learning	Essays, academic, and action research studies related to education.	http://www.iusb.edu/~josotl/	Yes.
Journal of Special Education Technology	Research, policy, and practice related to the use of technology in the field of special education.	http://jset.unlv.edu/	Yes.
Journal of Technology Education	Research, theory, and philosophy related to educational technology.	http://scholar.lib.vt.edu/ejournals/JTE/	Yes.
Journal of Vocational Education & Training	Articles on work-related education.	http://www.triangle.co.uk/	Yes.
Kairos	Research on teaching writing using the World Wide Web. Geared toward teaching writing at the college level.	http://english.ttu.edu/kairos/	Yes.
Language Arts	Articles pertaining to classroom strategies, methods, reports of research at the elementary school level.	http://www.ncte.org/pubs/journals/la	No. TC only.

(continued)

TABLE 3.1   Continued

Language Learning & Technology	Research related to teaching foreign languages.	http://llt.msu.edu/	Yes.
Learning & Leading with Technology	Articles emphasizing practical ideas about technology in the K–12 curriculum.	http://www.iste.org/LL/32/3/index.cfm	TC & selected FT.
The Mathematics Educator Online	Literature reviews, article critiques, academic and action research.	http://jwilson.coe.uga.edu/DEPT/TME/ TMEonline.html	Yes.
Mathematics Teacher	NCTM journal. Articles on improving math education in grade 8 and above.	http://www.nctm.org/publications/index. htm#journals	TC & selected FT.
Mathematics Teaching in the Middle School	NCTM journal. Provides teaching strategies for use with middle school students.	http://www.nctm.org/publications/ index.htm#journals	TC & selected FT.
National Forum of Educational Administration and Supervision Journal	Articles related to school administration and supervision.	http://www.nationalforum.com/	Yes.
National Forum of Special Education Journal	Articles related to special education issues.	http://www.nationalforum.com/	Yes.
Networks: An Online Journal for Teacher Research	Educational action research studies.	http://education.ucsc.edu/faculty/gwells/ networks/	Yes.
On-Math. Online Journal of School Mathematics	NCTM journal. Teaching resource for math teachers.	http://www.nctm.org/publications/index. htm#journals	TC & selected FT.
Ontario Action Researcher	Educational action research studies in Canada.	http://www.nipissingu.ca/oar/	Yes.
Phi Delta Kappan	Articles related to policy issues, research-based school reform, and controversial topics.	http://www.pdkintl.org/kappan/kappan. htm	Yes.
Primary Voices K–6	Articles written by teachers on teaching strategies.	http://www.ncte.org/pubs/journals	TC only.
Reading and Writing Quarterly:	Articles on causes, evaluation, and remediation	http://www.tandf.co.uk/journals/titles/ 10573569.asp	No. TC only.

TABLE 3.1   Continued

Overcoming Learning Difficulties	of reading and writing difficulties.		
Reading Online	Articles specific to methods for teaching literacy.	http://www.readingonline.org/	Yes.
Research in the Teaching of English	Academic research related to teaching English.	http://www.ncte.org/pubs/journals only.	Archived FT
Review of Educational Research	In-depth literature reviews on educational topics in any discipline.	http://www.aera.net/pubs/rer/	No. AB only.
School Library Media Research	Research on instructional theory, teaching methods, and critical issues relevant to school library media	http://www.ala.org/aasl/SLMR/ archived.	TC & FT
The Science Teacher	Issues related to teaching science in secondary schools.	http://www.nsta.org/highschool#journal	Yes.
Social Education	Theory and practical ideas related to teaching social studies.	http://www.socialstudies.org/publications/	TC & AB only.
Social Studies and the Young Learner	Practical ideas for teaching social studies K–6.	http://www.socialstudies.org/publications/	No.
Teachers and Teaching: Theory and Practice	Research on teachers' thinking, reflections, and work.	http://www.tandf.co.uk/journals/titles/ 13540602.asp	No. TC only.
Teachers College Record	Articles on education-related issues.	http://www.tcrecord.org/default.asp	*Yes.
Teaching Children Mathematics	NCTM journal on activities and strategies for teaching math.	http://www.nctm.org/tcm/	TC & selected FT
Teaching English as a Second Language	Research and literature reviews related to ESL teaching.	http://www-writing.berkeley.edu/TESL-EJ	Yes.
Teaching Exceptional Children	Articles on methods and materials for teaching exceptional children.	http://www.cec.sped.org/bk/abtec.html	No. Current TC only.
Technological Horizons in Education (T.H.E.) Journal	Issues related to technology in education.	http://www.thejournal.com	Yes.

(continued)

TABLE 3.1   Continued

Voices From the Field	Action research and topics related to classroom instruction.	http://www.alliance.brown.edu/pubs/voices/	Yes.
Voices from the Middle	Descriptions of classroom practices in the middle school English classroom.	http://www.ncte.org/pubs/journals	No. TC only.

Key: TC (Table of Contents), FT (Full-text), AB (Abstracts)

*Must be a member, but membership is free at the online site.

CHAPTER FOUR

INITIAL PLANNING OF THE ACTION RESEARCH STUDY

CHAPTER GOALS:

- Explain the process of articulating research questions that are action-oriented and outcome-based.
- Illustrate the process of planning and implementing the intervention that will be used.
- Describe the processes of choosing research participants and engaging in collaboration.
- Provide activities that guide practitioners through the planning and implementation phase of their studies.

After completing a review of the literature on the chosen research topic, the next step is to plan the intervention that will be used. The information learned in reviewing the literature is used to guide the creation of the implementation plan. For example, in Chapter 3, Jack, our middle school teacher interested in increasing student engagement with literature by implementing reading clubs, reviewed the literature and learned ways in which reading clubs impact student learning and motivation, the positive instructional benefits of utilizing reading clubs with students, methods for structuring reading clubs and evaluating their effectiveness, and ways to connect reading and writing activities through the reading club model. This information provides a way to structure and evaluate the effectiveness of the reading club intervention Jack will use.

At this stage of the action research process, the first step is to articulate research questions. Next, the intervention is planned based on what was learned from a review of the literature. Once the intervention plan has been formulated, participants must be chosen, and collaboration possibilities can be further explored. Activities are provided in this chapter to help you complete each of these important initial steps in the planning process.

ARTICULATING RESEARCH QUESTIONS

The first step in planning an action research study is to clearly articulate research questions. A primary research question that is based on the purpose of the study should be articulated at this stage. In Chapter 2, a reflection activity (Activity 2.2) was completed that included a detailed reflection on the area of research focus. The reflection also included an explanation of desired outcomes for the project. In Chapter 3, a literature review on the area of focus was conducted. At this point in the project, it is time to write a primary research question that is based on the purpose of the study described in the initial reflection statement *and* what was learned in the review of literature. Considering both the initial reflection and the information gathered in the literature review are key elements in preparing a study that is aligned with the area of focus and with best practices found in the literature. To illustrate how the process moves from reflection to theory/best practices to the intervention plan, consider this example: Rosario, a third-grade teacher, wrote this initial reflection:

> Each year I seem to spend a lot of time working with students on their writing. With my third-grade students this year, I am spending more time than ever helping students correct spelling and grammar mistakes in their written work. We seem to spend so much time on these basics that I have little time to focus on other important concepts in writing, like using compound sentences and using adverbs and adjectives to make writing more interesting. Also, my students seem really turned off on writing. They groan when I give a writing assignment, and they act as if their monthly book reports are absolute torture. For my action research study, I would like to find a way to improve students' writing. I would also like to see a positive change in students' attitudes about writing.

Rosario's reflection includes a clear statement of the problem (spending too much time with writing instruction that is not helping; students' negative attitudes toward writing) and plainly stated outcomes (improvement in student writing and a positive change in students' attitudes). In the early reflection stage, however, Rosario was not ready to write research questions. If she had simply written questions based on her reflection, they would have lacked a key element: the *action* part of the action research process. To clarify, if Rosario had written research questions prior to conducting the literature review, they probably would have been questions such as *How do I improve students' writing achievement? How do I improve students' attitudes toward writing?* These questions provide no indication of any action (such as an instructional method) that will be taken to increase attitudes about and achievement in writing. Thus, Rosario first needed to consult the literature to review interventions that could be used to achieve her desired outcomes. Studying best practices provided her with a strategy to improve students' writing achievement and attitudes about writing.

In Rosario's literature review, she read about an intervention that involves students and the teacher working together to create grading rubrics that are used for evaluating student writing. In her review, Rosario learned that in other studies, students' writing achievement and attitudes about writing increased when they were able to have a say in how their work was graded. The process of creating the rubric helped students better understand the elements of good writing and made them more responsible for the quality of their written work. Because improvement in writing, more positive attitudes about writing, and increased student responsibility and ownership of their writing were outcomes Rosario desired in her own students, she decided to study the rubric intervention in her action research study. With an intervention decided upon, Rosario wrote her primary research question: *Will the process of creating and using writing rubrics increase students' writing achievement?* Rosario also had secondary questions: *Will the process of creating and using writing rubrics increase students' attitudes toward writing? Will using the rubric make students feel more in control of their learning?*

By returning to her initial reflection, considering the best practices information gathered in the literature review (specifically the information on the intervention using rubrics), and focusing on her desired outcomes, Rosario was able to write well-articulated primary and secondary research questions. As you begin formulating research questions for your study, remember to consider the initial purpose of your study described in your reflection, the desired outcomes of your study, *and* what you learned in your literature review as you write your research questions. Research questions should include the intervention (the action that will be taken) and the desired outcome. Begin by listing a primary or main research

■ ■ ■ ■ ■

ACTIVITY 4.1
ARTICULATING RESEARCH QUESTIONS

Begin by referring to your reflection and purpose of your classroom-based action research study. Next, reread your literature review.

1. State your primary research question. Make sure that this question is aligned with your initial reflection and your literature review. Your question should include the intervention you will use and the outcome you desire.
2. State no more than three secondary questions. These questions should be aligned with your initial reflection and your literature review. Include the intervention and desired outcomes.

(?) Has the direction of your study changed after reviewing the literature? If so, rewrite your initial reflection to indicate this change and to ensure that it is aligned with your new purpose and desired outcomes. This kind of change is normal in action research.

Journal Activity: As new questions emerge during your study, write them in your journal. Mark all questions so that you can find them easily. Highlight these questions in the same color, use sticky notes, or utilize another method to mark and keep track of emerging questions.

Research Paper Activity: Write a paragraph on the purpose of your study followed by the primary and secondary questions that are the focus of your investigation. Label this section *Purpose and Research Questions* (or similar heading). Place this section of the paper after the literature review (Activity 3.1).

question. Next, list one or two secondary questions. As you begin your study, you do not want to focus on a lot of secondary questions. If there are too many secondary questions, it will be difficult to focus on the primary research question. Also, as the study progresses, many new questions will come up, and these questions are typically much more important in understanding the outcomes of the study than the scores of secondary questions that can be generated before the study even begins.

PLANNING THE INTERVENTION

After writing primary and secondary research questions, the next step of the action research process is to create the intervention plan, which should be based on the best practices reviewed in the literature. In the plan, you should clearly describe the intervention you will use and its relation to the literature reviewed, and the plan should be written with enough detail so that other teachers or administrators could read the plan and use it in their settings. It is important to describe the activities included in the intervention and the length of the intervention (How long will the intervention last? How long are individual sessions? How much time will be devoted to the activities in the intervention?). Look back to Rosario's reflection and research questions in the previous section. In planning and describing her intervention, Rosario needs to explain the rubric activity that students will engage in, and she needs to provide a timeframe for the study. Rosario's intervention plan might look like this:

> As described by Skillings and Ferrell (2000), when students are part of the process of creating scoring rubrics, they develop a better understanding of what counts as good work, and they are able to develop the metacognitive skills necessary to monitor their own learning and understanding. With this in mind, the students and I will collaborate in the creation of a rubric that will be used to evaluate the monthly book reports. During the first four days of the intervention, we will work on the rubric activities for approximately one hour per day. On the first day of the intervention, I will describe what a rubric is, and I will provide several examples of rubrics for students to study. Students will have copies of rubrics, and we will discuss the type of information included on a rubric. On the first day I will also explain that we will develop a rubric together that will be used to grade book reports. On the second day, I will ask students to provide suggestions about what categories should be incorporated on the book report rubric (such as capitalization, punctuation, spelling, description, etc.), and I will provide guidance to ensure that certain nonnegotiable categories are included. On the third day, we will work to create scoring levels in each category. On the fourth day, students will work in pairs to score their book reports from last month using the rubric. Students will discuss the way they scored their own work and their partner's work using the rubric. After this activity, we will work in a large group to discuss difficulties or questions using the rubric, and we will refine the rubric as needed. Approximately one week later, students will begin working on their October book reports. They will be instructed to use the rubric as they write their book reports. Two days before the book report due date, students will work in pairs to evaluate each other's book reports using the rubric, and then students will have the opportunity to seek guidance from me on unclear points. Students will make any necessary revisions to their book reports before turning them in. Students will be required to turn in a rubric with their own evaluation of their book report. These rubric activities (writing the book report with the rubric, reviewing reports with partners, and turning in a completed

rubric with the book report) will be required on each book report for the remainder of the school year.

Rosario's plan could also be graphically represented in a lesson plan format, as shown in Figure 4.1.

FIGURE 4.1   Rosario's intervention plan: Lesson plan format.

WEEK 1				
Monday 9:00–9:55	*Tuesday 9:00–9:55*	*Wednesday 9:00–9:55*	*Thursday 9:00–9:55 10:15-10:35*	*Friday 9:00–9:30*
Rubric description. Students will study example rubrics. *Goal explanation:* Students and I will create a rubric that will be used to grade students' book reports.	Review of rubric description. Students will review example rubrics. Students generate ideas about what to incorporate into book report rubric.	Review of rubric description. Review of student-determined rubric categories. Students review scoring levels on example rubrics. Students develop scoring levels for book report rubric.	Review of student-developed rubric categories and scoring levels. Students work in pairs to score last month's book reports using newly developed rubric. Rubric scoring discussion/ questions. Rubric refinement.	Additional time for rubric discussion and rubric refinement, as necessary.

WEEK 3				
Monday 9:00–9:55	*Tuesday 9:00–9:55*	*Wednesday 9:30–9:45 10:15-11:00*	*Thursday 9:00–9:45*	*Friday*
Review of student-generated book report rubric. Students begin October book report, using rubric to write and evaluate report.	Review of student-generated book report rubric. Book report writing.	Rubric review: using the rubric to score book reports. Students work in pairs to evaluate their partner's book report using rubric. Rubric conferencing.	Students revise book reports based on feedback on rubric scored by partner.	Book report and self-scored rubric due.

Rosario's plan includes an understandable intervention plan that could be used by another teacher wishing to use a similar rubric activity. An initial timeline is included that will help Rosario stay focused on her plan. It should be noted that the plan does not have to be laid out in precisely this way focusing on activities of each day. Instead, this is just one way of describing an intervention. Consider, too, that the daily interruptions faced by teachers may mean that Rosario will alter the plan as she goes, but that is a typical part of the action research process that will not interfere with Rosario's completing the intervention, even if it means taking a few more days to get through the activities.

Once you have designed a good research plan, but before implementing the plan, you need to consider who the participants will be and how (if at all) collaboration will occur during the study.

Participants

Who will be part of your research study? Will you conduct your action research study on all students, students in one class, a small group of students, teachers, staff, or others? In Rosario's study, her participants will be all the third graders in her class. As Rosario plans her study, she might also consider asking students' parents to participate in her study. For example, if Rosario wishes to determine whether students are more positive about completing their book report activities when rubrics are used, she could survey parents about their children's attitudes as they work on their book reports at home. She may also solicit information from parents about any comments their children have made outside of school about the rubric activity, writing the book reports, or writing in general. Parents could be a good source of information on the effects of the rubric activity beyond Rosario's classroom.

The teachers and administrators with whom I have worked frequently ask parents of students to be research participants in their action research projects. Parents can do more than simply provide a source of data. Sometimes they become part of the study itself, helping with classroom activities, planning with teachers, or offering input on interventions. When parents are asked to participate, they often become excited about their participation, which builds positive relationships between educators and parents and provides the educator with a valuable ally who is just as invested in student learning as the educator is.

As you consider who will participate in your study, remember that a participant is anyone who can contribute in any way to your study. This might include colleagues, parents, and students. Remember, too, that you are not just the researcher in your project; you, too, are a participant. Though you may believe at this early stage of the process that action research is about gathering information on others, a larger part of action research is learning about yourself.

One thing to be mindful of as you determine who will participate in your study is keeping your study manageable. If you are a teacher who has several different groups of students each day, you should think about focusing on just one class or one group of students for your first action research study. This will help to ensure that your study is manageable, which will increase your ability to conduct the study effectively. Often, teachers and administrators want to include large numbers of participants in their first action research studies. But having many participants means having to develop a more complicated research plan. It also means having more data to collect and analyze. If this is your first time conducting a study in your classroom, school, or district, focus this initial study on a small number of participants. This will help ensure that you are able to conduct your study the right way, which will allow you to learn how to do action research effectively. You will also have a better chance to develop a sense of the work and time commitments needed in the action research process. Once you are an experienced action researcher, you will be able to commit to larger projects with more participants.

Collaboration

As mentioned in Chapter 1, collaboration is an aspect of various forms of action research. In completing the reflection activities in Chapter 2, you may have engaged in reflective activities with colleagues, which is a collaborative act, and in reviewing literature you may have sought the assistance of colleagues, which is also a way of collaborating. There are several benefits of continuing the process of collaboration as you plan and implement your action research study.

- *Collaboration makes the work of educators a less lonely endeavor.* David Hobson (1996) and Anne Burns (1999) express concern over the isolation that many educators feel and suggest that collaborating on action research studies can serve to alleviate this sense of isolation. Hobson explains that collaboration in action research provides educators with the opportunity to work with colleagues to investigate problems and questions that have practical importance to them. Hobson, promoting the establishment of teacher research community groups, suggests that collaboration ". . .enables teachers to celebrate their successes with each other, create and re-create ways of helping groups of children, learn more effectively, and strengthen the connections teachers have with each other" (p. 96).
- *Collaboration encourages educators to engage in ongoing professional development.* Cole and Knowles (2000) explain that "collaboration is a powerful mode for the facilitation of learning and the propelling forward of professional growth" (p. 136). Thus, when educators engage in dialogue about improving teaching practices and when they work together to facilitate each other in moving conversations about best practices into their classroom activity, professional growth is a natural outcome.
- *Collaboration allows educators to gain multiple perspectives on critical educational issues.* In the action research courses I teach, I assign teachers to work in groups based on similar research interests. In a typical semester, there may be a group of teachers discussing using literature circles, another group discussing discipline programs, regular and special education teachers talking about ways to make inclusion work, and another group working on strategies to increase writing achievement. What I have found in my observations of these groups is that educators are often pleasantly surprised by the insight, experiences, and suggestions given by their peers. Colleagues can be an incredible resource when engaging in an action research project. You may find individuals who have attended inservice training on an instructional method you are interested in trying. You may find others who have read extensively on the topic you are investigating. Others may have found successful ways to deal with the research problem you wish to investigate. If you are a teacher, don't forgo

the possibility of collaborating with an administrator from your school or district. An administrator's broad range of experience and desire to assist teachers in engaging in best teaching practices make him or her a good ally and a good potential collaborator.

ACTIVITY 4.2
PLANNING THE INTERVENTION

1. Describe the intervention you will use in your study. Write in sufficient detail so a colleague could use your plan in his or her own setting.

Research Paper Activity: Provide a heading for the intervention (such as *Intervention, Research Plan, Innovation,* or something similar) and place this section after the section on participants (next activity).

Journal Activity: Keep a log of unexpected occurrences during the intervention (interruptions, extension or reduction of planned activities, etc.). These anecdotal notes may help explain outcomes as data are collected.

2. Describe the participants in your study. Start by describing your setting (school or district). Include information on the type of school or district, its size and location, and any other information that provides a snapshot of the setting. Next, describe the specific group of participants. Remember that context is important in action research. If you disseminate the findings of your study, it is imperative that you provide a detailed description of your participants to your audience. This will allow others to determine whether they might expect results with their own participants to be similar to your results. Consider including information on achievement or ability level, parental involvement, behavior, motivation, and engagement. When describing your school or district, consider including information on location (rural, suburban, urban), school climate, socioeconomic status, and special programs.

Research Paper Activity: Provide a heading for the participants (such as *Participants, Students, Sample,* or something similar) and place this section after the research questions (Activity 4.1) and *before* the intervention section.

3. If you are collaborating, describe who will be collaborating with you and the ways in which they will be contributing to your action research study. Explain each collaborator's role and how work will be shared in the collaborative group.

Research Paper Activity: Place this information in the intervention section. You may wish to use a subheading such as *Collaboration* or *Research Team.*

Journal Activity: Keep a record of collaboration efforts. Include information on collaborators, meetings, discussions, ideas generated, etc.

In addition to considering collaboration possibilities with individuals at your school, you may also consider working with a university faculty member or an educator from another school who you feel can assist you in your study. Cole and Knowles (2000) provide several benefits of working with outside researchers. First, levels of experiences and expertise are enhanced when outside researchers become part of your action research study. University researchers often can dedicate time and even financial assistance through grants to the project. Also, a university collaborator may be able to put you in touch with others around the world who are studying the same topic you are investigating (Cole & Knowles, 2000).

Yet another source of collaboration is having your participants serve as research collaborators. If you are a teacher, your students can be researchers with you. Instead of studying them, consider having them study themselves (much in the same way that you are now studying yourself in this action research process) and their classroom. If you are an administrator studying teachers, consider having the teacher-participants work with you as collaborators, rather than as only participants.

Cole and Knowles (2000) suggest several ways to involve students as research collaborators, and these methods can be extended to other types of participants—parents, teachers, staff—as well. First, participants can work with you to conceptualize the study, meaning they develop the area of focus for the study while you facilitate the process. Second, participants can become co-investigators, working with you collaboratively to develop an area of research focus. Third, you can take charge of identifying the area of focus for your study and then give partial responsibility for planning the study to participants. Participants can also become collaborators through helping with data collection (for example, conducting interviews or leading focus group discussions with peers), evaluating and interpreting the results of the study, and even helping plan future actions based on study results (Cole & Knowles, 2000).

The benefits of collaboration are extensive, and I hope that you have discovered in this section ways to make collaboration a part of your action research study. The books listed in the reference section for this chapter provide a wealth of information on effective collaboration. *Researching Teaching: Exploring Teacher Development through Reflexive Inquiry* by Cole and Knowles is a wonderful source of information in this area, and its authors provide sound suggestions for making collaborative efforts successful.

SUMMARY

The purpose of this chapter was to provide information on the steps of the action research process that occur during initial planning—articulation of primary and secondary research questions, choosing participants to be in the action research study, planning the intervention that will be used, and considering ways to collaborate throughout the study. Activities were provided to take educators through each of these steps of the process. In Chapters 5 and 6, the remaining steps of planning the study—including choosing data collection methods, gaining informed consent, and creating a timeline—will be described.

CHAPTER FIVE

STRATEGIES FOR COLLECTING DATA

CHAPTER GOALS

- Explain how collecting multiple forms of data increases credibility in action research studies.
- Describe various types of data—artifacts, observational, and inquiry—that can be collected to answer research questions.
- Illustrate ways to align data collection strategies with primary and secondary research questions.
- Demonstrate the ways in which baseline data can be used in action research studies.
- Provide activities to guide practitioners through the process of choosing data collection strategies that are aligned with the focus of their studies.

Before implementing the research plan developed in Chapter 4, you must decide on the data collection strategies you will use in your action research study. This process involves determining the types of data that must be collected to lead to meaningful, accurate, and appropriate conclusions regarding research questions. Also, multiple data collection strategies must be employed to establish the credibility of research findings. In this chapter, information is provided on ways to increase the credibility of your study through the collection of multiple forms of data and ways to align data collection with research questions. Numerous data collection strategies—organized in this text as artifacts, observational data, and inquiry data—are also included. The activities in this chapter are provided to help you choose the best data collection strategies for your study.

COLLECTING MULTIPLE FORMS OF DATA TO ESTABLISH CREDIBILITY AND VALIDITY

When planning ways to collect data to answer research question, a researcher must consider how to best ensure that the findings of study are credible and valid. Credibility can be established through **triangulation**, a process in which multiple forms of data are collected and analyzed. As David Clancy (2001) explains, looking at multiple forms of data when answering research questions helps the researcher fill in any gaps that occur if only one data source were used. Elliot Eisner (1991), who utilizes the terms *structural corroboration* when describing triangulation, explains that the purpose of triangulation is to ". . . look for recurrent behaviors or actions, like those theme-like features of a situation that inspire confidence that the events interpreted and appraised are not aberrant or exceptional, but rather characteristic of the situation" (p. 110).

To illustrate the importance of triangulation, consider an action research study conducted by a high school science teacher on increasing academic achievement in a college preparatory biology class by having students work in collaborative study groups. If the teacher reported that the use of collaborative groups was successful based on the fact that some students had higher test scores after participating in the groups than they did before participating in the groups, you would be wise to question the credibility of this finding. There are a multitude of reasons why test scores might have increased (for example, the unit studied during the intervention might have been easier or more interesting than previous units). If the teacher had collected multiple forms of data that all pointed to higher achievement during the collaborative groups intervention, then credibility of the findings would be increased. In this particular example, the teacher could have looked at many forms of student work in addition to test scores, and she could have observed the collaborative groups as they worked together. She might also have interviewed or surveyed students about their perceptions of the strengths and weaknesses of learning in collaborative groups. Analysis of various student work products (tests, papers, projects, etc.), observational notes, and interview or survey data would help the teacher determine the reasons the intervention was successful.

Consider the credibility of the results of the study if triangulation had been used and these were the findings:

- *Students' grades* increased, on average, by 7 points, and students with the lowest averages prior to the collaborative group intervention made the greatest gains.
- *Observations* of students indicated that peers were able to help each other understand difficult concepts, students asked more questions about unit content during the collaborative group work and during class lectures, and students were more interested and involved in learning during the unit than they had been when studying previous units.
- *Interviews* revealed that students felt like they were able to learn from their peers more easily than learning from the book or listening to a lecture, students spent more time preparing for class so they would be able to participate in their collaborative groups, and students studied for the unit test with their collaborative group outside of class.

Considering the results of these varied data collection strategies helps us feel pretty confident that the collaborative group intervention was successful and did indeed lead to higher

---

Triangulation: A method in which multiple forms of data are collected and compared to enhance the validity and credibility of a research study.

academic achievement for the participating students. Also, the observations and interviews help us understand why the intervention succeeded.

As you begin to think about ways to establish credibility in your own study, remember that it is imperative that you collect multiple forms of data to answer your research questions. You have probably inferred that triangulation involves having three data sources. In your own study, you may decide to collect more than three kinds of data, which is fine. The number of data collection strategies you will use will depend on the nature of your research question(s) and the number of research questions you are investigating. The more sources of data you have, the more likely it is that your findings will be credible. Keep in mind, however, that you don't want to collect too much data. Meaningful analysis of your data sources will take time, and if you have collected too many different types of data, you may have difficulty making sense of them.

Remember, too, that collecting multiple forms of data can help you answer the *why* questions in your study, which is an important part of any action research project. Look back at the collaborative groups study mentioned previously. Examining student work products helped the teacher conclude that the intervention was successful, but analysis of observational notes and the interviews were crucial for understanding why it was successful. In your own study, you may try an intervention that turns out to be unsuccessful. If this happens, looking at your varied data sources will help you figure out the reasons the intervention did not work, which is critical for ongoing reflective planning. Collecting multiple forms of data and triangulating them will help increase the credibility of your findings, and this will ultimately impact the validity of your study, which will be discussed in greater detail in Chapter 6.

METHODS OF DATA COLLECTION: ARTIFACTS, OBSERVATIONAL DATA, AND INQUIRY DATA

In this section three categories of data will be described: artifacts, observational data, and inquiry data. Artifacts include various types of student work and other items created by participants. There are many forms of observational data, including field notes, checklists, and photographs. Inquiry data are collected to elicit opinions, attitudes, and other types of feedback from participants. Surveys, questionnaires, interviews, and focus groups are typically used for collecting inquiry data. Table 5.1 includes the various forms of data collection strategies that will be described in this chapter for the three data types.

Artifacts

There are a variety of ways to use artifacts to answer research questions. Many action research studies conducted by teachers focus on increasing student achievement. If your study focuses on student achievement, you will want to choose student-generated artifacts, such as assignments, projects, tests scores, or other types of work, as a data source in your study. If you are an administrator and have decided to focus your study on teachers rather than students (for example, investigating the effectiveness of a new teacher mentoring program), there may be teacher-generated artifacts that would be useful sources of data in your study. These include lesson plans, teacher journals, and self-assessments. A third type of ar-

TABLE 5.1   Data Collection Strategies

ARTIFACTS	OBSERVATIONAL DATA	INQUIRY DATA
Student-generated: • teacher-made tests • standardized tests • written assignments • performances • artwork • projects • journals • self-assessment • peer review *Teacher-generated:* • lesson plans • journals • self-assessment • peer review *Archived:* • computer-generated reports • school records • documents	• field notes/observational records • logs • narratives • checklists • tally sheets • videotapes • photographs • audiotapes • organizational charts/maps • behavioral scales	• interviews • focus groups • conferencing • surveys/questionnaires • attitude scales

tifact—archived sources—may be useful if you wish to use school records in your study. A variety of archived information, such as computer-generated reports, attendance and discipline records, or standardized test scores, can be valuable data sources.

Student-Generated Artifacts.   There are many types of artifacts that can be used to measure students' attainment of learning objectives or students' progress toward nonacademic goals. Some artifacts can be used for formative assessment, which occurs during the instructional process to monitor the effectiveness of instruction or intervention. **Formative assessment** artifacts include *quizzes* and other written assignments such as *short papers* or *essays, homework,* and *worksheets.* Utilizing these formative assessments can help determine the effectiveness of an intervention continuously throughout the study. This is beneficial in two ways. First, if formative assessments reveal that the intervention is not working, reflective planning can occur during the study the intervention can be altered as necessary. Second, collecting various types of formative assessments provides an opportunity to see changes—in student learning or professional development, for example—over time. **Summative assessment** is used to measure instructional outcomes at the conclusion

Formative Assessment: A method of ongoing assessment used to determine whether progress is being made toward goals.

Summative Assessment: A method of assessment used at the conclusion of instruction or intervention to determine whether goals have been met.

of an intervention or intervention unit. Artifacts used in summative assessment include *projects, performances, papers,* and *teacher-made tests. Standardized tests,* which can also be considered a type of summative assessment, are not often used in action research studies, but they can be used if appropriate for the purpose of the study (for example, in a schoolwide study that involves utilizing a writing intervention for the purpose of increasing scores on the writing section of a standardized test).

Student *artwork* and student *performances* are often used in studies that take place in art, music, or physical education classes. For example, a band director interested in increasing his percussion students' ability to read music would use student performances as a measure of the effectiveness of his intervention strategy. Artwork can be used to measure both the acquiring of skill (understanding use of light and dimension in an art class) and changes in affective behavior such as how a student feels about him or herself. To illustrate this latter use of artwork, consider the example provided in Figure 5.1, which shows two pictures drawn by a first-grade student when he was asked to draw himself at school. In the first picture, which was drawn just prior to the action research study, the child drew his school and drew himself outside the school building. After an intense intervention aimed at helping this child succeed in school, he again was asked to draw himself at school. In the second picture, the boy has drawn himself smiling and inside the school building.

Other forms of student-generated data include student journals, self-assessments, and peer review. Student *journals* can be used for more than just recording feelings and emotions. Students can use journals to record learning struggles, successes, or personal accounts of growth and learning. When using student journals in a study, the first step is to think about the kind of information that the journals can provide. Students often need specific guidelines or prompts for journal writing, which can increase the chances that information in the journals will be useful. Here is an example: Consider an action research study that focuses on increasing writing achievement in a fifth-grade class. The teacher has decided to

FIGURE 5.1   Student artwork example.

utilize student journals for two purposes. First, the teacher will provide journal prompts to gather information about student perceptions of the writing intervention being used. Second, responses in the journals will be analyzed to determine whether writing achievement has improved. Some of the journal prompts used might be

- *The most difficult part of writing for me is*
- *Writer's workshop* [the intervention] *has helped me*
- *I still struggle with these things when I write*
- *Writing makes me feel*

To assess any changes in writing achievement from the journal entries, the teacher would need to use a standard form of assessment, such as a scoring rubric, to evaluate student work. The use of rubrics will be described later in this section.

Self-assessments are completed by students as they evaluate their own work or their progress toward a certain goal, which may be academic, motivational, behavioral, or affective. Self-assessments can be particularly useful as a type of formative assessment because they indicate students' perceptions of their progress toward learning objectives. If self-assessments reveal that students are struggling, the teacher can engage in reflective planning and make changes to the intervention as necessary. When self-assessments are used, the teacher must make clear to students that honesty and accuracy on the self-assessments are critical so that teaching activities can be planned to increase student learning or growth. This will help reduce the incidence of students providing positive, but inaccurate, self-assessments. Figures 5.2 and 5.3 provide examples of self-assessment. Figure 5.2 includes an example of an academic self-assessment.

In Figure 5.3 a behavioral self-assessment is displayed that includes a teacher assessment component. This type of assessment can be very useful for providing feedback to students showing how the teacher's assessment is similar to or different from the stu-

FIGURE 5.2   Academic self-assessment for reading comprehension (7th grade).

Rate your ability to do the following using a 0 to 3 scale. Your honest answers will help me figure out the best ways to teach you. (0 = I have a lot of difficulty; 1 = I am sometimes successful; 2 = I am often successful; 3 = I am always successful)

1. I can identify the main characters in a fictional story. _____
2. I can describe the plot of a fictional story. _____
3. I can use context clues to figure out words I don't know. _____
4. I can make predictions about what will happen in a story. _____
5. I can identify the conflict in a fictional story. _____
6. I can describe the differences between fiction and nonfiction stories. _____
7. I can identify the point of view from which a fictional story is written. _____
8. I can tell whether what I'm reading is a short story, novel, epic, drama, essay, myth, or poem. _____
9. I know what figurative language is. _____
10. I can interpret the meaning of figurative language. _____

FIGURE 5.3   Behavioral self-assessment for Johnny Vincent (Mr. Mathis, 4th grade).

Rate how you did in class today following the classroom behavioral objectives. Use this scale:

A = GREAT! B = Pretty Good; C = Could Use Some Work;
D = Could Use a Lot of Work; F = TERRIBLE!

STUDENT ASSESSMENT	BEHAVIOR	TEACHER ASSESSMENT
A B C D F	I stayed in my seat.	A B C D F
A B C D F	I raised my hand to speak.	A B C D F
A B C D F	I completed my work.	A B C D F
A B C D F	I paid attention to the lesson.	A B C D F
A B C D F	I did not disturb my classmates.	A B C D F

dent's assessment. It also allows the teacher to keep track of differences in student and teacher perceptions of assessment.

Peer review involves having a student evaluate the work of another student, which gives students an opportunity to provide and receive feedback from peers on their work or progress. Airasian (2000) explains that this process allows students not only to get feedback from their peers, but to also see another student's work, which serves as a model for comparison. Peer review can be especially useful when students are allowed to revise their work based on the feedback they get from peers. When peer review is used, standard criteria for assessment in the form of a scoring rubric should be used. Often, the same scoring rubric used by the teacher to grade students' work can be used in the peer review process.

No matter which types of student artifacts are used in the action research study, steps must be taken to ensure that the artifacts do indeed measure what they are intended to measure. For example, if a teacher-made test will be used as a type of summative evaluation in the study, the test must accurately measures what was taught during the intervention. So if a study focused on teaching students multiplication facts (2×9, 3×4, etc.), measuring their knowledge of multiplication facts using a word problem test (*Farmer John has three rows of corn with four seeds planted in each row. How many stalks of corn can he expect if all the seeds grow?*) would not accurately measure whether students know multiplication facts. Scrutinize your assessment methods to ensure that they are aligned with instruction. Ask collaborators or peers to look at your assessment methods and help you determine whether the methods measure what you want them to measure.

Also keep in mind that your assessment of student artifacts must somehow be standardized. Simply stated, this means that all work is assessed in the same way. For work that is considered subjective in nature, such as essays, papers, projects, performances, or artwork, steps will need to be taken to ensure that students are assessed in a standard way. The most efficient way to do this is to create a **scoring rubric**. Airasian (2000) defines a rubric as

---

Scoring Rubric: A guideline for measuring whether objectives have been met based on predetermined performance criteria.

. . . a set of clear expectations or criteria used to help teachers and students focus on what is valued in a subject, topic, or activity. Scoring rubrics are brief written descriptions of different levels of pupil performance based on the performance criteria. Rubrics can be used to score both performances and products. They are constructed by combining performance criteria into different levels of performance and ordering them in descriptive terms. (p. 166)

Thus, in creating a scoring rubric, the criteria by which students will be assessed must be determined, and then a decision must be made regarding how different levels of performance on these criteria will translate into an evaluation, score, or grade. If you will be creating a scoring rubric for your own study, there are several books on creating scoring rubrics that may be helpful to you, including:

- Airasian, P. W. (2000). *Assessment in the classroom: A concise approach* (2nd ed.). Boston: McGraw Hill.
- Arter, J., & McTighe, J. (2001) *Scoring rubrics in the classroom: Using performance criteria for assessing and improving student performance.* Thousand Oaks, CA: Corwin Press.
- Marzano, J. (2000). *Transforming classroom grading.* Alexandria, VA: Association for Supervision and Curriculum Development.
- Marzano, R. J., Pickering, D., & McTighe, J. (1993). *Assessing student outcomes: Performance assessment using the dimensions of learning model.* Alexandria, VA: Association for Supervision and Curriculum Development.

Also, there are some very useful websites for teachers who wish to create scoring rubrics, such as:

- *Kathy Schrock's Guide for Educators—Assessment Rubrics* (Available at: http://school.discovery.com/schrockguide/assess.html)
- *Designing Scoring Rubrics for Your Classroom* by Craig A. Mertler (Available at: http://ericae.net/pare/getvn.asp?v=7&n=25)
- *Rubrics: Scoring Guidelines for Performance Assessment* by Adele Fiderer (Available at: http://teacher.scholastic.com/professional/profdev/summerbookclubs/grade46/)

You may wish to conduct your own Internet searches using the keywords *rubric, scoring rubric,* or *grading rubric.* Two examples of scoring rubrics are provided in Figures 5.4 and 5.5. Figure 5.4 is a mathematics scoring rubric and Figure 5.5 is a public speaking performance scoring rubric.

Teacher-Generated Artifacts.   Many of the student-generated artifacts described previously are similar to the types of teacher-generated artifacts that can be used in a study in which teachers rather than students are the study participants. Journals kept by teachers are a good source of data, and they can be used to evaluate both affective and behavioral information. For example, if a principal or staff development specialist were interested in studying the effect of a mentoring program for first-year teachers, she might ask first-year teachers to keep a daily or weekly journal about meetings with mentors. As described in the

FIGURE 5.4   Math scoring rubric (Mr. Compton, 8th grade algebra).

SOLVING LINEAR EQUATIONS AND INEQUALITIES IN ONE VARIABLE.

	Advanced (4)	*Proficient (3)*	*Basic (2)*	*Emerging (1)*
Solution	Student demonstrates a thorough understanding of the concepts and provides correct solutions for all problems.	Student demonstrates good understanding of concepts and provides correct solutions at least 80 percent of the time.	Incorrect solution provided, but student demonstrates some understanding of concepts.	Student provides incorrect solution.
Procedure	Student uses correct procedures at all times.	Student uses correct procedures at least 80 percent of the time.	Student always or often uses incorrect procedures but demonstrates some understanding of how to use procedures.	Student uses incorrect procedures in an attempt to solve the problem.
Explanation of Solution	Explanation of solutions are correct and are provided for all problems.	Explanation of solutions are correct at least 80 percent of the time.	Explanations of solution are incorrect, but student can explain some procedures correctly.	Explanation of solutions are incorrect.

FIGURE 5.5   Public speaking performance rubric.

	Excellent (4)	*Good (3)*	*Adequate (2)*	*Poor (1)*
Clarity	Speaker clearly enunciates all words.	Speaker clearly enunciates most words.	Speaker enunciates some words.	Speaker does not enunciate.
Eye Contact	Speaker maintains eye contact with audience.	Speaker often makes eye contact with audience.	Speaker makes little eye contact with audience.	Speaker does not make eye contact with audience.
Grammar	Speaker makes no grammatical errors.	Speaker makes few grammatical errors.	Speaker makes some grammatical errors.	Speaker makes numerous grammatical errors.
Information	Speech includes many facts related to topic.	Speech includes some facts related to topic.	Speaker includes few facts related to topic.	Speaker includes no facts related to topic.
Volume	Speaker maintains appropriate volume level throughout speech.	Speaker uses appropriate volume level during most of the speech.	Speaker uses an uneven volume throughout the speech.	Speaker uses an inappropriate volume level throughout the speech speech.

previous section, journal prompts could be used to ensure that certain types of needed information are included in the journal. Prompts might include

- *The most useful information my mentor has shared with me was*
- *I wish my mentor would help me with*
- *My mentor has helped me with classroom management by*
- *My mentor has helped me with my instruction by*

Self-assessment and peer-review are other sources of teacher-generated artifacts. *Self-assessment* can be used to gather teachers' perceptions of their strengths and weaknesses, their understanding of state mandates, or their content knowledge. An example of a teacher self-assessment is provided in Figure 5.6. It should be noted that with self-report data such as this, respondents may provide answers that they think are expected of them or are socially desirable, rather than provide an honest and accurate self-assessment. With all types of self-assessments, it is imperative to explain to the respondents that honest responses are desired. Other methods, such as allowing respondents to remain anonymous or informing respondents that there are no risks in providing honest responses (and following through on this policy) may increase the likelihood that responses are honest.

Peer review as a teacher-generated artifact can be used to allow teachers to receive feedback from colleagues on various aspects of their teaching, which could include topics such as teaching effectiveness, participation in curriculum planning, communicating with parents, and classroom management. The self-assessment for first-year teachers provided in Figure 5.6 could also be used for peer review. For example, a mentor teacher or administrator could use the assessment to determine areas in which the new teacher needed mentoring.

Lesson plans are another type of teacher-generated artifact that can be useful in action research studies. For example, in an action research study that focused on training teachers to use a new method for teaching reading comprehension, the researcher would be interested in determining whether teachers were utilizing their training and using the new method during instruction. Evaluating lesson plans is one way the researcher can look for evidence that teachers are indeed incorporating the new reading comprehension strategy instruction into their lessons.

Archived Artifacts.   Archived artifacts, such as computer-generated reports, school records, and school documents can be useful sources of data in some action research studies, particularly those studies that are conducted at the school level. For example, a media specialist I recently worked with utilized *computer-generated reports* in an action research study she conducted on the use of the Accelerated Reader program at her school. In working with teachers, she observed that some teachers were not implementing the program—which assesses a student's reading level, allows the student to choose books to read on that level, and then assesses the student's success on a reading comprehension test—effectively or with much enthusiasm. The purpose of the media specialist's study was to train the teachers in the effective use of Accelerated Reader with the hope of getting them to buy into the program. One aspect of the Accelerated Reader program is that it generates computer reports for students and classes regarding each student's reading level and his or her rate of success on the reading comprehension tests. The media specialist was able to use these

FIGURE 5.6   Teacher self-assessment for first-year teachers at Griffin High School.

This self-assessment will be used to determine areas for mentoring during this school year. Our ability to provide the best and most useful mentoring for you relies on your honesty and candor as you complete this assessment.

Please rate your abilities in each of the following areas using the scale:
1 = I need a lot of help in this area
2 = I am making progress in this area, but I need some help
3 = I do not need help in this area

Also list your strengths and weaknesses in each area.

1. Classroom management   1   2   3

    Strengths:

    Weaknesses:

2. Use of class time   1   2   3

    Strengths:

    Weaknesses:

3. Lesson planning   1   2   3

    Strengths:

    Weaknesses:

4. Understanding the content I teach   1   2   3

    Strengths:

    Weaknesses:

5. Working with students who have special needs   1   2   3

    Strengths:

    Weaknesses:

6. Understanding school procedures   1   2   3

    Strengths:

    Weaknesses:

computer-generated reports to determine whether training the teachers to use Accelerated Reader had an effect on students' reading levels and reading comprehension. If you are utilizing software or computer program in your study, the software may generate reports on student progress that can be useful in your study.

School records are another source of archived data that may be useful in an action research study. School records can provide information on attendance, disciplinary actions, retention rates, or standardized achievement scores. Finally, *documents* such as PTA bulletins, committee meeting minutes, and school handbooks can be good sources of data, particularly if the action research study involves analyzing perceptions, goals, school culture, or procedures. For example, analyzing PTA bulletins can reveal issues that teachers and parents see as important. Analysis of the school handbook can reveal information on the culture, climate, and rules in a school. Studying committee meeting minutes can indicate how time is spent during meetings, what issues are seen by teachers and administrators as important, and how much progress is made toward achieving goals over time.

Observational Data

Observational data are the most important source of information in an action research study. Whereas artifacts can help decide whether an intervention has had an impact (for example, evaluating student work to look for gains in achievement), observational data can help determine why an intervention was successful or unsuccessful and how the context of the setting impacted the study. To illustrate, consider an action research study conducted by a principal on the use of teacher study groups to improve school climate. The principal could interview or survey teachers to determine whether school climate improved as a result of the intervention, but just knowing whether there was an improvement would greatly limit the credibility of the study. Observations of teachers as they worked in the study groups could reveal teacher attitudes and perceptions about the issues related to school climate. Continuing to observe the study groups throughout the study would allow the principal to see how attitudes and perceptions change over time, and the ongoing observations could provide the principal with the opportunity to understand how the complex issues dealt with by teachers interact to impact school climate. The deeper level of understanding that comes with good observational data collection leads to effective and ongoing reflective planning.

As you determine the best ways to use observation in your own action research study, you must consider how observational data will be used to inform your action research study, what it is you want to observe, who you want to observe, and what role you wish to play in the observation. First, how will observational data be used in your study? Is the purpose to evaluate how the intervention is working or how participant behavior is affected by the intervention? Deciding on the purpose of your observation will help you establish what it is that you want to observe. Good questions to ask yourself at this stage are:

- *How will observations help me answer my primary research question?*
- *How will observations help me answer my secondary research questions?*
- *What type of observations can best help me understand how the context of my setting affects the success of my intervention?*

Once you know what you want to observe, you must also determine who you want to observe. If you are conducting a study with a large group of students, it may not be possible to observe each participant. If this is the case in your study, how will you choose who you observe? Will you focus on those students who have struggled the most in the past? Will you choose only the high achievers? Will you randomly select a small number of individuals to observe? Will you systematically choose so that you are able to observe different types of participants? Will you simply make general observations of the setting? Once again, the best rule here is to focus on the purpose of your study and on your primary and secondary research questions. In order for you to answer your questions, who must be observed in your study?

Finally, you must consider the role you wish to play in observation. If you are a teacher studying your classroom, you will be a participant-observer. As a teacher, you cannot simply sit back and watch what goes on in your classroom. Even if you are observing students as they work in collaborative groups, you will still be teacher and facilitator—a participant in the classroom environment. In other types of action research studies, it is possible to be an observer without having to participate in the action. For example, a principal or administrator could observe a teacher study group without actually being a part of that group (though the nonparticipant status could change if the teachers attempted to bring the administrator into the discussion).

Although it is difficult to be anything but a participant observer in educational action research, the observer can engage in different levels of observation. For example, if it is critical to the purpose of your study that you engage in ongoing observation during your study, you will probably choose to make notes throughout the study, even during the intervention. If, instead, it is critical for you to stay focused on the intervention, it may be necessary to video- and/or audiotape during your study so that you can concentrate on teaching during the intervention and make observations from the videotape later. Finally, if it is important in your study to have some type of nonparticipant observation in order to get a different perspective of what is occurring during your study, you may wish to ask a colleague or collaborator to make some observations of your research setting. Comparing your observations with another colleague's observations is a method of peer debriefing, and it can be very useful for checking biases and getting a second opinion about what the observations indicate.

One method of collecting observational data is through *observational records* or *field notes*. Field notes are kept throughout the study and include detailed information about implementation of the intervention, participant responses, and surprising events. Field notes are best kept in a journal, and they should be entered each day of the study or each day the intervention takes place. Because you are both a participant **and** observer in your study it can be quite difficult to record detailed information as you are teaching or facilitating. It is more reasonable to jot brief notes as significant or noteworthy events occur, but it is critical that more detailed notes are made as soon as possible. Establish a time each day—during planning time, during lunch, or at the end of the day—to expand the notes made earlier. Remember, too, that it is not necessary to write down each and every event that occurred. Focus on making notes that are relevant to the study.

When you observe something that seems to be vital for describing or understanding aspects of your study, you may wish to write a *narrative* account of the event. A narrative is simply a detailed description of an event that is used to portray detailed contextual information. Consider this example: A fourth-grade teacher focused his action research study on a severely withdrawn and socially shy child whose withdrawal from peers was negatively affecting his classroom participation, acceptance by peers, and academic achievement. Here is the teacher's narrative account of Juan's activities after fourteen weeks of intervention:

Juan raised his hand, and when I called on him, he quietly asked me if he could work with Rita to complete his math sheet. Over the past three weeks, Juan has been requesting to work with Rita on some math assignments, particularly the ones he struggles with. Rita is a good math student but is quiet and reserved much like Juan, though she does participate in class and she has many friends. Each time Juan has worked with Rita, he has gone to her desk, watched her complete some math problems, and waited for her to say the first word. Usually Rita will ask Juan a question such as, "Which one are you stuck on?" or "What problem are you working on now?" Juan then points to the problem or quietly says the number of the problem. Of the several times Juan has worked with Rita, he has rarely said a word to her. Instead, he watches how she completes a problem, listens to her explanation, and then tries a problem himself as Rita shows him how to do it. Today, though, Juan went to Rita's desk and very quietly said, "I don't know how to do this problem [long division, worksheet 5.1, question 4]. I keep getting stuck here [what to do with the remainder]." Rita showed him how to work the problem and then asked him if he understood. This is the first time she has asked him a question like that. It appears that she took her cue from Juan. Because he was more vocal today—initiating a conversation—she was, too. Juan responded, "I think so," and then attempted to complete the next problem on his own. Rita watched without saying a word, and when he was done and had successfully calculated the answer, she looked at Juan, smiled, and said, "That's right! You did that really fast." This was the first time she had encouraged Juan in that way. Juan, who rarely looks his peers or me in the eye, looked at Rita, smiled, and said quietly, "Thanks." He then went back to his seat and completed his assignment. When he was done, which was much sooner than the majority of his classmates, Juan raised his hand. When I called on him, he came to my desk and showed me his paper, though students were not required or even asked to do this. I asked Juan if he wanted me to grade his paper then, and he nodded yes. I scored his paper and he missed only one problem, which was one of the most difficult. I showed Juan which answer was incorrect and he said, "What did I do wrong?" I showed him his mistake and explained how to fix it. Juan then went back to his desk with his paper, fixed his mistake, and then sat quietly. Marcus then came to my desk and said he didn't understand what to do. I asked Rita, Juan, and Melinda if any of them would be willing to help Marcus since they were already finished with their assignments. Even Juan said yes. Marcus chose to work with Rita, but when Samantha asked for help and I told her she could work with Juan or Melinda, she chose to work with Juan. Though he seemed a bit reluctant at first, Juan patiently showed Melinda how to work one of the problems. He spoke very quietly and at one point Melinda said she couldn't hear him. Juan spoke a bit louder then and continued to explain how to do the problem. After several minutes, Melinda said, "Oh! I get it!" She thanked Juan and sat down to complete her assignment. When I asked for volunteers to try some new problems on the board, Juan kept his head down, which is his usual behavior. However, he was attentive as his peers completed their work on the board, and he raised his hand to help Marcus when he was stuck on his problem.

This narrative was written from brief field notes (see Figure 5.8) jotted by a teacher during his action research study. Because it is difficult, if not impossible, to write detailed narratives during an observation, it is necessary to expand field notes soon after the observation to ensure that important details are remembered. Narratives such as these can provide much insight in certain action research studies. In the study focusing on Juan, the narrative account expresses the nuances of Juan's behavior that help us understand exactly how he is changing as a result of the teacher's intervention. The narrative is much more useful in understanding Juan as a person and in understanding the change in his behavior than a brief description such as, "Juan now works well with other children, asks questions in class, and has improved his grades from Ds and Fs to As and Bs." Keep in mind that writing numerous narrative accounts can be a time-consuming enterprise, so carefully choose the events that you wish to explain through a narrative.

Field notes and narratives are a great way to collect detailed information. However, it may be useful to make less detailed observations, in which case logs, checklists, and tally sheets can be utilized. A *log* is a running record of activities that is used to record events at specified intervals. To keep a log, you must first determine how often you will record events. For example, if you decide to record information every ten minutes, you must carefully observe the time and then each ten minutes write down what is occurring. A log is an effective way of keeping track of activities, but is not always useful to keep track of participant behaviors. Significant behaviors can happen at any time, not just every ten minutes. Figure 5.7 provides an example of a teachers' log.

FIGURE 5.7   Teaching log for Jurdell Jackson, Honors Biology, Period 2, 10/15/2003.

TIME	EVENTS
0900	Began class with focusing exercise on the amoeba. Assignment was on board: Draw and label all parts of an amoeba.
0910	Discussed collaborative assignment for today: In assigned groups of 5, students design a new single-cell life form.
0920	Students working in groups : reading assignment sheet, asking for clarification, making notes
0930	Students working in groups: Group 1: Students silently reading/skimming textbook Chapter 7. Group 2: Students engaged in debate about food source: Group 3: Group leader has assigned separate tasks to each group member. Group 4: Students discussing shape of their organism. Group 5: Students independently working quietly on sketches and ideas.
0940	Students working in groups: G1: Discussing all necessary elements to describe for project. G2: Discussing reproduction. G3: Still working on separate tasks; G4: Sketching life form. G5: Group members sharing sketches and ideas.
0950	Break for whole class question/answers.
1000	Each group completes progress sheet to turn in.
1010	Dismissal.

Logs can also be kept to record behaviors. Behavior logs are especially well-suited for studies that focus on increasing appropriate student behaviors. The log can serve as a running record of inappropriate behaviors and when the behaviors occur. For this type of log, behaviors are written down as they occur, and the time of occurrence is noted with each behavior. Behavior logs can also be used to simply record any type of observed behavior, which is illustrated in Figure 5.8. This log was later expanded into a narrative, which was presented previously.

Checklists and tally sheets are used to track types of behavior or events and their frequency. On a *checklist,* the researcher keeps track of behaviors that are exhibited or events that occur. A *tally sheet* is used to keep up with the number of times a behavior is exhibited. Both checklists and tally sheets are used to gather information at a point in time such as during a class period, at lunch or recess, during a group activity, or during a performance. Checklists and tally sheets can be combined, as can be seen in Figure 5.9.

Figure 5.10 includes an example of a checklist that could be used to monitor activities during collaborative work. An effective and useful checklist should include those behaviors that are deemed to be important in relation to the intervention or the desired effects of the intervention. Thus, in the example in Figure 5.10, the teacher has listed the desirable traits of effective collaboration (the intervention), and he uses the checklist to monitor which groups exhibit those traits. Analysis of the checklists and other forms of data that may be collected (student work, field notes, surveys) will help the teacher determine the traits that are necessary for collaborative group work to be most effective.

FIGURE 5.8 Behavioral log for Juan R., 4th grade, Mr. Brindle.

DATE	TIME	BEHAVIOR
Oct. 16, 2003	0946	Juan asked to work with Rita (math worksheet 5.1)
	0948	Juan initiated conversation with Rita: "I don't know how to do this problem [5.1, #4]. I keep getting stuck here [Remainder]".
	0950	Rita showed Juan how to work the problem and asked if he understood [new behavior/conversation]. Encouraged Juan. Juan made eye contact, said, "thanks."
	1002	Juan asked me to review his problems [new behavior]—only 1 wrong answer. Juan asked me to explain his mistake.
	1005	Juan offered to help Marcus and Samantha [new behavior]. Juan worked with Samantha. Samantha asked Juan to speak up.
	1018	Juan helped Marcus with problem on board.

FIGURE 5.9   Checklist and tally sheet for persuasive speech.

Student Name: Jonathon Thurman

Student maintained eye contact:	Yes	No
Student's speech was engaging:	Yes	No
Speech was organized:	Yes	No
Number of times student said "uh" or "um."	✔ ✔ ✔ ✔ ✔	
Number of times student looked at note cards.	✔ ✔ ✔ ✔	

Figure 5.11 shows an example of a tally sheet used to monitor behaviors. In this example, the teacher is studying the effects of a behavioral intervention for a child with autism who is mainstreamed in a regular fourth-grade classroom. Using tally sheets in a study such as this can help the researcher see how behavior changes over time during and after the intervention process. The tally sheet is different from a behavior log. On a behavior log, behaviors are written down as they happen. On a tally sheet, common behaviors—particularly those that are focused on in the study—are listed on the sheet prior to the observation. Marks are made during the observation time to note how many times, if any, the behavior occurred.

Behavioral scales, like tally sheets, checklists, and behavioral logs, are used to provide an assessment or evaluation of behavior. A behavioral scale is used to determine a general assessment of behavior rather than keep track of the number of times a behavior occurs. A number of behavioral scales have been created to allow teachers, counselors, administrators, and other school staff to provide data that can be analyzed to determine whether a student exhibits signs of attention deficit disorder, hyperactivity, characteristics of autism or Asperger's syndrome, developmental delays, behavioral problems and so on.

Video- and *audiotapes* are not observational methods but are tools for observation. Often, as a participant as well as observer in your study, you will lack the time to make observational notes on the spot. Also, as you teach or facilitate during the intervention phase

FIGURE 5.10   Collaborative groups checklist, Honors Biology, 2nd Period, Mr. Jackson, 10/22/03.

BEHAVIORS/ACTIVITIES	GROUP 1	GROUP 2	GROUP 3	GROUP 4	GROUP 5
All members actively participate.	✔		✔		✔
Group members are respectful of one another.	✔	✔		✔	✔
Group members attempt to complete work on their own before asking me questions.	✔		✔	✔	
Group stays on task.	✔		✔	✔	
Group completes and turns in progress sheet.	✔	✔	✔		✔

FIGURE 5.11   Tally sheet for Micah R., fourth grade, Mrs. Ellison's class.

Observed Student: Micah R. Date: March 15, 2002 Time: 0830 - 0930

Undesired Behaviors		*Desired Behaviors*	
Tapping pencil:	✔✔✔✔✔	Asking for help with work:	✔✔
Spinning pencil:	✔	Raising hand for attention:	✔
Mumbling:	✔✔✔✔✔✔✔	Responding when spoken to:	✔✔✔
Talking out in class:	✔✔	Following oral directions:	

Notes: Micah responded three times when spoken to (out of seven opportunities). Micah was given oral directions five times during this period, but did not follow directions at any time. Micah was asked three times to stop mumbling, once to stop tapping his pencil, and once to begin his work. He responded once with "OK" when I asked him to stop mumbling, but he did not stop.

of your study, it will not be possible to see and hear everything that is occurring. For these reasons, you might wish to consider videotaping and audiotaping parts of your study. You and your collaborators—as well as a peer reviewer—can make observations from video. Audiotapes are useful, too, but they do not allow the researcher to see what is occurring. Audiotaping can be very helpful, though, particularly if the intervention involves collaboration on the part of participants. A principal investigating teacher study groups or a teacher studying the effects of collaborative learning cannot observe all groups at once. If each group is audiotaped, however, the principal or teacher can go back and listen to a record of events for each group.

As you determine whether you will use video- and/or audiotape in your study, you need to consider several things. First, it is imperative that you have permission from participants, their parents (if participants are minors), and your school before you video- or audiotape participants; this process will be discussed in further detail in Chapter 6. You also must decide what you will tape and how often you will tape. Keep in mind that you will need to make observational notes from videotapes and transcriptions from audiotapes, and both of these activities are extremely time consuming. For that reason, take time to think about how taping can help you answer your research questions. It is unlikely that you need to tape every event during your entire study in order to get useful information. Come up with a plan for taping that is reasonable and that will provide the kinds of data needed to answer research questions. The last thing you need to consider is choosing taping equipment. Video- and audiotaping can be frustrating, especially when equipment does not work properly. Make sure to do a test run prior to using any taping equipment. If groups of participants will be audiotaping themselves, make sure they practice taping and listening to themselves so they will know how loudly to speak so that the tapes are clear. Finally, clearly mark all tapes with dates, times, and participant information. You should plan to look at videos or listen to audiotapes as soon as you can after taping.

Photographs are another tool for data collection. Though photos do not provide the kind of detailed information that a video can provide, they do offer a point-in-time reference, and they can be very useful when included in a publication or presentation of an action research study. Burns (1999) provides a number of ways photos can be used in action research, including for illustration of the intervention strategy used, for presenting a lasting visual reference of classroom tasks and activities, and for personalizing the participants in the study. Consider the effectiveness of using photographs in the study about Juan, the shy and withdrawn student who was described earlier in a narrative. Including pictures of Juan before the intervention to compare to pictures during and after the intervention could be a very powerful indicator of how Juan's behavior changed over time. Early pictures might show Juan away from others during classroom activities whereas pictures taken during and after the intervention might show Juan working with other students. Pictures such as these, in addition to the narrative and other sources of data, would be powerful evidence of the change in Juan after the intervention phase.

Photographs can also be useful to show what an intervention "looks like" or to provide examples of student work. For example, a teacher studying the use of Reader's Workshop could use a series of pictures to show the different types of activities that are part of the intervention. She could also take pictures of student work or student performances (book reports, students engaged in debate about an issue from a book, oral presentations, dioramas relating to a story) to graphically illustrate the type of work and the quality of work that students provide. Photos used in these ways are very useful when included in publications or presentations of the action research study. Be sure to secure permission from participants (and their parents if they are minors) before using photographs in your study.

Organizational charts or *maps* are used to provide various types of data related to the layout of an environment (the classroom, media center, playground) and the interactions of individuals in that environment. A media specialist, for example, could use a map of the media center to evaluate its layout. To begin, the media specialist would create a floor plan of the media center. Once the floor plan was created, the media specialist would make several observations of students and teachers as they used the media center, making notes on the floor plan. In Figure 5.12, an example of an organizational map is provided.

Inquiry Data

Inquiry data are used to gather information from participants about their knowledge, values, beliefs, past experiences, feelings, opinions, attitudes, or perceptions. In action research studies, inquiry data can provide a researcher with participants' perceptions about the effectiveness of an intervention, ways the intervention could be improved, and feedback regarding positive and negative aspects of the intervention. Consider the example provided at the beginning of this chapter about a biology teacher's study of collaborative study groups. Collecting inquiry data in the form of interviewing students revealed to the teacher the students' attitudes about learning in collaborative study groups. Students expressed that it was easier for them to learn from peers than from the textbook or class lecture. Further, students said that they spent more time preparing for class because they wanted to contribute to their collaborative group. In the interviews, students also explained that they

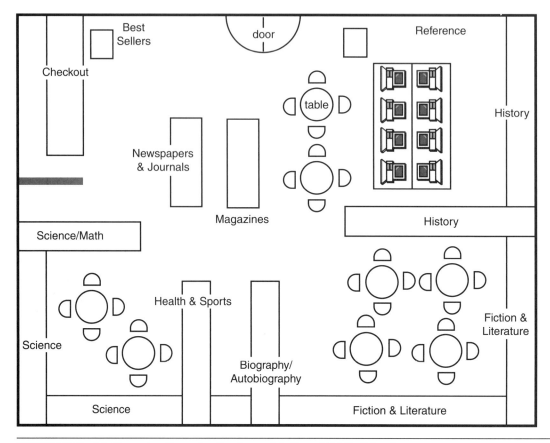

FIGURE 5.12   Media center floor plan for James Madison Middle School.

studied for tests with their collaborative group outside of class, which is something they had not done in the past.

Allowing participants to express their ideas and opinions about various aspects of your study is a good way to add to the richness of your investigation. Inquiry data can help you answer the *why* questions in your study by providing you with your participants' assessment of the effectiveness of the intervention. This leads to a thorough understanding of reasons the intervention was successful (or unsuccessful). Further, analysis of the inquiry data that participants provide is important in the ongoing process of reflective planning.

Inquiry data can be collected verbally in face-to-face meetings with participants through interviewing, holding focus groups, or by conferencing. There are many benefits to collecting these types of verbal data. One benefit is that participants have the opportunity to provide detailed feedback. Another benefit is that the researcher can shift the focus of the inquiry meeting based on participants' comments and the researcher can ask questions as they arise in conversation with participants. Though verbal inquiry data are a rich source of information, there are negative aspects of collecting this type of data. First, if you wish to interview participants individually, the process of interviewing, transcribing the interviews, and analyzing the interview data can be very time consuming. Also, you must be able to facilitate your meetings with participants so that you maintain some measure of control in the meetings (you don't want it to turn into a free-for-all gripe session) while allowing participants freedom to express what they think is important for you to know. Finally, you must be able to listen to *criticism*—in both ways this term is defined: as a disapproval and as an assessment or analysis—without penalizing, denigrating, or reprimanding the critic. In action research, one of the most difficult aspects of data collection, particularly with inquiry data, is that participants may be reluctant to provide honest responses. Students may find it difficult to tell teachers how they honestly feel about the teacher's instruction or the way the teacher interacts with students. Teachers also may worry about providing their principal or another administrator with honest answers to interview questions. Thus, it is important to make your interviewees feel at ease. You must inform your interview participants that you cannot improve your practices without their honest answers, and you must assure them that there will be no penalty for answering honestly. Though it may be hard for you to receive negative feedback, always keep in mind that any information that participants provide is useful for helping you understand how to improve your practice. If eliciting honest answers is problematic in your particular study, consider having a colleague or collaborator collect inquiry data for you.

Interviewing participants can occur through a structured or unstructured process. In a *structured interview,* the researcher prepares a list of specific questions prior to the interview that guides the process. In an *unstructured interview,* the researcher asks broad questions and then lets the interview proceed on its own course. A *semi-structured interview,* which involves asking some planned questions and then allowing participants to speak about related issues that are important to them, can be very useful in action research. Using a semi-structured interview is a good way to make sure that questions important to the researcher are answered while providing participants with an opportunity to add other useful information.

If you will use interviewing as a method for collecting inquiry data in your study, there are several steps to take in the planning process. First, determine the purpose of the interview. Think about how interview data will help you answer your primary and/or secondary research questions. Second, you must decide who you will interview. If you are a teacher conducting a study in your classroom, you may not be able to interview all students because of the time needed. If, instead, you will interview only some participants, how will you decide who the interviewees will be? Will you choose randomly from the entire class? Will you choose systematically—for example, a few high-achieving, average-achieving, and low-achieving students or a few students who responded well to the intervention and some who responded poorly to the intervention—so that you get multiple perspectives? Be sure to carefully choose interviewees, keeping in mind that various perspectives may be important to help you find meaningful and credible answers to your research questions.

The third consideration in planning your interview is to determine whether you will conduct a structured, unstructured, or semi-structured interview. To help you decide, consider the purpose of interviewing in your study. If, for example, you are a teacher who wishes to elicit students' opinions about a new teaching strategy and their perceptions about its effectiveness, a semi-structured interview is a good choice. Specific questions, such as *How did working in the collaborative groups affect your learning? Do you prefer learning on your own, listening to class lectures, or working in a collaborative group?* and *In what ways is learning in a collaborative group different than learning in other ways?* could be followed with more open-ended questions such as *Tell me why you think learning in collaborative groups was so helpful to you* (following a participant's response that learning in the groups was helpful) and *How could I make the collaborative groups better?* Throughout the semi-structured interview you should ask follow-up questions based on the student's responses.

In some cases, an unstructured interview is the best way to gather information. This is particularly true early in the action research process if you are collecting baseline data, if you want to use participant feedback as you plan your intervention, or if you want to know how participants feel the intervention is going. For example, a principal interested in investigating the use of teacher study groups might choose to begin his study by interviewing teachers about their opinions of the study group concept. Information provided would be very useful in planning how best to implement the study groups. If, for example, most interviewed teachers expressed that teachers should volunteer to be in study groups rather than be forced to participate in them, the principal would be wise to begin the study group intervention phase by asking teachers to participate. Once the volunteer study groups were formed, the principal could use unstructured interviews at the end of early study group sessions asking a broad question such as *In what ways, if any, is participation in this study group helping you in your classroom?* Feedback could be used for ongoing reflective planning for future study group sessions.

Structured interviews do not allow for the depth of responses and information that is so useful in action research studies. In fact, an interview that is too structured—one that allows for only *yes* and *no* answers, for example—is not much different from a survey. At times, though, a structured interview can be useful. A kindergarten teacher I worked with used a structured interview at the beginning of her study to determine her students' attitudes about writing. In the interview she asked questions such as *Do you like to write? Do you like working in our writing center?* and *Why do people write?* The teacher was able to determine students' attitudes about writing and their perceptions about the uses of writing before the study began. This provided her with baseline data, which was later used to compare students' attitudes about writing after the intervention had been utilized. It also provided her with information about students' perceptions of the purposes of writing, which guided the initial reflective planning as she prepared the intervention.

If you plan to interview participants in your action research study, consider these interviewing strategies provided by Seidman (1998):

- **Listen more and talk less.** Listen to what the interviewee is saying and make sure you understand it.
- **Follow up on what the interviewee says.** When you ask questions in an unstructured interview, make sure the questions are related to what the participant has said. Ask for clarification on points you do not understand, and ask the interviewee to provide a story or example to illustrate his or her point.

- **Avoid asking leading questions.** Don't use words or tones that imply the correct response. For example, don't say, *Why are study groups more fun than studying by yourself?* Instead say *Tell me about working in the study group.*
- **Keep interviewees focused and ask for specific details.** If an interviewee gets off the topic, guide him or her back to it. Ask for specific, concrete details about experiences (*Describe the activities you engaged in during the collaborative group exercises*).
- **Do not reinforce interviewees' responses.** Agreeing or disagreeing with an interviewee's response implies that there are correct and incorrect answers to your questions, which may impact the way he or she answers subsequent questions.

Focus groups are used for interviewing groups of participants. There are several advantages to using focus groups. One advantage is that focus groups allow for interviewing many participants at one time. Also, as Fontana and Frey (1998) explain, focus groups are "data rich, flexible, stimulating to respondents, recall aiding, and cumulative and collaborative" (p. 55). In a focus group interview, responses of one participant can help other participants recall important information that they wish to share. Members of the focus group respond not only to the researcher, who moderates the discussion, but to other individuals in the focus group. Thus, responses to questions build on others' responses, which can result in much richer data than that collected in individual interviews.

Moderating a focus group discussion involves more work on the part of the researcher than conducting individual interviews. Fontana and Frey (1998) provide several useful suggestions for moderating focus groups:

- *Do not allow a person or a small group of people to dominate the discussion.*
- *Encourage participation from silent focus group members.*
- *Obtain responses from all members of the focus group.*
- *Balance the task of moderating the group and asking structured questions with allowing for evolving questions and interactions.*

Also, follow the guidelines for interviewing listed earlier. Make sure to ask questions and guide the focus group discussion to elicit responses that will help answer primary and secondary research questions. Listen more than you talk. Ask for clarification. Emphasize the importance of honest responses.

Conferencing involves in-depth conversation between the researcher and a participant relating to some aspect of the action research study. Often, conferencing is used by a teacher in conjunction with a student work product. For example, a teacher studying ways to improve writing achievement could conference with a student about an essay written for class. The point of the conference would be to obtain information about the process of writing the essay. Questions such as *How did you choose your essay topic? What strategies did you use to organize your paper?* and *How did you come up with the thesis for your paper?* are a few examples of the kinds of questions that could be asked during the conferencing session. Conferencing used in this way can be instructional because it allows for conversation and discussion of the elements of writing, and it can be informational because it provides the teacher with data regarding the strategies the student used during the writing process.

A teacher I recently worked with conducted an action research study on the effectiveness of her mentoring of a first-year teacher. Throughout the study the mentor teacher used conferencing to discuss with the new teacher the effectiveness of various strategies the mentor had shared (classroom management techniques, instructional strategies). The conferencing sessions provided the mentor with a rich source of data: The mentored teacher gave feedback on the effectiveness of the mentor's strategies and her perceptions of why they did or did not work. The mentored teacher also shared information about difficulties she was still encountering in the classroom and asked for assistance in some of those areas, which provided the mentor with data for ongoing reflective planning. Finally, the mentor teacher was able to analyze the exchanges made during the conferences with the mentored teacher, which provided an illustration of the relationship between the two teachers.

If you decide to collect verbal inquiry data, either in the form of interviews, focus groups, or conferencing, be sure to audio record all sessions. This will allow you the freedom to actively listen during conversations with interviewees without having to take detailed notes. Follow the suggestions for audio recording provided in the section on observations. Remember that you will need to transcribe the audiotapes prior to analyzing the verbal inquiry data, which can be a time-consuming task. If a large amount of audiotape is to be transcribed, consider hiring a professional transcriber.

Inquiry data, in addition to being collected through conversations with participants, can be collected in written form using surveys/questionnaires or attitude scales. The benefit of these methods is that information can be collected from many participants at one time. It can take hours or even days to interview all students in a class, but a questionnaire can be given to that same class and completed in just a few minutes. Analyzing written inquiry data also takes less time than analyzing verbal inquiry data. The disadvantage of written inquiry data is that it does not allow for the depth of response that verbal inquiry data allows. Further, it is much easier to get participants to verbally answer questions and provide detailed responses than it is to get participants to provide detailed written information on open-ended questions.

Surveys or *questionnaires* are a good alternative to the structured interview. Questions asked during a structured interview can instead be written on a survey and distributed to participants—providing that participants are able to read the survey. In the earlier example of the kindergarten teacher's structured interview, it would not be wise to use a survey instead of an interview because children would not be able to read the survey. Keep in mind that if you use a survey in your action research study that your participants' reading ability must be high enough so they can understand your written questions. Ensure that the reading level of your survey matches the reading level of your participants.

Surveys and questionnaires are good alternatives to interviews and focus groups when time constraints are such that interviewing is impossible or when the researcher is seeking responses to a predetermined set of questions. In some cases, participants may feel more comfortable providing honest answers to an anonymous survey as opposed to being subjected to an interview in which their identity is known. Consider, though, that sometimes it is critical that names are included on surveys. For example, you may want to compare multiple sources of data for each individual participant to determine whether a participant's work, your observations of the participant, and the participant's answers on a survey are related. If this is the case in your study, you should have participants include their names on surveys. If matching different types of data is not important in your study, using an anonymous survey is fine.

If you plan to use a survey in your action research study, first consider how data from the survey will help you answer your primary and/or secondary research questions. Refer to your research questions as you plan questions for your survey. Consider this example: A middle school language arts teacher is interested in studying the effectiveness of literature circles for increasing student achievement and interest in reading. His primary research questions are: *Does the use of literature circles increase students' reading achievement?* and *Does the use of literature circles increase students' interest in reading?* Secondary questions relate to *why* questions: *Why are literature circles effective (or ineffective) for increasing achievement and interest in reading? In what ways does participating in literature circles change students' attitudes about reading?* The teacher could use a survey to measure students' perceptions of literature circles. An example is included in Figure 5.13.

FIGURE 5.13   Student survey on literature circles (Mr. Kaston, 7th grade).

Students, please complete this survey on literature circles. Answer each question and provide as much information as you can on the open-ended questions. It is important to be honest in your answers because I will use the information you provide to help me plan future language arts lessons. You do not have to put your name on this survey. Thanks for helping me with this important project. Mr. K.

1. What have you learned about reading as a result of participating in your literature circle?

2. After participating in your literature circle, do you feel you are a better reader, a worse reader, or about the same kind of reader you were before working in the literature circle? (circle one)   Better   Worse   Same

   Why?

3. Has participating in the literature circle changed the way you feel about reading for school? (circle one)   Yes   No

   If yes, how has it changed the way you feel about reading for school?

4. Has participating in the literature circle changed the way you feel about reading for fun? (circle one)   Yes   No

   If yes, how has it changed the way you feel about reading for fun?

5. What activities during the literature circle have been most helpful to you?

6. What activities during the literature circle have been least helpful to you?

7. How can we improve the literature circle activities?

8. Is there anything else you would like to say about literature circles? If so, please write your comments here.

The literature circle survey provided in Figure 5.13 is aligned with the teacher's research questions. Survey question 2 relates to students' perceptions of how their reading achievement has changed as a result of participating in literature circles. Question 1 provides students with an opportunity to explain how literature circles have helped them develop reading skills. Questions 3 and 4 are concerned with students' attitudes about reading and how the literature circles have impacted those attitudes. The remaining questions allow students to express ways the literature circles have been effective and ineffective and provide students with an opportunity to give feedback on ways to improve the literature circle activities. Notice, too, that the survey begins with a request to provide detailed information. The teacher has also explained the importance of providing honest responses and has increased his chances to get honest responses by telling students they do not have to write their names on the survey.

Surveys have a variety of uses in action research studies. They can be used with different types of participants—students, teachers, parents, school staff, administrators—and they are a simple way to collect data on large groups of participants. Here are several suggestions for those interested in using surveys or questionnaires in action research studies:

- **Ensure that survey questions are aligned with research questions** (Burns, 1999). It is critical that you create your survey so that it will provide the kinds of information you need to answer your research questions. Refer to your primary and secondary research questions often as you work on your survey items.
- **Pilot test the survey before administering it to participants** (Burns, 1999). Pilot testing the survey with a small group of participants or having colleagues or collaborators evaluate the survey before it is administered is a good way to identify any problems. The pilot test or collaborator review can help identify reading level problems, ambiguous questions, redundancies, instructions that are unclear, and unnecessary questions.
- **Keep your survey brief and to the point.** The longer your survey, the less likely that your participants will complete it. Also, participants generally will not provide in-depth responses to open-ended questions on a long survey.
- **Do not ask questions that are unrelated to your primary or secondary research questions.** Often researchers will include questions on their surveys because they think responses will be interesting. For example, the language arts teacher who created the literature circle survey in Figure 5.13 may be interested in whether students' parents read at home and in fact may hypothesize that his best readers come from homes where reading is valued. But including a question on parents' reading habits will in no way help the teacher answer his research questions. Avoid including questions in your survey about gender, race, or other demographic variables unless they are specifically related to your research questions. Avoid any other questions that are only tangentially related to your study.

Attitude scales are surveys that focus on the way participants feel about certain topics. They are useful to researchers in a variety of ways: to measure students' attitudes about school, their abilities, or their self-concept; to measure teachers' attitudes about school policies, school climate, mentoring activities, or professional development activities; and to measure parents' attitudes about school rules, or availability of teachers, staff, and administrators (to name just a few). Attitude scales typically contain close-ended questions to which participants choose a response—such as *I am confident in my ability to multiply fractions: strongly agree, agree, disagree,* and *strongly disagree*—although open-ended items are also occasionally included.

The guidelines for creating an attitude scale are similar for the survey guidelines listed previously. In addition, a number of attitude scales have been published in the literature that may be useful in your study. These include the School Achievement Motivation Scale (Chiu, 1997), the Teacher Rating of Academic Achievement Motivation (Stinnett, Oehler-Stinnett, & Stout, 1991), the Reader Self-Perception Scale (Henk & Melnick, 1995), the Writer Self-Perception Scale (Bottomley, Henk, & Melnick, 1998), the scale for Teacher-Perceived Student Behaviors: Disrespect, Sociability, and Attentiveness (Friedman, 1994), and the Early Adolescent Self-Esteem Scale (DuBois, Felner, Brand, Phillips, & Lease, 1996). A number of other attitude scales are also available, and they can be found in academic journals and teacher magazines. Conduct an online search and library search to locate scales in your area of research.

If you use an established or published attitude scale, make sure the reading level is appropriate for your participants. You may need to make changes to the scale so that items align with the purpose of your action research study. If you plan to create your own attitude scale, make sure that the response choices on the scale are appropriate for the questions. For example, appropriate response choices to the prompt *I am confident in my ability to multiply fractions* are *strongly agree, agree, disagree,* and *strongly disagree.* It would not be appropriate to use responses choices such as *always, frequently, sometimes,* and *never* for the prompt unless the purpose of the study is to measure *how often* students are confident in their ability to multiply fractions. Be sure to pilot test the scale or have a collaborator review it before administering the scale. An attitude scale for math is included in Figure 5.14. This attitude scale could be used in a study by a teacher who wished to determine students' confidence in completing certain math tasks before and after implementing an intervention.

THE IMPORTANCE OF COLLECTING BASELINE DATA

The preceding section introduced a number of ways to collect data in your action research study: through artifacts, observations, and inquiry. As you decide on the best ways to collect data to answer your research questions, you may need to think about collecting baseline data before beginning your intervention. Baseline data are collected before the implementation of an intervention, and they are used to make comparisons of participants before and after the intervention occurs. If you are a teacher interested in examining the ways a strategy for teaching the writing process impacts students' writ-

FIGURE 5.14   Mathematics attitude scale, Mrs. Cho, 5th grade.

Students, please complete this attitude scale. Please write your name on this sheet because I will use it to plan activities to help you improve your achievement in math. It is important that you are honest in your responses. Your honesty will help me plan the best instructional activities for you.

Rate your confidence in completing each activity by circling one of the choices (very confident, somewhat confident, not confident at all).

1. I am confident in my ability to add fractions that have the same denominator.

very confident   somewhat confident   not at all confident

2. I am confident in my ability to add fractions that have different denominators.

very confident   somewhat confident   not at all confident

3. I am confident in my ability to multiply simple fractions (such as $\frac{1}{2} \times \frac{1}{4}$).

very confident   somewhat confident   not at all confident

4. I am confident in my ability to multiply complex fractions (such as $2\frac{1}{2} \times 3\frac{1}{4}$).

very confident   somewhat confident   not at all confident

5. I am confident in my ability to divide simple fractions (such as $\frac{1}{2} \div \frac{1}{4}$).

very confident   somewhat confident   not at all confident

6. I am confident in my ability to divide complex fractions (such as $8\frac{1}{2} \div 2\frac{1}{4}$).

very confident   somewhat confident   not at all confident

ing achievement, it would be a good idea to collect writing samples from students before the implementing the strategy intervention. Collecting writing samples during and after the intervention would allow you to determine the ways in which students' writing improved. If, instead, you only measured student writing after the completion of the intervention, it would be impossible for you to determine the ways that students' writing was impacted by the intervention.

As you plan ways to collect data to answer your research questions, think about whether baseline data are important in your study. If you wish to determine ways in which an intervention impacts achievement or attitudes, you will need to measure these constructs before beginning the implementation phase of your study. Artifacts created by participants before intervention implementation are one source of baseline data. You may be able to use existing artifacts, or you may need to have participants create certain artifacts to produce baseline data. You can also make baseline observations, conduct baseline interviews, or collect baseline surveys prior to implementing your intervention.

ALIGNING DATA COLLECTION STRATEGIES WITH RESEARCH QUESTIONS

Aligning data collection strategies with research questions has been stressed throughout this chapter, and it will be repeated here one last time. It is absolutely essential that you refer to your primary and secondary research questions as you determine the best ways to collect data for your study. Ask yourself these questions:

- What types of data should I collect to answer my primary research question?
- What types of data should I collect to answer my secondary research questions?
- What types of data should I collect to help answer the *why* questions in my study?

Work with a collaborator as you work through this critical step of determining ways to collect data to answer your research questions. If you are able to bounce ideas off of a collaborator—or even a peer who is not formally collaborating in your study—you have a better chance of choosing appropriate data collection techniques for your study.

Here are some suggestions for making sure data collection strategies match research questions:

- Refer to your primary and secondary research questions as a first step in choosing data collection strategies.
- If the purpose of your study is to increase student achievement, be sure to choose several types of student-generated artifacts to examine as one data source.
- If the purpose of your study is to examine changes in attitudes, feelings, or opinions, use verbal and/or written inquiry data as one data source.
- Regardless of the purpose of your study, it is critical to utilize observational data. In rare instances, observational data are not useful, but in most action research studies utilizing observational data is essential for understanding the reasons why an intervention was successful or unsuccessful.
- Choose multiple data collection strategies so that you will be able to triangulate data.
- Work with a collaborator or peer in the data collection development process.

In Activity 5.1, you will complete several activities that will assist you in creating your data collection plan and ensuring that the chosen data collection strategies are aligned with your primary and secondary research questions.

■ ■ ■ ■ ■ ■ ━━━━━━━━━━━━━━━━━━━━━━

ACTIVITY 5.1

CHOOSING DATA COLLECTION STRATEGIES

1. Write your primary and secondary research questions. Leave several lines of open space between questions.
2. Under each question, write at least three (but no more than five) data collection strategies that can help you answer the research question. Provide examples of the specific kinds of information you plan to obtain (for example, instead of writing *I will use student-generated artifacts* write something more specific such as *I will have students complete persuasive essays as a form of student-generated artifact*).
3. Determine whether baseline data are important in your study. Write a justification for your determination. If you do plan to collect baseline data, explain which data collection strategies you plan to use and provide examples of the specific types of baseline data you plan to obtain.
4. In a sentence or two, write an explanation of how the data collection strategies (including baseline strategies, if appropriate) will provide you with the data you need to answer your research questions.
5. Share your data collection ideas and the information you have written thus far for this activity with a collaborator or peer. Obtain feedback and suggestions on ways to improve your data collection plan. Write down feedback provided.

Research Paper Activity: Based on collaborator/peer assistance and your reflections on your answers to the previous questions in this activity, write a data collection plan for your study. For each research question, write a detailed explanation of the types of data you will collect (including baseline data, if appropriate) and a timeline or timeframe for collecting data. Provide a justification for your data collection plan that explains how your plan will help you answer your research questions. Place this information under a heading such as *Data Collection Plan* or *Data Collection Strategies* and have it follow the section on the intervention.

Journal Activity: Use your journal as a place to make or keep observational records. Make a commitment to write in your journal each day that the intervention is implemented. Make notes on the way you are implementing your intervention as well as the way participants respond to the intervention.

SUMMARY

This chapter explained the importance of triangulating data sources to increase credibility in action research studies. It also focused on describing multiple ways to collect artifacts, conduct observations, and acquire inquiry data, and an explanation of how to collect baseline data was provided. Finally, methods for ensuring that data collection strategies are aligned with research questions were described. Activity 5.1 led you through the steps of creating a data collection plan. Once your plan is in place, you will be ready to complete the final steps of research planning and then begin implementation of the intervention phase of your study. Chapter 6 focuses on these final steps of the planning process—increasing validity of the study, engaging in continuous reflective planning, following ethical guidelines for research, and establishing a timeline for the research project.

CHAPTER SIX

FINAL PLANNING BEFORE IMPLEMENTATION OF THE STUDY

CHAPTER GOALS

- Explain ways to define validity in action research and suggest ways to align methods of increasing validity with the nature and purpose of the study.
- Describe procedures for following ethical guidelines in action research studies.
- Illustrate the process of ongoing and continuous reflective planning.
- Demonstrate ways to create timelines for action research projects.
- Provide activities to guide practitioners through the processes of increasing validity, following ethical guidelines, creating a project timeline, and engaging in action planning.

Chapters 4 and 5 provided guidelines for planning an intervention and collecting data to determine the effectiveness of the intervention. Prior to beginning the intervention, however, it is necessary to finalize the research plan, which includes planning ways to increase validity of the research results, following ethical guidelines for research studies, creating a timeline for the completion of the action research project, and engaging in continuous reflective planning throughout the study. This chapter provides information in each of these areas and includes activities that will guide these final planning activities.

DEFINITIONS OF VALIDITY

The term *validity* has a number of meanings in educational research. In quantitative research, validity can refer to the degree to which results are true for the participants (*internal validity*), the degree to which the results can be generalized beyond the participants in the study (*external validity*), or the degree to which a test or assessment measures what it is supposed to measure (*test validity*). Different types of validity that are appropriate for qualitative studies have been described by a number of qualitative researchers. For example, Maxwell (1992) described the need for qualitative studies to have descriptive, interpretive, and theoretical validity. These criteria refer to the accuracy of facts portrayed in the study (*descriptive validity*), the researcher's accurate interpretation of data (*interpretative validity*), and the accuracy of the theoretical model postulated by the researcher to explain the findings (*theoretical validity*). Three similar types of validity have been suggested by Eisner (1991). The first type, *consensual validity,* is defined as "agreement among competent others that the description, interpretation, evaluation, and thematics of an educational situation are right" (p. 112). *Structural corroboration,* which can also be defined as triangulation (described in Chapter 5) is the extent to which analysis of multiple forms of data lead to conclusions about the study. Finally, *referential adequacy* is the ability of a study to bring about understanding.

Perhaps the most widely referenced validity criteria in qualitative research are the four trustworthiness criteria described by Lincoln and Guba (1985), who explain that the validity of a qualitative study can be increased by (1) establishing the verisimilitude of the research findings for the context that was studied (*truth value validity*), (2) determining the extent to which results of a research study are applicable to other contexts and other individuals (*applicability/transferability*), (3) establishing whether research results would replicate with the same or similar participants and/or contexts (*consistency/dependability*), and (4) showing that results are an accurate representation of what occurred rather than the result of the researcher's bias, motivation, or interest (*neutrality/confirmability*).

Among proponents of action research, there has not been much discussion about how to best define validity in action research. However, Anderson, Herr, and Nihlen (1994) have suggested five distinct criteria for assessing validity in action research, and some action research theorists have supported these criteria. According to Anderson et al., *democratic validity* is the extent to which stakeholders in the research area have collaborated in the research process. *Outcome validity* is the degree to which there has been a successful resolution of the research problem. *Process validity,* which is closely aligned with the notion of credibility, refers to the use of appropriate processes for studying the research question. A fourth type of validity, *catalytic validity* (from Lather, 1991), is the extent to which the research transforms and changes the researcher's views and/or practices. Finally, *dialogic validity* refers to the sharing or disseminating of research findings with other practitioners or peers. Table 6.1 illustrates types of researcher behaviors that can both enhances and diminish these forms of validity. In the next section of the text, specific strategies for increasing validity will be described.

TABLE 6.1   Researcher Behaviors That Enhance/Diminish Validity

TYPE OF VALIDITY	BEHAVIORS THAT INCREASE THIS TYPE OF VALIDITY	BEHAVIORS THAT LESSEN THIS TYPE OF VALIDITY
Descriptive validity	A teacher accurately and completely describes the intervention in her study, including detailed information on instructional strategies and frequency and intensity of the intervention.	A counselor provides little information on the behavioral intervention used in his study and has not kept field notes so that he can accurately describe how often and in what capacity the intervention took place.

[handwritten annotations: "Complete info." and "Not clear. Not enough info."]

TABLE 6.1   Continued

Interpretive validity; Structural corroboration; Truth value validity	A school principal collects multiple forms of data on teacher study groups, triangulates information from observations, interviews, and teacher journals, and asks teacher participants to check the interpretations of his data for accuracy.	A teacher studying ways to increase writing achievement collects two forms of data—essays and student journals—and makes all judgments about the effectiveness of the intervention by looking only at these two sources.
Theoretical validity	A counselor has collected multiple forms of data on her career counseling intervention, has triangulated data sources, and has asked participants to confirm her results. All results suggest that the intervention was not successful at helping students choose a career, and the counselor concludes that the intervention failed.	A media specialist concludes that his study on teaching high school students about computer copyright laws was a success, even though there is a discrepancy among the various data sources. Tests he administered reveal that students understand computer copyright laws, but in interviews and observations it is clear that they still believe it is OK to download music and movies.
Consensual validity	A *media* specialist studying the Accelerated Reader (AR) program collects data that includes teacher interviews, observations of students, student interviews, computer-generated test reports. After analyzing the student observations and student interviews, he discusses the interpretations of his data with a randomly selected group of students, asking them if they believe his interpretations of their attitudes about AR are correct. He also conducts a focus group interview with teachers to discuss their views on his interpretations of student observations, student interviews, and teacher interviews. The media specialist incorporates student and teacher feedback in his results and conclusions.	An assistant principal investigates the effectiveness of a bullying prevention program in her middle school. She analyzes and interprets data from student interviews, observations, and surveys and determines that the program has been effective for preventing bullying and the students like the program. In sharing her results with students, several students respond that there has been a decrease in bullying, but that the principal misinterpreted their responses about the program itself. These students claim that the program is effective because students fear the consequences of bullying. However, they also state that the definition of bullying has become blurred and some students threaten to turn each other in for bullying even when there has been no bullying behavior. Although the principal politely listens, she does not incorporate these concerns into her analysis or conclusions.

(continued)

TABLE 6.1   Continued

Referential adequacy	A school district administrator presents the results of his study on teacher attrition, describing in detail the setting, participants, intervention, results, and conclusions. Members of the audience are provided with sufficient information to replicate his study in their own districts.	In describing her study to colleagues, a science teacher is unable to describe the elements of her collaborative group intervention that were most helpful to students. Though she knows student achievement increased, she is unsure how the intervention may have affected achievement.
Applicability/transferability; Consistency/dependability	A band instructor studies a method for increasing students' sight reading ability. She includes detailed information on her intervention (its length, duration, intensity), participants, and setting, which increases the replicability of her study. In addition, she works with a colleague in another school, replicating her study with different students in a setting very different from her own. Based on her analysis and interpretation of data in each setting, the band director is able to conclude which aspects of the intervention are effective in both settings and which must be altered based on differences in students and in the settings.	A teacher of students with behavior disorders studies the effectiveness of a behavior intervention strategy. In describing his study, he does not fully explain each activity in the intervention, which makes it difficult for another teacher to try the intervention. Further, he provides only surface descriptions of his students and setting (three male students in an inner-city school). In describing his study to classmates in a Masters program, his peers are unable to conclude how his results may apply to their settings and their students because they do not have a clear picture of the teacher's own students or setting.
Neutrality/confirmability	Throughout her study, the art teacher asks a respected and forthright colleague to read through her data analysis notes (based on student projects, observations, interviews) and discuss the analyses. In these discussions, the colleague asks clarifying questions that help the art teacher focus on what the data reveal, rather than what she hopes they reveal.	A principal buys an expensive software program that all students in grades 2 through 5 use to improve and track their reading comprehension. In analyzing its effectiveness, the principal focuses on computer-generated reports that show gains in comprehension. However, she disregards several teachers' complaints that students have figured out how to pass the tests without reading the books.
Democratic validity	A principal interested in building a sense of community in his school invites teachers, staff, parents, and students to actively be part of his research study. They are part of intervention planning, data collection, and data analysis.	A school district administrator brings new principals together to work as a professional learning community, but does not allow the members to plan activities. Further, when the principals suggest ways to evaluate the effectiveness of the learning community, she tells them she has predeveloped surveys that she plans to use.

TABLE 6.1 Continued

Outcome validity	A math teacher studies the effectiveness of using manipulatives to teach students how to solve word problems. Although the intervention is not as effective as the teacher had hoped, her results provide data that can be used to alter the intervention (adding other teaching strategies). The teacher uses the data to redesign the intervention, and over time there is a definite increase in students' ability to solve word problems.	A school counselor implements an intervention aimed at decreasing discipline referrals for students who receive multiple in-school suspensions. The intervention is unsuccessful, and although there is a wealth of data from her study that suggests ways the intervention could be strengthened, the counselor continues using the ineffective intervention.
Process validity	To study the effectiveness of literature circles on increasing reading achievement, a middle school teacher spends significant time reading about literature circles and designs an intervention based on best practices and on other studies of literature circles. The teacher ensures that research questions and data collection strategies are aligned, and he uses appropriate strategies in data analysis.	An instructional lead teacher (ILT) decides to start a teacher study group with the teachers she supervises. The ILT designs the study group intervention based on what she has heard about study groups. She reviews no literature on study groups, nor does she discuss the study group concept with knowledgeable colleagues.
Catalytic validity	For several years, a high school English teacher has been having students design web pages on various literature topics to improve their research writing ability. After three years, he decides to conduct an action research study on the effectiveness of this instructional strategy. In analyzing the data, the teacher determines that although students like to design web pages, they tend to focus on making their sites look good, rather than on ensuring that included information is correct and cited properly. Based on these results, the teacher decides to stop using the web design activity and to look for ways to improve students' research abilities while valuing their desire to use technology in their projects.	A physical education teacher tries a new strategy for engaging students with special needs. Though the strategy is a success, he does not use it in the future because it requires 30 extra minutes of planning per week.
Dialogic validity	A principal studies ways to improve teacher mentoring, has much success with her intervention, and shares results with other principles in a districtwide training session.	A teacher finds that the reading program used in his school does not help students in his class develop reading comprehension strategies. He does not share results with teachers or administrators at his school.

DETERMINING WAYS TO INCREASE VALIDITY

Thus far fifteen types of validity for qualitative or action research studies have been presented and, incredibly, even more types of validity have been proposed for qualitative research (for other validity terms, see Lather, 1993; LeCompte & Goetz, 1982; Wolcott, 1994). As illustrated in the discussion of reflection (Chapter 2), the process of action research often involves making decisions (e.g., *Should I engage in autobiographical, collaborative, or critical reflection?*) that are based on the purpose of the study. In determining ways to increase validity in your action research study, you will need to consider the nature of the study, its purpose, and the audience with which you will share your results. Criteria for validity may be established for you if the study is intended for a particular audience. Whereas colleagues may expect information regarding descriptive validity, truth value validity, transferability, and outcome validity, a professional organization or a journal's review board may expect Lincoln and Guba's trustworthiness criteria to be followed. If the purpose of the study is purely to inform your own educational practice, you may wish to focus on truth value validity, outcome validity, and catalytic validity. Research that is collaborative or communal should include democratic validity as one way to establish the study's credibility.

As you determine which ways to increase validity in your own study, think back to your goal as you began to conceptualize the study: Did you wish to conduct a study of your own practice, did you wish to conduct a collaborative study within a critical community, or did you wish to be part of a communal study that focused on issues of social justice? As you answer this question, consider the various forms of validity presented and choose methods for increasing validity that are aligned with your initial goal. For example, a counselor who conducts a study on implementing a schoolwide study of racial inequity in the school's discipline procedures could choose to focus on *truth-value validity* (Are we confident that the findings presented are accurate?), *neutrality/confirmability* (Are the results presented free of biased interpretation?), *democratic validity* (What was the extent of stakeholder collaboration?), *outcome validity* (Has the problem been successfully resolved?), and *catalytic validity* (Has the study resulted in changed practices at the school?). If these conditions of validity are agreed upon as being necessary for this particular study (by stakeholders, collaborators, or other appropriate audiences), *and* if the questions associated with each condition are satisfactorily answered in the study, the counselor can say with confidence that validity has been established.

Once you have determined which validity conditions are necessary for your study, the next step is to choose specific methods for increasing validity. Strategies for increasing the different forms of validity are described here. In Table 6.2, these strategies are graphically aligned with the various forms of validity described in this section.

Steps for increasing validity:

- **Utilize peer debriefing** (Lincoln & Guba, 1985). Peer debriefing involves discussing your study with a colleague or peer who is not invested in the study (not a collaborator). During the debriefing session, you discuss with your peer your interpretations of collected data. The peer debriefer can provide alternative interpretations, help point out your biases and the way your values may be coloring your interpretations, and assist you in formulating new directions for ongoing study.

TABLE 6.2   Strategies for Increasing Validity

TYPE OF VALIDITY	FOCUS	STRATEGIES
• Descriptive validity • Structural corroboration • Truth-value validity • Process validity • Interpretive validity • Theoretical validity	Accuracy of facts and findings; correct interpretations made and correct conclusions reached.	• Persistent and prolonged observation. • Triangulation. • Accurate data recording. • Member checks. • Peer debriefing. • Negative case analysis. • Biases made clear.
• Consensual validity	Agreement among others that interpretations and conclusions are accurate.	• Peer debriefing. • Member checks. • Audit trail.
• Referential adequacy • Outcome validity • Catalytic validity	Ability of study to increase understanding, resolve problems, and transform practices.	• Presentation of results. • Continuous, ongoing reflective planning.
• Applicability/transferability • Consistency/dependability	Usefulness of the results in different settings and contexts and with different individuals.	• Thick description of setting, study, and participants.
• Neutrality/confirmability	Evidence that results are accurate and are not a result of researcher bias.	• Peer debriefing. • Accurate data recording. • Member checks. • Triangulation. • Biases made clear. • Audit trail.
• Democratic validity	Evidence that stakeholders collaborated in the research process.	• Peer debriefing. • Member checks. • Audit trail.
• Dialogic validity	Sharing or disseminating research findings.	• Peer debriefing. • Member checks. • Presentation of results.

■ **Engage in persistent and prolonged observations** (Lincoln & Guba, 1985). The longer you are able to collect data, the more likely you are to see the true effects of your intervention. Prolonged observation will help you determine whether the intervention is effective after the newness of it wears off. Persistent observation will allow you to gather enough data to add to the credibility of your study and help answer the *why* questions.

■ **Be sure to record data accurately** (Maxwell, 1992; Wolcott, 1994). Accurate recording during your action research study is critical. You must plan for ways to record as much information as possible when important events occur. Also, sufficient detail should be included in observational records, field notes, and notes from interviews. It can be very helpful to record parts of your study, using either audio- or videotape, so that you can revisit events and conversations and record them accurately.

- **Use member checks** (Lincoln & Guba, 1985). Also known as *respondent validation* (Hitchcock & Hughes, 1995), member checks are a useful way to reduce bias and increase credibility in your study. Member checks involve discussing your interpretations of data with the participants of your study. This allows you to determine whether your findings accurately represent participants' actions and responses.

- **Triangulate data sources** (Anderson, Herr, & Nihlen, 1994; Eisner, 1991; Lincoln & Guba, 1985). As described in Chapter 5, collecting multiple sources of data is a necessary step in action research. When the researcher uses multiple sources to corroborate findings (for example, teachers' self-reports indicated that they implemented a new policy for ensuring discipline procedures consistently for all students, percentages of discipline referrals for each ethnic group were similar, and conferences with teachers at each grade level revealed that teachers believed the new discipline policy was fair and necessary and they were committed to following it), the credibility of the findings is increased.

- **Provide thick description of the setting and study** (Geertz, 1973; Lincoln & Guba, 1985). Providing thick description means describing in detail the setting, participants, intervention, and research methods employed in the study (completed in Chapter 4 activities). Portraying the setting and study in this way provides an audience or readers with the information needed to determine whether the study is generalizable, transferable, or useful in their settings. When the research setting shares characteristics with the audiences' or readers' setting, generalizability is increased.

- **Employ techniques in negative case analysis** (Lincoln & Guba, 1985). Negative case analysis involves qualifying research findings by analyzing data that are not supported or corroborated by other sources of data. Data that do not "agree" with the majority of the other data collected are considered the negative case. In the example just cited about the new discipline program aimed at ensuring equitable treatment of students in different racial groups, the three sources of evidence—teachers' self-reports, percentages of discipline referrals, and conferences with teachers—corroborated the finding that the new policy was in place and working effectively. If, however, there was a negative case, such as an area in which the policy did not seem to be working well, the case would need to be analyzed to determine why the policy wasn't working. Then the results could be refined to explain that, overall, the policy was effective, but under certain conditions (which would be described) the policy was less effective.

- **Make clear any researcher bias** (Merriam, 1998). It is important as you plan your study that you consider any biases that you have at the outset. Engaging in reflection at the beginning of the research process is one way to clarify any initial biases. Bias here is defined as any preconceived ideas about the participants, setting, intervention, or the research process itself. Although the word "bias" has many negative connotations, in the case of research you can be biased if you believe with certainty that your intervention will be successful. As you prepare to begin the intervention phase of your study, consider any preconceived ideas that you have and note them in your journal. Referring to these biases as you collect and analyze data will help keep biases in check. In addition, include information on biases—and how you dealt with them—in the research report.

■ **Make available an audit trail** (Halpern, 1983; Lincoln & Guba, 1985). An audit trail is simply a record of data analyzed in the study. This may include analyzed artifacts, video- or audiotape, transcribed notes from observations or interviews, fieldnotes, records of ways data were analyzed and interpreted, the timeline of the study, and the researcher's journal. When the audit trail is made available, it is possible for the audience and/or stakeholders to look at both the researcher's results and the actual data to see if results and interpretations are accurate. Making audit trails available is particularly important in larger studies that involve policy, program, or curricular decisions.

■ ■ ■ ■ ■ ▬▬▬▬▬▬▬▬▬▬▬▬▬▬▬▬▬▬▬▬▬▬▬▬▬▬▬▬▬▬▬▬

ACTIVITY 6.1
CREATING A PLAN FOR INCREASING VALIDITY

1. Refer to your response to Activity 2.2 to determine your initial goals in conducting your action research study.
2. Determine the types of validity that are applicable in your study. Consider the purpose of your study, the nature of your reflective activities in planning the study, and your audience.
3. Create a plan for increasing validity that is aligned with the types of validity you deemed applicable for your action research study.

Journal Activity: Include in your journal issues related to validity in your study. Your journal is a place to record information from peer debriefing and member checks. You can also refer to previous journal entries related to bias, descriptions of the setting and events that have occurred, and negative cases. The journal is one potential source of data that can be part of the audit trail. In addition, reflections written in the journal—on the intervention, data, and the progress of the study—can be used for ongoing reflective planning.

Research Paper Activity: Under the heading *Plan for Increasing Validity* (or a similar heading such as *Validity Issues, Validity of the Study,* or another appropriate heading), write a section that explains the types of validity chosen for your study, a justification for choosing those types of validity (with a link to the purpose, nature of reflection, and audience of the study), and the methods used for increasing those types of validity. It may be necessary to complete this section of the paper after the conclusion of the study so that the methods used and the results of using those methods can be described in detail. This section should follow the section on data collection strategies employed (see Activity 5.1).

■ **Present results to key audiences** (Anderson, Herr, & Nihlen, 1994). Anderson et al. suggest engaging in dialogue with peers as a way to increase dialogic validity. In sharing results with others, peers are able to review each others' work and provide feedback on the soundness of both the research process and the researcher's conclusions. Key audiences can include colleagues as well as stakeholders in the process (e.g., parents, students, teachers, administrators).

■ **Engage in continuous, ongoing reflective planning.** In the process of action research, a researcher continually reflects on what is occurring during the study and makes changes to the research plan as necessary. For example, a principal engaged in project on teacher study groups may determine to alter the intervention plan if sources of data indicate that changes are warranted. If the principal's observations lead her to believe that the groups need more than one week to prepare for their study group meetings, she would be wise to alter the intervention plan to allow for a longer period of preparation time between meetings. Ongoing reflective planning also allows a researcher to change data collection strategies based on experiences during the data collection phase. If the principal investigating study groups determines that observing the study groups for the first 15 minutes of each group session is not resulting in useful observation data, she could plan to spend longer periods of time observing the groups.

ETHICAL GUIDELINES FOR ACTION
RESEARCH STUDIES

Historically, individuals engaging in academic educational research, including higher education faculty, advanced graduate students, and others involved in educational research, have been bound by ethical guidelines that protect the rights of human subjects/participants. These guidelines have been put into place to ensure that participants are not harmed or deceived, that they have been informed regarding what participation entails, that they have agreed to participate, and that they have been assured that confidentiality of their responses and their participation will be maintained.

There has been a great deal written about whether these ethical guidelines are necessary and/or appropriate for research conducted by practitioners. As Zeni (2001) explains, guidelines for educational research are based on those established for quantitative research and thus are not well-fitted to the type of research conducted by practitioners. For example, ethical guidelines for educational research require that the researcher explain precisely which types of data will be collected before the study begins. However, as Zeni explains, the action research process is one that can change along the way as ongoing reflective planning takes place; practitioners who conduct research often decide during the study which types of data should be collected as new questions and new directions emerge.

Although a number of suggestions have been put forth regarding ethical guidelines for action research, a procedure has not yet been agreed upon by the professional community. So, for the time being, guidelines for quantitative educational research must be observed. You need permission to conduct an action research study if the data you are collecting on human participants will be disseminated (including as research paper for a course, as a presentation at your school or district, as a conference presentation, or through publication). Most school districts require individuals—even teachers and administrators in the district—to obtain permission before conducting any type of research. If you are completing your action research project as part of a university requirement, the university also has its own procedures for approving research involving human participants.

When conducting an action research study in a school or school district (not in a college or university), the first step is to contact the district office and inquire about the approval process for research studies. Obtain necessary paperwork and begin completing it as soon as possible. If completing the study is also a university course requirement *or* if the project will take place in a college or university setting, contact the university's Institutional Review Board (IRB). It is necessary to obtain an IRB application and complete it before formally beginning the study.

Although the process of obtaining permissions can be burdensome, it is a necessary and important step of the action research process. Obtaining permissions will protect you, your participants, your school, and your university. If you are a parent, you probably would not want your child's teacher to conduct a research study that involves your child without telling you and obtaining your permission. You also probably would not want the teacher to report information about your child without your written permission. Always extend the courtesy of obtaining permission from the participants in your study, regardless of whether they are children or adults.

All participants must agree in writing to be part of the study. If the study includes individuals younger than 18 years of age, a requirement is to obtain their parents' permission to use data obtained on them in the study. Consent can be obtained using an informed consent form. On an informed consent form, it is imperative to explain the purpose of the study, the nature of participation in the study, that confidentiality will be maintained, and that participation is voluntary. Further, a statement must be included that says that there will be no penalty for withdrawing from or not participating in the study. Figure 6.1 is an informed consent template for minors that can be adapted for use in most studies. If your study includes adult participants, alter or adapt the form accordingly. Each participant and/or parent should sign two copies of the form. One is kept by the participant or parent and the other should be returned to you and filed in a safe place.

If you are a teacher, you may be required by your district or university IRB to have written permission from the school or school district where your study will take place. Check the procedures in your school system and/or university IRB before collecting any data for your project. If a school or school district consent form is required, you may be able to use the consent template authorizing a school to participate in a study, which is included in Figure 6.2.

Occasionally, parents will return a consent form in which they have indicated that they do not want their child to be part of a research study. When this happens, educators often get confused as to whether this means that the child cannot be part of the instructional activities in the action research project. For this reason, make it clear in the consent form that the intervention is part of your normal instructional activities that all students will be a

FIGURE 6.1   Informed consent template for minors.

Informed Consent Form

*Authorization for a Minor to Serve
as a Research Participant*

Dear Parents,

I will be conducting a study in our classroom to determine [include purpose here]. I am writing to ask permission to use the data I collect from your child during this process. Participation in this study involves only regular classroom activities. You may contact me at any time regarding your child's participation. My phone number is [include phone number here]. The principal of the school has approved this study.

The purpose of the study is to [briefly describe purpose here]. The study will take place at [name location] and will last for [give time frame]. [Briefly describe the procedures you will follow]. During the study, I will collect various forms of data to determine whether [name of intervention] was successful. Possible types of data I will collect include [list data collection strategies such as samples of student work, surveys/questionnaires, interviews, observations, test scores, etc.]

Benefits of participating in this study include [describe the benefits]. Only [name(s) of researcher and collaborators] will have access to the data collected in this study. Your child's participation in this project is strictly confidential. Only I [and names of collaborators and/or supervising professor if study is part of a university assignment] will have access to your child's identity and to information that can be associated to your child's identity. [If applicable, state when data or documentation will be destroyed].

Use of data from your child is voluntary. You may contact me at any time if you do not wish to have your child's data included in the study.

Please check the appropriate box below and sign the form:

☐ I give permission for my child's data to be used in this study. I understand that I will receive a signed copy of this consent form. I have read this form and understand it.

☐ I do not give permission for my child's data to be included in this project.

_____   _____
Student's name   Signature of parent/guardian

_____
Date

FIGURE 6.2   Authorization for a school to serve in a research study.

Authorization for a School to Serve in
a Research Study

Project: The purpose of this study is to examine the effects of

Researcher:

Employment Affiliation: Phone Number:

Location of the study:

Supervising University Professor (if applicable):

Purpose of the study:

Procedures to be followed:

Time and duration of the study:

Benefits of the study:

Persons who will have access to the records, data, tapes, or other documentation:

When the records, data, tapes, or other documentation will be destroyed (if applicable):

I understand that participation in this project is voluntary, and I understand that a parent or guardian may withdraw his/her child from this study at any time by notifying the researcher.

Statement of confidentiality:

The participation of the students in this project is confidential. Only the researcher, collaborators, and supervising professor [if appropriate] will have access to the students' identities and to information that can be associated with their identities.

Please check the appropriate box below and sign the form:

☐ I give permission for my school to participate in this project. I understand that I will receive a signed copy of this consent form. I have read this form and understand it.

☐ I do not give permission for my school to participate in this project.

_____   _____
        Signature of principal   Date

■ ■ ■ ■ ■

ACTIVITY 6.2
GAINING INFORMED CONSENT

1. Contact the review board that oversees research studies. If you are conducting your study in a K-12 school/district setting, contact the school district office to locate the individual or board that reviews research studies. If you are conducting your study as part of a university's requirement (or in a university setting), contact the university's Institutional Review Board (IRB). Contact both the school district IRB *and* the University IRB if your study is both in a K-12 school/district setting and is part of a university requirement. Once you have made contact, request information on the review process(es).
2. Complete and submit paperwork to applicable IRBs.
3. Once the study is approved, distribute informed consent forms to participants. Keep returned forms in a safe place. Be sure to analyze data on only those individuals who have granted consent.

part of and that you are only seeking permission to *use/report* data collected on participants. Follow up with parents who have any questions or concerns about the study.

ENGAGING IN CONTINUOUS, ONGOING REFLECTIVE PLANNING THROUGHOUT THE STUDY

A key element in the action research process is reflecting throughout the process. This act of reflection goes beyond simply revisiting or thinking about what is occurring during the intervention. Reflection in action research means considering actions taken throughout the study and altering those actions as necessary. This may mean altering an intervention plan, changing data collection strategies as the study progresses, or modifying the project timeline. Consider, for example, a career counselor studying an intervention focused on working with ninth-grade students to establish academic and personal goals for structuring high school activities (courses taken, extracurricular participation, community service) aligned with students' postsecondary goals. If, in the third week of her intervention, the counselor determined that many participating students had clear career aspirations but that the students did not understand the realities of their chosen professions, she would probably want to provide time for instruction, discussion, and research on the day-to-day activities of the professions of interest to the students. She might determine that adding a "shadow day" in which participating students spend a day with an individual from the community in the student's chosen profession would help students understand what certain professions are really about. Additional intervention activities such as this would need to be planned and implemented as the counselor collected formal and informal data to determine what was and was not working in her intervention. Altering the plan would help the counselor make steady progress toward her goal of helping students prepare for life beyond high school. Making changes to the intervention would alter the timeline (additional time would need to be added to the intervention), and it might also mean adding data collection strategies. In this case, the counselor could choose to collect data on the new intervention phase focusing on <u>observations</u> of students researching and discussing chosen professions, <u>journal entries</u> about students' shadow days, and <u>student conferences</u> about what was learned in researching chosen profession and spending a day with someone in that profession.

Remember as you begin your action research study that ongoing reflection is an important element of your project. As the intervention or innovation begins and you look at the various sources of data collected, reflect on what is working and what isn't working. When a certain strategy isn't effective, use the different sources of data you are collecting to determine why the strategy isn't working, and then alter the intervention plan using your best judgment (based on the data and what was previously learned in reviewing the literature) about how to make the strategy more effective. Collect additional data on these changes, analyze the data, and keep working to make the intervention as effective as possible. This may mean making drastic changes such as restructuring the entire intervention. More often, though, it will mean making small changes along the way, such as adding strategies to help a few struggling students or changing/adding to data collection strategies. Be sure to record any and all changes in your journal. If you are writing up your results (for a paper, presentation, or publication, for example) you will be able to use the record in your journal to write about what actually occurred in the study rather than simply what was planned at the beginning of the study.

CREATING A TIMELINE FOR THE PROJECT

Once an intervention plan has been created and data collection strategies have been decided upon, the next step is to create a timeline for the action research project. Creating a timeline will help you sketch a plan for when activities and the intervention will take place, when data will be collected and analyzed, and when you will begin writing results. The timeline will help you maintain your research focus and will give you some indication of how much time should be planned for each phase of the research process.

Provided here are two types of timelines. Both timelines show activities for a research project on using student contracts. Figure 6.3 displays the timeline in list form, providing activities for each date listed. Figure 6.4 displays the timeline in a Gantt chart, which is a method borrowed from the business world to graphically display activities for certain dates. You may wish to use both types of timelines. Using a list-form timeline will enable you to include detailed information about what will happen on each date or time period during the study. This should be written like a lesson plan and should include enough information to help ensure that you complete each planned step of the intervention. Supplementing a list-form timeline with a Gantt chart can provide you with a visual depiction of events for each phase of the study. This type of display works well in keeping you on track regarding upcoming intervention steps, data collection stages, and dates for analysis and writing.

FIGURE 6.3   **List-form timeline for student contract project.**

September 2–September 9: Initial reflection.

September 9–September 30: Review of literature.

October 1–October 8: Contact principal, school district, and university Institutional Review Board to secure permissions for study.

October 1–October 25: Gather baseline data (student work samples, observational notes) Conference with students on October 23rd.

October 7–October 31: Phone parents to discuss action research study. Send home permission forms. Collect permission forms. Follow-up phone calls to parents if necessary.

November 1–November 29: First contract phase.

   November 1: Discuss contract procedure with students.

   November 4: Conference with students to establish first contracts.

   November 5–6: Work with students to create rubrics for contract grading.

   November 14–15: Contact parents to discuss student progress on contracts.

   November 27–28: Student presentations (videotaped).

   November 29: Conference with students to discuss accomplishment toward contract goals.

January 16–February 14: Second contract phase.

   January 17: Conference with students to establish contracts.

   January 19–20: Creation of rubrics for contract grading.

   January 31: Contact parents to discuss student progress on contracts.

   February 12–13: Student presentations (videotaped).

   February 14: Conference with students to discuss accomplishment toward goals.

February 17–March 14: Third contract phase.

   February 17: Conference with students to establish contracts.

   February 18–19: Creation of rubrics for contract grading.

   March 3: Contact parents to discuss student progress on contracts.

   March 12–13: Student presentations (videotaped).

   March 14: Conference with students to discuss accomplishment toward goals.

March 17–April 1: Data analysis (observation notes in journal, videotapes, transcripts from student and parent conferences, rubrics, artifacts).

April 2–April 15: Writing results and putting the action research report/paper together.

April 16–April 30: Revisions of the paper.

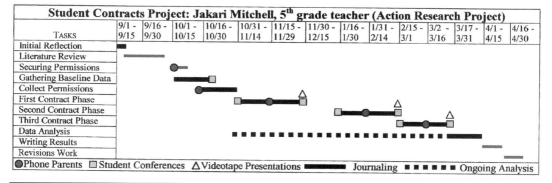

FIGURE 6.4   Gantt chart for student contracts project.

■ ■ ■ ■ ■ ■

ACTIVITY 6.3
ONGOING REFLECTIVE PLANNING AND CREATING A TIMELINE

1. Create either a list-form timeline *or* a Gantt chart for your action research study. Include a detailed plan for implementation of your intervention and the dates the intervention will take place. The plan should also include information on when data will be collected and when (if at all) meetings will collaborators will take place. Include when analysis of the data will occur.
2. Share your timeline with a collaborator or colleague and seek feedback on the feasibility of your plan. Make changes to the timeline as necessary.
3. Begin the intervention phase of the study.

Journal Activity: Keep track of changes to the research plan in your journal. Describe how ongoing reflection shapes changes to the research plan.

Research Paper Activity: Make changes to previously written sections of the paper if/when ongoing reflective planning leads to changes in the project. If the intervention changes, reflect these changes in the intervention plan (see Activity 4.2). If the data collection plan changes, add these changes to the data collection strategies section of the paper (see Activity 5.1).

SUMMARY

This chapter described the final steps of planning an action research study (increasing validity of the study, following ethical guidelines, engaging in continuous reflective planning, and creating a timeline) prior to implementation of the intervention or innovation. Fifteen types of validity relevant in action research studies were described and methods for choosing ways to describe validity—based on the nature and purpose of a particular study—were presented. Guidelines for ensuring the ethical treatment of research participants and gaining their consent were provided. In addition, the importance of engaging in ongoing reflective planning to increase the effectiveness of interventions was illustrated. Finally, both a list-form timeline and a Gantt chart were provided as methods for displaying a study timeline.

As you complete this chapter, it is time to begin the implementation phase of your study and begin the intervention or innovation you have chosen to study. In Chapter 7, methods for analyzing data are presented. It is important to begin reading this chapter as the intervention begins so that you can analyze data throughout the study. This ongoing analysis will make it possible to engage in continuous, ongoing reflective planning.

CHAPTER SEVEN

STRATEGIES FOR DATA ANALYSIS

CHAPTER GOALS:

- Explain the process of interim analysis and its importance in action research.
- Illustrate ways to analyze, report, and display results for quantitative data.
- Illustrate ways to analyze results for qualitative data using thematic analysis.
- Describe the process of triangulating data sources.
- Illustrate ways to draw conclusions from data.
- Provide activities to demonstrate the ways to analyze various data sources, triangulate them, and make conclusions about the effectiveness of interventions or innovations.

INTERIM DATA ANALYSIS

In Chapter 5 a number of strategies were presented for collecting data during your action research study. At this point in the action research cycle, you should be implementing your intervention and collecting multiple forms of data to answer your research questions. You need to begin making sense of data *as you collect the data.* The analysis of data is an on-going process that should occur throughout the study rather than at the end of it. Huberman and Miles (1998) define the collection and analysis of data during the study as **interim analysis**. Interim analysis, they explain, allows the researcher make changes to data collection strategies during the study based on problems or questions that arise when analyzing the data. Thus, interim analysis is part of continuous, ongoing reflective planning, which was described in Chapter 6.

You may be thinking that it would be much easier to analyze all the data from your study after they have all been collected. But waiting until the end of your action research

---

Interim Analysis: Analyzing data throughout the research study for the purpose of enhancing data collection strategies based on emerging problems or questions.

study—remember, in this cycle there really is no end—lessens your ability to gather the information you need to make your study credible and valid. Consider, for example, an action research study conducted by a teacher studying the impact of using student learning contracts. During the teacher's first interview with a student, the teacher concludes the semi-structured interview by asking the student if there is anything else she would like say about learning contracts, to which the student replies, "Some of the smart kids think it's unfair that some of us who don't get such good grades have raised our averages now that we have the contracts." This comment, though based on only one student's interview, may deserve to be further investigated as a negative consequence of or negative attitude toward using learning contracts. In future observations of students as they work on their learning contracts and discuss them with each other, the teacher may choose to look for evidence of this negative attitude. Further, during future interviews, the teacher could ask structured questions such as *Have you heard any positive or negative comments from other students about using learning contracts?* and *Do you feel that using learning contracts is a fair way to evaluate all students?* These added interview questions, in addition to formal observations related to students' attitudes about the learning contracts, may result in data that are important for understanding reasons the learning contract intervention is successful or unsuccessful. If the teacher had not engaged in interim analysis, she would have missed the opportunity to collect information critical to the study.

Interim analysis is an informal process of ongoing data analysis and reflective planning, which means that all that is required is looking at and thinking about data as it is collected and then making changes or additions to strategies if necessary. The more structured and formal data analysis process will indeed occur once all data have been collected. At that point, the process of data analysis is one of reducing data, interpreting it, and drawing conclusions. Strategies for data reduction of quantitative forms of data, which include reporting, comparing, and displaying information, are much different than the strategies used to reduce qualitative forms of data, which involves studying the data to find patterns and themes.

In this chapter, data analysis strategies for quantitative and qualitative data are presented. Keep in mind that the techniques explained in this chapter are organized differently than the way data collection strategies were organized in Chapter 5. The methods used to analyze artifacts are not separate or distinct from the methods used to analyze observational data. To clarify, some artifacts are analyzed using quantitative techniques, whereas other types of artifacts are analyzed using qualitative techniques. The same holds true for observational data and inquiry data.

Also presented in this chapter are methods used for drawing conclusions from data, which involve triangulating data sources to determine valid and credible answers to research questions. Ways to verify findings and increase validity of the study will be described as well. Activities that will help you analyze your data are presented in this chapter.

USING SOFTWARE PACKAGES TO ANALYZE LARGE AMOUNTS OF DATA

Although it is beyond the scope of this book to describe the ways in which software can be used to analyze quantitative and qualitative data, you should be aware that several software packages are available. For individuals interested in statistical analysis of quantitative data, SPSS, SAS, Minitab, and even Excel can be used to determine statistical differences or relationships in data. For those interested in using qualitative software to analyze large amounts of qualitative data, NVivo, QSR N6 (formerly NUD*IST), and ATLAS.ti, are just a few of the many software packages available. To learn more about how these different types of software can be used to analyze data, visit the links provided in Table 7.12 on page 150. Other useful links include:

- **Gene Glass's Online Data Analysis:** http://glass.ed.asu.edu/stats/online.htm
- **Electronic Statistics Textbook:** http://www.statsoft.com/textbook/stathome.html
- **VassarStats:** http://faculty.vassar.edu/lowry/VassarStats.html
- **Bobbi's Place—Qualitative Research Software:** http://kerlins.net/bobbi/research/qualresearch/researchware.html

ANALYSIS OF QUANTITATIVE DATA: REPORTING, COMPARING, AND DISPLAYING

Quantitative data can be generated from test scores, rubric-scored work (written assignments, performances, artwork, projects), closed-ended self-assessment items, computer-generated reports, school records, checklists, tally sheets, behavioral scales, attitude scales, and closed-ended survey items. Specific data from some of these data gathering tools, however, is not quantitative in nature, although the data can be analyzed quantitatively. For example, in Table 7.1, items from self-assessments, peer reviews, rating scales, and surveys are provided. Although the *responses* to these items are not quantitative, the data can be described by counting or averaging the number of responses for each item. For example, analyzing a closed-ended self assessment item in which students indicated whether they were a strong, average, or weak readers would involve counting the number of students who chose *strong,* the number who chose *average,* and the number who chose *weak* (for example, in Mr. Phillips' class, five students said they were strong readers, three students said they were average readers, and two students said they were weak readers). Numbers of responses could also be counted for the closed-ended peer review items, the attitude scale items, and the closed-ended survey item.

For the behavioral scale item, which includes numerical responses, the actual number chosen for each item could be tallied, as in the previous example, but numbers could also be averaged to describe results. For example, a teacher of a self-contained class for students with behavior problems could look at her five students' average number of physical outbursts (Jim = 2, Sherian = 1, Paul = 1, Beth = 0, Trey = 1) and report that, on average, students exhibited one to two physical outbursts per day. This was determined by calculating the average ($[2 + 1 + 1 + 0 + 1]/5 = 1$) and then looking back at the scale to determine what the average (1) means.

The steps of analysis for quantitative forms of data include reporting, comparing, and displaying data. The first step in the analysis process is to look at various data sources and determine which can be analyzed quantitatively. Next, follow the guidelines given in the following subsections for *tests, closed-ended items, checklists and tally sheets,* and

TABLE 7.1   Examples of Quantitative Items for Self-Assessments, Peer Review, Rating Scales, and Surveys

Closed-ended self assessment item	*Circle your response:* 1. The type of reader I am: **Strong Average Weak** 2. The type of writer I am: **Strong Average Weak**
Closed-ended peer review item	*Evaluate your mentor teacher in the following areas:* E = excellent, G = good, A = average, P = poor 1. Assisting with instructional planning: **E G A P** 2. Assisting with classroom management: **E G A P**
Behavioral scale items	*Evaluate the frequency of the following behaviors.* 0 = never, 1 = up to 2 times per day, 2 = three + times per day 1. Defying authority. **0 1 2** 2. Physical outburst. **0 1 2**
Attitude scale item	*Circle your response:* SA = strongly agree, A = agree, D = disagree, SD = strongly disagree 1. I'd rather read than watch TV. **SA A D SD** 2. I am a good reader. **SA A D SD**
Closed-ended survey item	*Circle your response:* SA = strongly agree, A = agree, D = disagree, SD = strongly disagree 1. I like deciding how my work will be evaluated. **SA A D SD** 2. Learning contracts are a fair way to evaluate students. **SA A D SD**

computer-generated reports and school records. These guidelines suggest ways to organize data, report in written form what the data indicate, and graphically illustrate results.

Tests

A number of different test formats can be analyzed quantitatively. First, follow guidelines for the recording of data based on if the test was teacher-made, a standardized test, or some type of work scored using a rubric:

- **Teacher-made tests:** Score tests and record scores for each student. Consider looking for patterns of errors, which can indicate what students know and can do as well as any areas where they may be lacking.
- **Standardized tests:** Use score reports to record scores for each participant. Record a standard score such as normal curve equivalent (NCE) score, percentile rank, or stanine. If scores are broken into subcategories (for example, the reading section

includes a vocabulary subsection and a reading comprehension subsection), record subsection scores as well. If you are conducting a schoolwide action research study with a large number of participants, you may want to look at scores for classes or grade levels rather than for individual students.

■ **Rubric-scored work** (written assignments, performances, artwork, and projects): Score each student's work using the rubric. Record a score for each student. If the rubric contains subsections (for example, a writing rubric that includes a separate score for thesis development, transitions, audience, and mechanics), record a score for each subsection.

Record scores in a grade book or in research journal. If you are familiar with spreadsheet programs, you can input grades on a spreadsheet and then generate graphical displays of the data from the spreadsheet program. Other software programs that are used for statistical data analysis, such as SAS or SPSS, can also be used if you are familiar with the programs and have access to them. Keep in mind, though, that unless you are analyzing a large amount of data (such as in a schoolwide study), inputting information on a spreadsheet or in a statistical program is not necessary. In fact, in action research studies that involve a small number of participants, using software can be more work than making calculations by hand.

Whether you record data by hand or use a computer, you should record the data so that each row contains data for one student, which is the way grades are recorded in a grade book. Also, using numbers as codes for responses (1 = *emerging,* 2 = *basic,* 3 = *proficient,* 4 = *advanced* or 1 = *strongly disagree,* 2 = *disagree,* 3 = *agree,* 4 = *strongly agree*) will allow you to find averages for responses and create charts with computer software. Averaging can produce strange results, such as a score that is between points. This is true for ordered data that is not quantitative. For example, averaging an essay score for a student could result in a score of 2.75, which is a point not represented on the four-point rubric described previously. However, the score can be interpreted as between the basic and proficient level. An example of how to record data is provided in Table 7.2.

Once data have been recorded, you can report, display, and/or compare data. Reporting the data simply means providing an explanation of what is found. For example, average total scores for each of the four essays in Table 7.2 could be reported in this way: *The average score on the persuasive essay was 6.4 points. On the Hero essay, the average score was 7 points, on the My Perfect World essay the average score was 8.1, and on the My Worst Day essay, the average score was 9.5.* These averages were calculated by adding Total Scores for each essay and dividing by the number of scores. For example, the average for the persuasive essay was determined by adding the ten students' scores (6 + 6 + 6 + 7 + 6 + 8 + 4 + 9 + 3 + 9), which equaled 64, then dividing by the number of scores (10 students' scores) to arrive at an average score of 6.4. Data from Table 7.2 could also be graphically displayed in chart form. An example is provided in Figure 7.1. This chart was created in Microsoft Excel.

Another way to report data is to make comparisons across different data points. For example, the data provided in Figure 7.1 could be compared in this way: *The average total score on the persuasive essay, which students wrote before we began the Writer's Workshop intervention, was 6.4. Scores increased throughout the intervention phase of the study. On the second essay, average total scores rose to 7 points, and on the third essay, total*

TABLE 7.2 **Rubric Scores for Writer's Workshop Study**

	Persuasive Essay (Baseline)				Hero Essay				My Perfect World Essay				The Worst Day Essay			
	C	M	T	TS	C	M	T	TS	C	M	T	TS	C	M	T	TS
Abdullah, Momar	3	2	1	6	3	2	2	7	3	2	3	8	3	3	4	10
Adams, Jason	2	3	1	6	3	3	1	7	3	2	2	7	3	3	3	9
Crenshaw, Mandi	2	2	2	6	3	2	2	7	3	2	3	8	4	3	3	10
Davidson, Bakari	3	3	1	7	3	3	2	8	3	3	3	9	4	3	4	11
Gonzales, Jorge	3	2	1	6	2	2	2	6	3	2	2	7	3	3	2	8
Huynh, Sarah	4	2	2	8	3	2	3	8	3	3	3	9	4	3	3	10
Timmons, Freda	2	1	1	4	3	1	1	5	3	2	2	7	3	2	2	7
Vinson, Cyndi	3	4	2	9	2	4	2	8	3	4	3	10	4	4	4	12
Warren, Robert	1	1	1	3	2	1	1	4	2	2	2	6	2	3	2	7
Whaley, Donetta	3	3	3	9	3	3	4	10	2	4	4	10	3	4	4	11

Key: C = Content M = Mechanics T = Transitions TS = Total Score 1 = emerging 2 = basic 3 = proficient 4 = advanced

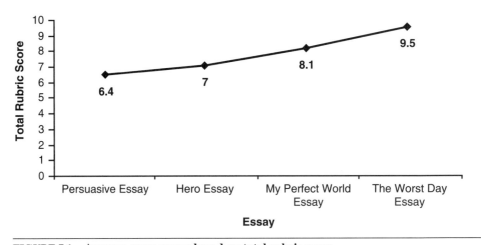

FIGURE 7.1 **Average essay scores based on total rubric score.**

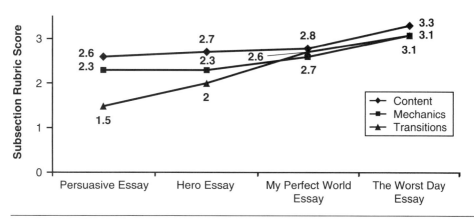

FIGURE 7.2   Subsection rubric scores for essays.

scores rose once again to 8.1. On the final essay, students' average total score was 9.5—just over a three-point gain compared to the baseline data.

If you are analyzing test scores or rubric-scored work in your action research study, begin by recording the data, averaging scores when appropriate, and thinking about ways to display data. Choose strategies that will help you learn as much as you can about your data and that will help you explain your results to others in a way that is simple and understandable. Look back at Table 7.2. There is much more data displayed than what has been described in the previous examples of reporting, displaying, and comparing data. The teacher who collected these data may also be interested in seeing how students' writing skills increased in the three areas measured on each essay—content, mechanics, and transitions. This deeper level of analysis can help the teacher determine whether the Writer's Workshop intervention is more helpful to students in some areas but not others, which is critical for ongoing reflective planning. Figure 7.2, which was created using Microsoft Excel, contains a chart display of average scores on the four essays for each subsection of the rubric.

This chart is useful for seeing where students made the greatest gains. A teacher reading this chart could report and compare data in this way: Throughout the Writer's Workshop intervention, students improved in content, mechanics, and transitions. Their greatest gains, however, were in the area of transitions. Baseline data indicated that the average score for students in this area was 1.5, which was just below the basic level. Students' scores gradually increased during the intervention, and on the last essay, students' average score on transitions rose to 3.1, which is at the proficient level.

Closed-Ended Items

When analyzing closed-ended items from self-assessments, peer reviews, behavioral scales, attitude scales, or surveys, first record data by participant for each close-ended item in a grade book or journal or use a spreadsheet or statistical software package. An example of how to record data for closed-ended survey items is provided in Table 7.3.

TABLE 7.3   Student Survey Data for Writer's Workshop Study

	I know how to use correct grammar when writing essays.		I know how to use transitions in my writing.		I like to write.		I am a good writer.		Writer's Workshop has helped me become a better writer.	
	B	F	B	F	B	F	B	F	B	F
Abdullah, Momar	4	4	3	4	3	4	4	4	na	4
Adams, Jason	1	3	2	3	2	2	2	1	na	2
Crenshaw, Mandi	1	3	1	2	2	3	2	3	na	4
Davidson, Bakari	2	3	1	3	1	3	2	3	na	3
Gonzales, Jorge	2	3	2	3	2	3	3	4	na	3
Huynh, Sarah	1	3	2	3	3	3	2	3	na	2
Timmons, Freda	2	3	1	2	1	3	2	2	na	3
Vinson, Cyndi	2	4	3	4	1	3	3	3	na	4
Warren, Robert	2	2	2	2	1	1	2	3	na	1
Whaley, Donetta	1	3	2	3	1	2	3	2	na	3

Key: B = Baseline Survey   F = Final Survey   1 = strongly disagree   2 = disagree   3 = agree   4 = strongly agree

Once data have been recorded, think about the best ways to report, display, and compare the data. As you look at your data, remember that you want to explain results in a way that helps you answer your research questions. You also want to explain the data in a way that is understandable so that others can learn from the outcomes of your study. There are several ways to report, display, and compare the data presented in Table 7.3. In fact, the table itself is a display of the data. Other graphical displays could be created from the data as well. The chart provided in Figure 7.3 is one way to display the data.

Figure 7.3 displays data from the closed-ended items on the Writer's Workshop survey, and because results are included from the baseline survey and the final survey, it is easy to compare differences between the two. The researcher displaying this chart could explain it in this way: *Student responses to the survey items were averaged and comparisons were made between responses on the baseline survey and responses on the final survey. For each of the four closed-ended survey items, students' confidence in their writing abilities and attitudes toward writing improved. On the baseline survey, most students strongly disagreed or disagreed that they knew how to use correct grammar and transitions when writing essays. On the final survey, most students agreed or strongly agreed that they could use correct grammar and transitions when writing. There was also a change in students' attitude toward writing. On the baseline survey, the average response to the prompt* I like to write *was between* strongly disagree *and* disagree. *On the final survey, more students*

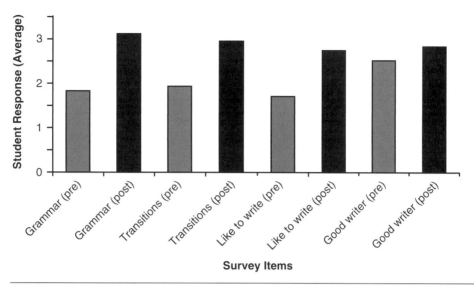

FIGURE 7.3 **Baseline and final survey comparisons of students' responses to the survey on Writer's Workshop.**

agreed that they like to write. Although students' confidence in their writing abilities and their attitudes about writing increased, there was little change in students' responses to the prompt I am a good writer. *On both the baseline and final surveys, the average student response was between* disagree *and* agree.

Another way to display the data shown in Table 7.3 is to record changes in survey responses for each student. This would be appropriate in a study in which the teacher wished to analyze changes in achievement, attitudes, and confidence in writing for individual students. Table 7.4 displays changes in survey responses for each student.

Displaying data in this manner provides the teacher with information regarding individual students. Looking at the data this way, it is clear that Robert's confidence using correct grammar and transitions has not been affected by his participation in Writer's Workshop. His negative attitude toward writing also has not changed. Notice that Momar's survey responses show that he hasn't changed much either, but in his case his writing confidence and attitude toward writing were good prior to the Writer's Workshop intervention. The teacher might conclude from these data—especially if confirmed by other sources of triangulated data—that Momar should continue participating in the Writer's Workshop, but different strategies should be used with Robert.

Checklists and Tally Sheets

When analyzing data from checklists and tally sheets, the first step is to record behaviors or events and, for checklists, the number of times they occur. An example of one way to record data from a checklist is provided in Table 7.5.

TABLE 7.4   **Changes in Students' Self-Assessment of Writing**

	I know how to use correct grammar. . .			I know how to use transitions. . .			I like to write			I am a good writer		
	B	F	C	B	F	C	B	F	C	B	F	C
Abdullah, Momar	4	4	0	3	4	+1	3	4	+1	4	4	0
Adams, Jason	1	3	+2	2	3	+1	2	2	0	2	1	−1
Crenshaw, Mandi	1	3	+2	1	2	+1	2	3	+1	2	3	+1
Davidson, Bakari	2	3	+1	1	3	+2	1	3	+2	2	3	+1
Gonzales, Jorge	2	3	+1	2	3	+1	2	3	+1	3	4	+1
Huynh, Sarah	1	3	+2	2	3	+1	3	3	0	2	3	+1
Timmons, Freda	2	3	+1	1	2	+1	1	3	+2	2	2	0
Vinson, Cyndi	2	4	+2	3	4	+1	1	3	+2	3	3	0
Warren, Robert	2	2	0	2	2	0	1	1	0	2	3	+1
Whaley, Donetta	1	4	+3	2	3	+1	1	2	+1	3	2	−1

Key: B = Baseline Survey F = Final Survey C = Change

1 = strongly disagree 2 = disagree 3 = agree 4 = strongly agree

TABLE 7.5   **Collaborative Groups Checklist, Honors Biology, Mr. Jackson**

Behaviors/Activities	First Activity					Second Activity					Third Activity				
GROUP NUMBER →	1	2	3	4	5	1	2	3	4	5	1	2	3	4	5
All members actively participate.			✔		✔			✔		✔	✔		✔		✔
Group members are respectful of one another.	✔	✔		✔	✔	✔		✔	✔	✔	✔		✔	✔	✔
Group members attempt to complete work on their own before asking me questions.	✔		✔	✔		✔		✔	✔	✔	✔			✔	✔
Group stays on task.	✔		✔	✔		✔		✔	✔		✔		✔	✔	✔
Group completes and turns in progress sheet.	✔	✔	✔		✔	✔	✔	✔	✔	✔	✔	✔	✔	✔	✔

TABLE 7.6   Tally Sheet for Micah R., Fourth Grade, Mrs. Ellison

DATE	2/1	2/2	2/3	2/4	2/5	2/8	2/9	2/10	2/11	2/12	2/15	2/16	2/17	2/18	2/19
UNDESIRED BEHAVIORS															
Tapping pencil	5	6	4	6	4	7	4	5	3	3	4	3	2	1	3
Spinning pencil	1	4	3	3	4	6	2	3	4	2	3	1	0	2	1
Mumbling	7	9	5	4	4	8	4	4	3	2	5	2	2	3	2
Talking out	2	2	0	3	3	4	2	2	1	1	3	0	1	1	1
DESIRED BEHAVIORS															
Asking for help	2	0	1	2	3	1	2	2	3	4	2	4	4	5	3
Raising hand	1	0	0	2	2	0	1	1	2	3	0	3	2	3	4
Responding	3	3	5	4	5	3	5	5	6	5	4	5	6	6	5
Following directions	0	0	1	0	0	0	1	1	3	2	1	3	3	2	4

This record is a useful display of the behaviors and activities for each group during the three collaborative group activities. Based on this record, the teacher could identify several important pieces of information:

- Group 2 did not work well together and made no improvement between the first collaborative activity and the last collaborative activity.
- Groups 1 and 3 worked well together consistently from the first activity through the third activity.
- Groups 4 and 5 improved their collaboration between the first and third activities.
- More emphasis must be placed on all group members participating in the collaborative activity and completing activities on their own.

This information, particularly when considered with other data sources, can provide useful information about differences in increased achievement between and among groups. For example, if there are no changes in achievement in Group 2, a possible explanation is that because the group did not work well together and were not collaborative, there was little opportunity for learning. When data can be used to help understand reasons why an intervention is unsuccessful, there is an opportunity to look for ways to improve the intervention.

A method for recording tally sheet information is provided in Table 7.6. These data represent a behavioral tally sheet for one student over several days. The recorded data on the tally sheet could be displayed a number of ways, which is illustrated in Figures 7.4 and 7.5. Figure 7.4 displays the number of occurrences for mumbling and talking out between February 1 and February 19. In Figure 7.5, the number of occurrences of desired behaviors between February 1 and February 19 are displayed.

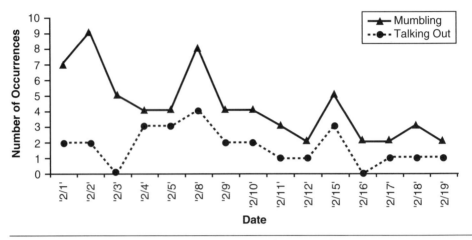

FIGURE 7.4   **Behavioral chart for Micah R. (undesired behaviors).**

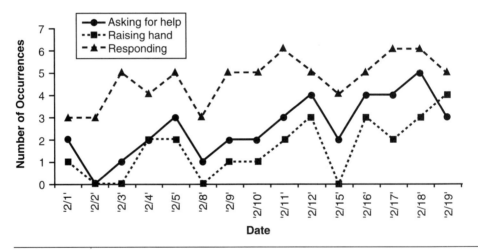

FIGURE 7.5   **Behavioral chart for Micah R. (desired behaviors).**

These figures, which were created in Microsoft Excel, do not display all recorded data because the charts were difficult to read when I attempted to display four behaviors on each one. As you determine the best ways to display the data in your study, always attempt to create graphical displays that can be easily read and understood, even if it means creating a number of separate charts to display the data.

Displayed data such as those provided in Figures 7.4 and 7.5 are easier than recorded data (Table 7.6) to understand and describe. The data in Figures 7.4 and 7.5 could be described this way: *There was a decrease in Micah's mumbling over the three-week intervention period. In the first week, Micah mumbled an average of 5.8 times per day, which decreased to 4.2 times per day the second week and 2.8 times per day the third week. During the second and third weeks, Micah's mumbling was greater on Monday and tended to decrease throughout the week. Micah's talking-out behavior did not decrease as much as his mumbling. In the first and second weeks, Micah talked out an average of 2 times per day, which decreased to 1.2 times per day the third week. During the second and third weeks, Micah talked out more often on Mondays than on other days. As the second and third weeks progressed, Micah's talking-out behavior decreased.*

Desired behaviors increased over the three-week intervention period. The first week, Micah asked for help an average of 1.6 times per day, which increased to 2.4 times per day the second week and 3.6 times per day the third week. There was less of an increase in raising his hand for attention and responding when spoken to, however. The first week Micah raised his hand for attention once per day, on average, which increased to 1.4 times per day the second week and 2.4 times per day the third week. Micah responded when spoken to an average of 4 times per day the first week, 4.8 times per day the second week, and 5.2 times per day the third week. [*Note*: Only some data have been described here, based on the displays in Figures 7.4 and 7.5. Other information on pencil tapping, pencil spinning, and following oral directions should be provided to give a complete explanation on how behaviors changed during the intervention.]

Computer-Generated Reports and School Records

When analyzing data from computer-generated reports and school records, first record information relevant to your action research project as you review reported/recorded data. Consider the best way to record the information, whether it is by student, grade level, teacher, year, or another method. Computer-generated reports, as well as some school records such as discipline reports, retention rates, and attendance can be displayed, reported, and compared in much the same way as checklist and tally sheet data are.

An example of a data record from a computer-generated report is provided in Table 7.7. The record includes the number of books read, the average reading level of the books

TABLE 7.7   Data from Computer-Generated Reading Report for Third-Grade Teachers

	Week 1			Week 2			Week 3			Week 4			Week 5			Week 6		
TEACHER	N	R	C	N	R	C	N	R	C	N	R	C	N	R	C	N	R	C
Jimenez	0.5	2.3	70	1.0	2.5	68	1.3	2.1	72	1.7	2.4	73	2.1	2.2	75	2.8	2.0	80
Southe	1.5	3.1	70	2.5	3.0	75	5.8	3.2	70	6.2	3.4	76	5.5	3.8	80	6.1	3.8	82
Reynolds	1.2	2.8	68	1.2	2.7	72	1.5	2.5	74	3.0	2.2	76	3.2	2.8	82	3.8	3.1	80
Johnson	4.1	3.1	80	3.8	3.4	82	5.2	3.6	84	6.2	3.5	82	6.5	3.7	83	6.3	3.8	85

Key: N = Average number of books read per student

R = Average reading level

C = Average reading comprehension score

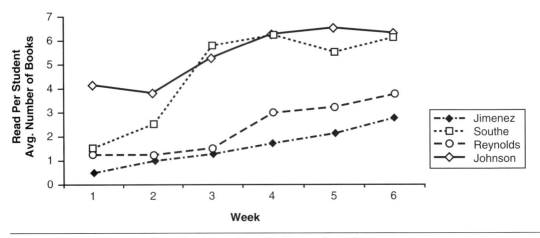

FIGURE 7.6   Average number of books read per student each week.

read, and the average reading comprehension score for each of four third-grade classes over a six-week period.

There are a variety of ways these data can be reported, displayed, and compared. For example, the average number of books read per student per week could be displayed on a chart like the one shown in Figure 7.6.

This graphical display shows that there were increases in the number of books read per student each week for each of the four teachers' classes. Figure 7.6 can be used to explain the gains made by students in each class, and it can be used to compare gains between classes. Other graphical displays could be created for the computer-generated data to show differences and gains in reading levels of books and reading comprehension scores.

To use information from school records, first record the data by hand or input the data into a spreadsheet or statistical software package. An example of how to record data is provided in Table 7.8. These data are from school records on discipline referrals, and they have been recorded for five sixth-grade teachers over a ten-week period.

TABLE 7.8   Number of Discipline Referrals for Sixth-Grade Classes

	Week									
	1	**2**	**3**	**4**	**5**	**6**	**7**	**8**	**9**	**10**
Bridges (6A)	4	2	3	4	5	3	4	4	3	2
Reinhardt (6B)	9	12	8	6	7	4	3	3	1	0
Gregory (6C)	15	9	6	8	6	3	0	1	2	1
A. Lewis (6D)	5	4	5	6	3	1	2	3	1	2
J. Lewis (6E)	7	6	9	5	5	4	3	2	0	0

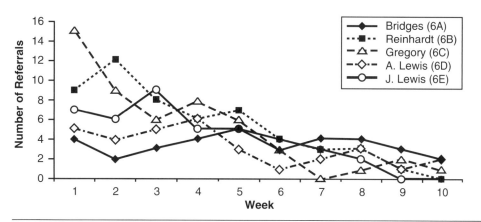

FIGURE 7.7 **Sixth-grade discipline referrals during ten-week intervention.**

A description of these data can be made from the recorded information provided in the table, but they can also be displayed to show whether there were changes in the number of discipline referrals over the ten-week period. Displaying the data makes the job of reporting and making comparisons a much easier task. An example of one way to display the data is provided in Figure 7.7.

Figure 7.7 displays a large amount of data, and it is a bit hard to read printed in black and white. However, it is clear from the graph that the number of discipline referrals decreased in each of the sixth-grade classes over the ten-week period. The largest decrease occurred in Mrs. Gregory's class, and the smallest decrease occurred in Mr. Bridges' class. A graphical display such as this one is very helpful for reporting changes in the number of discipline referrals and comparing changes among the five classes.

In this section, several examples were provided on ways to record, report, and display quantitative data. Explanations and examples were also included on methods for making comparisons with data. The examples provided show just a few of the many ways to explain and display results of your research study when quantitative data are used to answer research questions. As you begin the process of organizing and analyzing your quantitative data, follow these steps:

- **Gather together quantitative data sources and record information.** Record data in a grade book, journal, or computer spreadsheet. Double-check information as you record it to prevent data recording mistakes.
- **Create graphical displays of data.** Work with a collaborator or noncollaborating peer to brainstorm ways to display data. Display data using several methods, if possible, to ascertain the display method that is easiest to understand.
- **Examine displayed data to determine the best ways to explain results.** Study displayed data and then verbally describe important points. Reread your written explanations while looking at your records and graphical displays to ensure that you have accurately described data and data comparisons.

- **Share your analyses and graphical displays with collaborators or peers.** Colleagues can help you determine whether your analyses, charts, figures, and graphs make sense.
- **Make notes in your journal about how your analyses can be used to answer research questions.** Often, researchers become so involved in experimenting with different ways to make sense of their data that they lose sight of the research questions they are trying to answer. As you work on your data analysis, refer often to your primary and secondary research questions. Make sure to analyze your data in ways that can help you answer your research questions. Once that is accomplished, analyze the data in different ways, based on the questions that have arisen as your study has progressed, so that you can try to answer your *why* questions. Activity 7.1 is provided to take you through the steps of analyzing quantitative data.

ANALYSIS OF QUALITATIVE DATA: LOOKING FOR THEMES AND PATTERNS

The analysis of qualitative data is a process of making meaning from data sources that can be interpreted in a number of ways. Qualitative data sources—which in this text include field notes, logs, interviews, focus groups, conferences, documents, journals, and open-ended items from surveys, scales, self-assessments, and peer reviews—can only be explained and used to answer research questions after they have been interpreted. This process requires deeper analysis of data than those processes used to explain quantitative data sources.

Berg (2001) explains that the interpretation of qualitative forms of data involves analyzing "social action and human activity" as if it were text (p. 239). What this means is that in order to understand data based on observations, interviews, or conversations, we must first convert the data to text. Obviously, some forms of qualitative data are already in textual form (journals, responses to open-ended survey items), but with other forms of data, we must record the data in text form to make it ready for analysis. Once qualitative data have been recorded in text form, the text is analyzed to search for patterns or themes in the data. Shank (2002) calls this process, which involves building general themes from specific examples in the data, **thematic analysis**. Although a number of qualitative researchers and qualitative theorists have explained that themes "emerge" from data, Shank's explanation of emerging themes is closer to what actually happens in the analysis process:

> . . . themes do not really emerge from data. What emerges, after much hard work and creative thought, is an awareness in the mind of the researcher that there are patterns of order that seem to cut across various aspects of the data. When these patterns become organiza-

---

Thematic Analysis: Analyzing specific examples in qualitative data to discover general themes.

■ ■ ■ ■ ■ ■

ACTIVITY 7.1
ANALYSIS OF QUANTITATIVE DATA

1. Write your primary and secondary research questions. Keep them in sight as you work through the analysis of your quantitative forms of data.
2. Gather all quantitative data sources that will be analyzed in your study. Match each quantitative data source to the primary or secondary research question it will be used to answer. *Note*: Remember that some data sources will be used to answer more than one question.
3. Create records for each data source. Use a computer spreadsheet if you would like to create computer-generated figures or charts.
4. Display results for each data source. Share your displayed data with a collaborator or peer and ask for feedback on the appropriateness and understandability of the displays. Rework displays based on provided feedback.
5. Produce a written description to explain displayed data. Share descriptions and graphical displays with a collaborator or peer. Rework explanations based on provided feedback.
6. Answer any research questions that can be answered with your quantitative data sources. For example: My primary research question was Will students' achievement in writing increase as a result of the *Writer's Workshop* intervention? Based on analysis of student essays, writing achievement did improve throughout the intervention. The average total score on the persuasive essay, which students wrote before we began the Writer's Workshop intervention, was 6.4. Scores increased throughout the intervention phase of the study. On the second essay, average total scores rose to 7 points, and on the third essay, total scores rose once again to 8.1. On the final essay, students' average total score was 9.5—just over a three-point gain compared to the baseline data. Students improved in each of the three areas we tackled during the intervention: content, mechanics, and transitions. The greatest gains were in the area of transitions. Baseline data indicated that the average score for students in this area was 1.5, which was just below the basic level. Students' scores gradually increased during the intervention, and on the last essay, students' average score on transitions rose to 3.1, which is at the proficient level.

⊘ **What if I don't find what I expect?** As you begin analyzing your data, you may discover that your results are not what you expected. This is a normal part of the research process. Remember this: No matter what you find, your results will help you inform and improve your practice and will make you a better educator. Often, beginning action researchers are frustrated when they discover that their intervention has not produced the results that were expected. But even when this occurs, using data to answer the *why* questions can help the researcher reach conclusions about ways to improve the intervention to attain desired outcomes.

✎ **Journal Activity:** As you analyze quantitative data sources, make notes in your journal about results that are unexpected. Your analysis of data is likely to bring about new research questions (for example, *Why does the intervention seem to work better for some kids but not others?*), so keep track of new questions as they arise.

tionized, [SIC] and when they characterize different segments of data, then we can call them "themes." (p. 129)

The process presented in this text for analyzing qualitative forms of data, which is based on the process described by Berg (2001) includes several steps:

Step 1 Data that are not in textual form must be written so they are recorded as text. This means that audiotapes of interviews, focus groups, and conferencing sessions must be transcribed word for word. Data that are already in textual form (from lesson plans, journals, self-assessments, peer reviews, documents, observational or field notes, logs, narratives, organizational charts, scales, and open-ended survey items) should be assembled or gathered together. Videotaped observations must be described in written form or transcribed.

Step 2 Textual data are studied for patterns to determine ways to code the data.

Step 3 Textual data and codes are analyzed so that patterns and themes can be developed.

Step 4 Answers to research questions are offered based on themes found in the data.

Several examples of coded textual data will be presented in this section. Keep in mind that the examples are based on excerpts from much larger textual documents. They are provided to show the ways in which codes are constructed and themes are established from codes.

Interviews, Focus Groups, and Conferences

Data should be audio recorded and then transcribed. There are several ways to transcribe data, and one example is provided in Table 7.9, which displays an excerpt from an interview transcription from a principal's action research study about teacher study groups. On the left side of the table, the interview has been transcribed word for word. In the column to the right of the transcribed interview, the researcher has coded the interview.

As you read the transcript and reviewer's codes in Table 7.9, you may determine other ways the interview could be coded. This is what makes the analysis of interview data a subjective process. One person's interpretation of these data may be much different from another person's interpretation. Notice in the example that several codes, based on the patterns that emerged in the interview, have been developed: *study group behavior, topics discussed, ideas from colleagues, benefits of study groups,* and *barriers to study group participation.* As other interviews are analyzed, these codes would be applied to the transcripts and new codes would be added as the researcher identifies areas where additional codes are needed. Part of this process is one of negotiation. As you become more familiar with your data, some codes will be combined into a new code, some codes will be deleted, and new codes will emerge.

Ryan and Bernard (2000) suggest that a researcher develop a codebook once all texts have been analyzed. In the teacher study groups example, this would occur after all interviews had been transcribed and analyzed and codes have been applied. Include in your

TABLE 7.9   Coded Interview Transcription for Teacher Study Groups Project

March 6, 2002. Interview with Ms. Aronson. [interview begins 2:45]	Researcher notes and codes
Principal: *After participating in your study group with other teachers for the last six weeks, do you think that the study group has benefited you in any way?*	
Mrs. A: Yes. In our group we have all sixth-grade language arts teachers, and it's been great to be able to talk about the kinds of problems we have. Like the transition period the kids go through when they first get here. Their first few weeks of middle school . . . it's just tough. They have no idea what the expectations are. We talked about that the first couple of times the study group met. It was great just to get a chance to talk about the frustrations. I think that some of the teachers in the study group like having a place just to vent their frustrations. But for me, I liked brainstorming ways to make the transition time easier. Some of the other teachers had really good ideas, like giving students written information about procedures for class work and homework. Georgetta, who is also my mentor teacher, said that she makes each student keep an agenda. She checks it every day. The kids know what's due and when. They have to have their agendas signed by their parents every week. Her kids understand the expectations right from the start, so it seems that they have an easier transition.	[study group behavior: *discussing similar problems*] **positive**[*] [topic discussed: *transitioning for sixth-grade students*] [study group behavior: *sharing frustrations*] **positive**[*] [study group behavior: *venting*] **negative**[*] [study group behavior: *brainstorming*] **positive**[*] [ideas from colleagues: *written procedures* and *using agendas*]
Principal: *So the study group has been beneficial to you because you get to exchange ideas with other teachers?*	
Mrs. A: Yep, that's a big part of it. It's beneficial, I think, just to get a chance to gripe sometimes. And it's good to talk to your colleagues and find out that most people are in the same boat. Another thing is that when we talk in our study group, I get to learn stuff about the other teachers.	[benefits: *a place to gripe, not alone, getting to know colleagues*]
Principal: *Can you give me an example of the kind of stuff you learn about from other teachers?*	
Mrs. A: Yeah, I mean when I listen to the others talk, I can see who's got classroom management down, who has good ideas for group work, who I just really want to avoid because they're negative about everything. I guess part of the study group is having the opportunity to identify who can help you with different things. Like I now know to go to Jerry about special ed because he knows all about working with IEPs and the legal stuff. Plus, he has some really good ideas about what kinds of activities work well with inclusion kids.	[benefits: *learning from colleagues with special knowledge. Learning who to avoid.*] [study group behavior: *negative colleagues*] **negative**[*] [ideas from colleagues: *classroom management, group work, working with students who receive special education services*]

(continued)

TABLE 7.9   Continued

March 6, 2002. Interview with Ms. Aronson. [interview begins 2:45]	Researcher notes and codes
Principal: *Are there negative aspects of being in the study group?*	
Mrs. A: Some, I guess. For one thing, I hate to hear people go on and on about their problems and never once say anything about how to fix the problem. And I don't want my time wasted by people who want to talk about their personal problems. I mean, that's for the teacher's lounge, not for the study group. And sometimes it's hard to find the time to prepare for our study group meeting, especially when we're supposed to read before we go.	[study group behavior: *colleagues who go on and on about problems, wasting time, talking about personal problems*] **negative**[*]

[barriers to study group participation: *preparing, reading*] |
| **Principal:** *What can you tell me about the reading your group has done?* | [benefits: *reading topics are chosen by participants*] |
| **Mrs. A:** Well, it's all been good. Based on topics that we've decided we want to know more about—like transitioning. Our study group leader finds some articles or book chapters for us to read on the topic. We usually have a week or so to do the reading. It's not a lot of reading really, but sometimes it's hard to find the time. | [procedures: *group chooses topic, leader finds reading materials*]

[barriers to study group participation: *finding time to read*] |
| **Principal:** *Is the reading helpful?* | |
| **Mrs. A:** Yeah, most of it is. Sometimes when I haven't had time to do the reading, I've gone to the study group and then decided I had to do the reading. Like when the reading was on using cooperative groups. I didn't do that reading, but when I went to the group, the people who had read were talking about all these ideas from one of the book chapters, and they were really excited. So that made me want to read what I'd missed. And I did read it that night. There were some really good suggestions in that reading. | [study group behavior: *colleagues excited about reading, excitement is inspiring*] **positive**[*]

[benefits: *reading topics are useful*] |
| **Principal:** *Is there anything else you'd like to tell me about the study groups?* | |
| **Mrs. A:** Well, in our group last week we talked about the idea of getting professional development credits for our study group work. I mean, what we're doing is really working on professional development, so it would be nice to get credit for it. A lot of us feel like it would be more helpful to get credit for what we're doing than to go to those staff development things at the district office that really don't help us. Maybe if we got credit for it and people could choose whether they wanted to be in a study group or go to a staff development thing. . .I mean, maybe that would be best. Then those of us who like the study group could continue and get credit. And the others who don't like the study group could quit the group and just do staff development stuff. It's just an idea. | [improving study groups: *give professional development credit for participation, let colleagues who don't like the study group go to staff development*]

[benefits: *study group is more useful than staff development activities*]

[study group behavior: *negative colleagues*] **negative**[*] |
| **Principal:** *Thanks for the information you have provided. I appreciate your time.* [**Interview ends 2:56 p.m.**] | |

codebook an explanation of each code and any quotes or examples that powerfully illustrate the code. An entry in the codebook might look like this:

CODE	DESCRIPTION	QUOTE/EXAMPLE
SGB	Study group behavior [ways study group members interact]	I've gone to the study group and then decided I had to do the reading. Like when the reading was on using cooperative groups. I didn't do that reading, but when I went to the group, the people who had read were talking about all these ideas from one of the book chapters, and they were really excited. So that made me want to read what I missed.

Once you have created a codebook, review codes, descriptions, and examples, the next step is to organize codes to determine what is revealed in the qualitative data and to use this information to answer research questions. For example, if the principal investigating study groups is interested in answering the question *How does participation in a study group improve or change teachers' practices?* the information provided in the interviews might lead to several themes related to changing teachers' practices: Teachers can share ideas, they are able to brainstorm solutions to problems, they learn from each others' areas of expertise, and they learn from reading and discussing books and articles about teaching.

Observational Records and Field Notes

Analysis of observational records and field notes is identical to the process described for interview data. If the observation has been videotaped or audiotaped, it should be transcribed so the text can be analyzed. If observations are in the form of field notes, then the text is ready for analysis. In Chapter 5, the importance of expanding each day's field notes was described. As a reminder, this means that at the end of each day of observation, you read the comments you were able to jot down that day and then expand them while the day's events are fresh in your mind. Expanding field notes is critical for gathering useful observational data that can help answer research questions. Remember to analyze your *expanded* field notes. Table 7.10 includes an example of a method for recording and coding observational data. The technique used here is identical to the method used for recording and coding interview data illustrated in Table 7.9. On the left side of the table are the written observational notes made by the teacher as she watched students working in collaborative groups. The teacher has written notes and codes on the right side of the table.

Once observational data have been coded in this way, codes and notes should be added to your codebook. Remember that it is important to review your codes as you analyze more sources of data. This ongoing analysis and review will help you figure out how to organize the themes that emerge and to determine how best to explain what was learned from the data in answering research questions. During the process you will probably collapse some codes as you realize there is overlap. New codes and categories will emerge, whereas others may be dropped. As you build the categories and codes, themes and patterns will develop in the data. These themes will help you answer your research questions, and they will provide you with the information you need to answer the *why* questions in your study.

TABLE 7.10   Recorded and Coded Observational Records (Collaborative Groups)

Observational notes made on 10/18/2002 4th period. Observation began 1:20 p.m.

Group 1: (members—Sam, David, Joanna, Takesha, and Leigh). After I passed out the group assignment, each member of this group spent about a minute looking over the assignment. Takesha spoke first, asking if everyone understood what was supposed to be done. David said he didn't get the part about cell division, and Takesha asked him if he had done last night's reading. David said no and Joanna replied, "You have to do the reading, David, especially when you know we're going to have a group assignment. If you don't do it, it hurts all of us." David said he'd had football practice and had to study for a hard test in trigonometry. Leigh replied, "Well, I had band practice **and** I had to study for that test, but I did the reading. It didn't take that long."

I am observing Group 1 today. This is my first formal observation of the group. Informally, I have noticed that this group works pretty well together.

Group Dynamics: Takesha takes the lead in getting the group members ready to work. . . speaks almost like a teacher. Directs others.

Group Dynamics: Expectations are clear: Everyone does the reading and comes prepared. No excuses.

At this point, Sam said they all needed to do the reading, but that they were wasting time continuing to talk about the problem. Leigh said she would explain cell division to David after they decided how to do the activity.

Group Dynamics: Sam gets the group to move on (gender playing a role here?).

Group Dynamics: Leigh offers to help David catch up.

Takesha looked at the assignment and said that there were four areas the assignment covered and asked if they should do the assignment by the "divide and conquer" method. Sam said he felt sure he could answer the first problem, and Joanna said she could do the second one. Leigh suggested that she and David take the problem on cell division if Takesha could do the third problem. There were some nonverbal affirmations of this plan. . . nods by Leigh and David while Sam and Joanna opened their books to start working. Leigh and David got up to find another place to work [perhaps so they wouldn't disturb the others]. Before they left, Takesha said, "I think we should all just make some notes but not answer the questions all the way." She suggested that they come back as a group and talk about their answers and then work together to write answers to the questions.

Group Dynamics: Takesha leading again. Offering way to tackle the assignment.

Division of Labor: All members equally contribute, volunteer to tackle certain problems.

Group Dynamics: Each member begins work. No prodding.

Group Dynamics: Takesha leading.

Division of Labor: All will come back and share information, then group will work together to answer problems.

Takesha, Sam, and Joanna each worked quietly at the table. Takesha and Joanna used their notes and the textbook and jotted notes. Sam used his textbook only.

Problem-Solving Strategies: Use textbook and notes.

TABLE 7.10   Continued

Observational notes made on 10/18/2002 4th period. Observation began 1:20 p.m.

David and Leigh: Working in a corner with two desks pulled together. Leigh is reading the question and looking in her notes as David quickly skims the textbook section on cell division. When he's done, he tells Leigh he thinks he has it. She asked him how he would answer the activity question. He read the question and said he wasn't sure. He looked through the textbook section on cell division again and he seemed to be reading more carefully. David then looked at Leigh with a confused look on his face. Leigh said, "The answer isn't in the book. That's the whole point. We have to use what we know about meiosis and mitosis to answer this problem. It's like a brain teaser."	Group Dynamics: Leigh seems to be leading here. . . she leads David in the same way that Takesha leads the group. Problem-Solving Strategies: Don't rely on the book. Problem is like a 'brain teaser.'
Observation shifting back to Takesha, Sam, and Joanna. Sam said that he couldn't find the answer in his book. Takesha said he should look at his notes and think about what's in the book and then "get creative." Takesha and Joanna both write notes in their notebooks for a minute or so. Sam says, "I still don't get it." Joanna shows Sam the question she is answering. She explains that the answer isn't in the book or notes, but that the answer can be figured out from what's in the book and notes. Joanna: "See, there are things I know about asexual reproduction. I have to think about what I know about that. Then I write all that down. When I look at the question, it's like I have to guess how to answer it based on what I know. See?"	Problem-Solving Strategy: Use book and notes and 'get creative.' Group Dynamics/Problem Solving: Joanna models how to solve the problem. Using what is known to solve what is unknown.
Sam makes notes in his notebook for a minute or two. David and Leigh come back to the group. David says they figured out how to answer their question. Takesha suggests that they take turns talking about each question. Sam read the first question and then began to explain his answer.	Group Dynamics: Takesha in leadership role.
At this point, Group 2 called me over for help. I was helping other groups for about 15 minutes and then went back to observing Group 1.	
Takesha has written responses to questions 1, 2, and 4. The group is working on question 3 now. Sam, David, Joanna, and Leigh have each written notes in their notebooks. I looked at Joanna's notes and saw that they contained detailed answers to the activity questions. They appear to be word-for-word what Takesha has written on the group sheet. [**Question 3 is about differences in chromosomal mutations during mitosis and meiosis.**]	Group Dynamics: Takesha takes responsibility to recording group's answers. Joanna keeps her own record in her notebook.

(continued)

TABLE 7.10 Continued

Observational notes made on 10/18/2002 4th period. Observation began 1:20 p.m.

David is speaking, "Well, we know about how meiosis and mitosis work, and that must be important, right?"	*Problem-Solving Strategy*: David uses strategy Leigh explained earlier. Group members take turns explaining what they think is important.
Joanna: "Yeah, I think so. The question is about mutations in meiosis and mitosis. It has those two words, so that must be part of the puzzle."	"Part of the puzzle" Leigh, Joanna, and Takesha appear to think of the activities as puzzlers or brain teasers.
David asked Leigh what she thought. He said she seemed to understand mitosis and meiosis pretty well, so she might have some ideas.	Group Dynamics: David suggests to Leigh that she offer some input because she understood the concepts [smoothing things over?].
Leigh looked through her notes again and began describing the differences between mitosis and meiosis to the group. When she said that meiosis only happened in cells that form gametes, Joanna and Sam both began talking at the same time, indicating that they had found the important information. Joanna told Sam to go on. He explained that the chromosomal mutations that happen in meiosis affect the gametes so they appear in the offspring. Joanna agreed with this answer saying, "That's exactly right!"	Problem-Solving Strategy: Leigh looks through notes, verbalizes what she knows, Joanna and Sam have an "aha" moment simultaneously. Group Dynamics: Joanna defers to Sam. Don't know why. Joanna is usually very verbal. Perhaps to give him a chance to contribute?
Takesha wrote down an answer for question 3, and then she read it to the group. Sam changed some of the wording to "be more precise." Takesha then read aloud each question and the group's answers. The group members seemed pleased with the responses. Joanna copied down the answer to number 3 in her notebook, and then she compared her notes on the other answers with the group's sheet. Takesha handed me the assignment and then asked if there was a reading assignment for tomorrow. I said they were to read the next section in the chapter. As I left the group to go to Group 2, I heard Leigh say to David, "Did you write that down?" [in reference to the reading assignment].	Group Dynamics: Sam's suggestion for precision is interesting. He often misses points on assignments for his lack of providing enough information. He seemed pretty proud when he offered the solution to question 3, especially when Joanna reinforced his answer. Group Dynamics: Still hounding David about the reading.
As I collected papers from the rest of the groups, I heard Takesha, Joanna, and Leigh talking about getting together to study for the unit test, which is a week from today. Joanna said she would bring copies of the notes she'd taken today. David and Sam asked for copies of the notes, but did not indicate that they would study with the rest of the group.	I don't know how to code this yet, but there seems to be a positive benefit of this particular grouping—students getting together to study outside of class. Very uncommon for students to study together at this competitive school.

Documents and Journals

Because documents and journals are in text form, no recording is necessary. The text sources should be gathered, and if multiple sources will be analyzed (for example, several students' journals or sets of meeting minutes from different groups) all sources should be analyzed together. To clarify, if you are analyzing the journals of all students in your class, you need to be able to look at them together—even with several journals open at once as you look through them. This strategy will help you see patterns in the data. As categories or codes emerge, make notes in your journal or codebook. Be sure to make notes about where in the data to find the codes. For example, next to a code you may want to write where to find a data example (*Julie's journal, page 3, first paragraph*). It may be helpful to make copies of certain documents so that you can write codes on the copies or highlight information, which will help you find it easily. An example of coding document sources is provided in Figure 7.8. The figure includes data from the Study Groups project. The documents analyzed are three sets of minutes from one study group's meetings.

Open-Ended Items (Surveys, Scales, Self-Assessments, Peer Reviews)

The first step in analyzing open-ended items is to record responses from all participants. This involves gathering the data sources (for example, a set of surveys) and recording responses on the open-ended questions. Responses are counted or tallied, and these responses are reviewed and studied to identify codes and themes. As responses are counted, notes should be made of quotes that illustrate the coded response. An example based on student responses to a survey on cooperative group activities is provided in Table 7.11. The question is listed first and then responses and the number of times each response was made is listed. Quotes taken directly from surveys are included. If surveys are anonymous, they should be identified by a number to make it easier to find recorded quotes.

In this section, methods were presented for analyzing qualitative data. This process involves evaluating and analyzing text to identify themes and patterns in the data. The steps of the process are reviewed here again:

- **Record qualitative data in text form.** If data are audio- or video-recorded, they must first be transcribed so that the textual data can be analyzed.
- **Analyze multiple texts from different participants or sources together.** If analysis is of journals or documents, look at sources together rather than separately.
- **Study the text and make codes for categories as they emerge.** Patterns in data will reveal codes, which should be recorded on the text documents.
- **Create a codebook.** Codes should be recorded, described, and illustrated in a codebook. As more data sources are analyzed, codes may be combined or eliminated and new codes may be added.
- **Analyze codes to find patterns and themes in the data.** Once all qualitative data sources have been analyzed, patterns in the coded data will reveal ways to organize the information by themes.

Minutes 2/2/02

Members Present: Aronson, Mitchell, Stevens, and Little (Young absent)

Discussed transitioning for sixth grade. All agreed it's a big problem for our kids.

Mitchell (group leader) agreed to find some articles on transitioning for the group to read.

Stevens suggested we try to come up with a transitioning program to use next school year. All agreed it's a good idea.

Minutes 3/2/02

Members Present: Aronson, Mitchell, Stevens, Little, and Young

Discussed transitioning articles and brainstormed how we might create a transitioning program. All members agreed that it's something we need. Little suggested that we develop a plan like the one in the article by McKenna. Consensus reached. Mitchell suggested we put together the plan and share it with the entire sixth-grade team at our April faculty meeting. Aronson, Stevens, Mitchell, and Little will work on the plan.

Minutes 4/19/02

Members Present: Aronson, Mitchell, Stevens, & Little (Young absent)

Discussed presentation made to sixth-grade team (yesterday). Consensus reached by group to rework the plan based suggestions from team members and principal. Worked through transitioning plan and made requested changes. Plan will be presented at faculty meeting next week. Little suggested that we ask whether meeting with fifth graders at Kerry Elementary School can occur in May. If so, who will be on team?

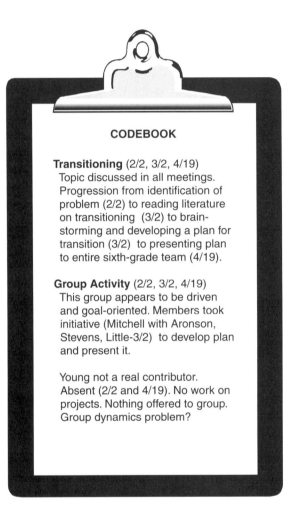

CODEBOOK

Transitioning (2/2, 3/2, 4/19)
Topic discussed in all meetings. Progression from identification of problem (2/2) to reading literature on transitioning (3/2) to brain-storming and developing a plan for transition (3/2) to presenting plan to entire sixth-grade team (4/19).

Group Activity (2/2, 3/2, 4/19)
This group appears to be driven and goal-oriented. Members took initiative (Mitchell with Aronson, Stevens, Little-3/2) to develop plan and present it.

Young not a real contributor. Absent (2/2 and 4/19). No work on projects. Nothing offered to group. Group dynamics problem?

FIGURE 7.8   Document analysis from teachers' Study Groups project.

TABLE 7.11   Responses to Open-Ended Survey Items—Cooperative G

Survey Question 10: *What are the benefits of working with your cooperative gr*

— **People in my group explain things in a way that I can understand** (10 stud
responded this way). Quote from David: "I don't always get it in class, even wh
question. But the people in my group can explain things so I get it. It's like they ta
language."

— **Solving problems together** (5 students responded this way). Quote from Chantal:
"Sometimes it's hard to understand the concepts when I'm just listening to a lecture. I'm
trying to take notes, and I have no time to think. But in my group, when I have a question,
just ask, and there's usually someone who knows the answer. And if no one does, we talk it
out until we get it. We get to all use what we know to solve the problems together."

— **It makes me study more because I have to prepare** (4 students responded this way).
Quote from Takesha: "I know that when I have a group assignment the next day, I have to
prepare before I go. I don't want to look dumb. I study more and my grades are higher."
Quote from Darren: "My average is higher since I'm doing the reading at home."

Survey Question 11: *What are the negative aspects of working with your cooperative group?*

— **Sometimes people don't participate** (8 students responded this way).

— **I have to read more than I used to** (6 students responded this way). Quote from Michelle:
"I liked just coming to class, taking notes, and studying. I did better. There's too much
reading now."

— **I don't like people (or a person) in my group** (4 students responded this way). Quote from
Maria: "There's one boy in my group who teases me all the time. I hate saying anything in
my group."

■ **Make notes in your journal about ways to explain the themes to answer research questions.** Maintain a focus on your research questions and look for answers
to those questions in the themes that emerge from the data.

Once these steps have been completed, you must write up your results in relation to the answers they provide to your research questions. Further, you should include any additional
information that can inform your practice as an educator, even if the information is only
tangentially related to your research questions.

Writing results, especially results based on qualitative data, can be a difficult task.
Often researchers feel like they have so much information that there is no way to coherently
explain it all. This is why it is critical that you stay focused on your primary and secondary
research questions as you analyze data. Make note of important information that is only peripherally related, but stay focused on the information that provides answers to your research questions.

One strategy that I ask the beginning researchers I work with to use is to begin by
writing the research question and then to provide the answer to that question based on

irces appropriate for answering that question. An example is pro-

tion in my study was Will the use of cooperative group activities fourth period advanced biology class? Analysis of student work d improve during the eight-week intervention. Baseline data .e implementation of the intervention showed that the average .erage quiz grade was 75, and the average lab grade was 85. Scores over the eight-week period, and at the end of the data collection period, .ose to 88, average quiz grades rose to 95, and average lab grades rose to 91. .vs conducted with students in the seventh week revealed that most students felt like y were learning more and doing better in class because of participation in the cooperative group activities. Eighteen of the 25 students said improvement in their work was a direct result of working in the cooperative groups. Benefits of the intervention went beyond simply completing class activities with peers. Half of the students said they were studying more in order to prepare for their group work, and responses on student surveys corroborated this. On one survey, a student wrote, "I know that when I have a group assignment the next day, I have to prepare before I go. I don't want to look dumb. I study more and my grades are higher." This attitude was fairly typical of the students who said they were preparing more for class. When asked why they were preparing more, most students said it was because they didn't want to look dumb in front of their group. Additionally, about half of the students said during the interviews that they were studying for tests and completing assignments outside of class with people from their cooperative groups, although only two students said they had worked with classmates before the cooperative group intervention. In my observations, I did note that students in some groups frequently made plans to get together to study for tests. This is a behavior I had not witnessed before the intervention.

This example, which is just a short selection of a much more detailed answer to a research question, is provided to illustrate one way to answer research questions based on analysis of data. In the example, results from analysis of both quantitative (test scores and assignment scores) and qualitative (observations, interviews, open-ended survey responses) forms of data are included. The quantitative data—test scores, quiz scores, scores on lab assignments—provide a direct answer to the question *Will the use of cooperative group activities increase achievement in my fourth period advanced biology class?* Qualitative forms of data help to explain the increases in student achievement. The analysis of the qualitative data—interviews, observations, open-ended survey question responses—helps answer the *why* questions. The intervention was successful, but *why* was it successful? In this example, it appears that the cooperative group intervention was successful because students prepared more for class and studied together outside of class. Notice, too, that in the example there is evidence of triangulation. Data sources have been used to corroborate one another. For example, students reported that they were studying together outside of class, and the teacher observed students planning to get together to study outside of class for a test.

Activity 7.2 is provided to help you complete the steps for analyzing qualitative data. After quantitative and qualitative data sources have been analyzed, the next step is to evaluate both forms of data together to determine answers to research questions. Data should be

■ ■ ■ ■ ■

ACTIVITY 7.2
ANALYSIS OF QUALITATIVE DATA?

1. Write your primary and secondary research questions. Refer to these questions often as you go through the process of qualitative data analysis.
2. Gather qualitative data sources. Transcribe any data from audiotapes or videotapes.
3. Read text sources several times and over several days. Code data (use examples provided in Tables 7.9, 7.10, 7.11, and in Figure 7.8).
4. Create a codebook. Define codes and illustrate them with quotes or examples from text sources.
5. Write the major findings from the analysis of the qualitative data in your study. Describe the patterns and themes specifically related to your research questions that emerged.
6. Refer to your responses to Activity 7.1. Look for ways that the results of the different types of data you have collected (artifacts, observations, and inquiry data) support each other.

Journal Activity: Use your journal as a place to write about the process of qualitative data analysis. You may also maintain your codebook in your journal. Make notes about ways to triangulate your data sources.

triangulated during this process. More information on triangulation and drawing valid conclusions is presented in the final section of this chapter.

TRIANGULATING DATA SOURCES AND DRAWING CONCLUSIONS FROM DATA

Recall from Chapter 6 the importance triangulating or corroborating multiple sources of data, which increases various types of validity related to the accuracy of the results of a study. Corroborating data sources simply means supporting results from one data source with results from another data source. For example, in the cooperative groups study described previously, the actual gain in scores was corroborated by students' reports of increased achievement. Further, reasons for the increased achievement—more preparation for class and studying with peers outside of class—were provided. Students' responses in interviews regarding studying more were supported with survey data that indicated more study time. Interview data in which students indicated they studied with peers outside of class was corroborated by observations of students making plans to get together to study. When multiple data sources are triangulated and point to the same result, confidence about the accuracy of the results of the study (which is connected to descriptive, truth-value, process, interpretive, and theoretical validity, as well as to structural corroboration and neutrality/confirmability) is increased.

As you begin the triangulation process, determine whether data sources corroborate one another. For example, if you have analyzed student artifacts such as tests, quizzes, and written assignments and have noted an increase in achievement, look at other data sources to see whether there is other supporting evidence that achievement did increase as a result of the intervention. If observations reveal an increase in students' motivation, a higher completion rate on class work, and greater student participation, these behaviors support or corroborate the improvement in achievement. If inquiry data were collected, say in the form of interviews, and most students said they felt better about their learning, were more interested in the lessons, and were working harder than they had before, this would also support the other data sources. Triangulating data in this example would allow a teacher to say *Student achievement increased, which was evident when looking at their tests, quizzes, and written assignments. This increase in achievement is supported by observations that revealed higher student motivation, students working harder to complete class work, and an increase in classroom participation during lessons. Further, students said that because of the new teaching strategy they felt they understood the lessons better, were more interested in the information we were studying, and were spending more time working on assignments and studying for the class.*

As data sources are triangulated and answers to research questions are postulated, conclusions are made about the effectiveness of the intervention or innovation that was implemented. In action research studies, conclusions are used for ongoing and continuous reflective planning. Based on the conclusions you reach (Was the intervention effective? Why or why not? What would you do differently?), you need to make future plans regarding how you intend to use the results and conclusions of your study to inform your practice. During the reflective planning stage, the researcher steps back and says *How can I use what I learned in my study and the conclusions I made to inform my practice as an educator?* For example, in the collaborative group study described previously, the teacher could plan to continue using collaborative groups but structure each group so that there is strong leadership and more time on task in each group.

Reaching valid conclusions in your study is a critical step in the action research cycle. Conclusions must be reasonable in light of the results obtained. It would be unreasonable, for example, to state *Although the writing intervention resulted in a decline in students' writing achievement, it is still a good method for teaching writing and I will continue to use it.* This is an extreme example, but it is included as a caution. Very often beginning researchers reach conclusions that are beyond what can be supported by the data. When this occurs, results can inform practice in a detrimental way. One way to prevent that from happening is to focus on increasing the validity of the study and the results of the study by following the guidelines presented in Chapter 6. As a reminder, those strategies include:

- Peer debriefing
- Persistent and prolonged observations
- Accurately recording data
- Member checks
- Triangulating data sources
- Providing thick description of the setting and study
- Negative case analysis

- Making biases clear and keeping them in check as data are
- Constructing an audit trail
- Present results to key audiences and eliciting their feedback
- Continuous, ongoing reflective planning

Activity 7.3 is provided to take you through the steps of pulling together the results of data analyses, writing results, and reaching conclusions.

■ ■ ■ ■ ■ ▬▬▬▬▬▬▬▬▬▬▬▬▬▬▬▬▬▬▬▬▬▬▬▬▬▬▬▬▬▬▬▬▬▬▬

ACTIVITY 7.3
ANSWERING RESEARCH QUESTIONS AND REACHING CONCLUSIONS

1. Write your primary research question. Look at all data sources, both quantitative and qualitative, that will be used to answer the question (refer to your responses to Activities 6.1 and 6.2).
2. Triangulate data sources and then construct a written answer to your research question. Support the answer with data. Use graphical displays, examples (of interview comments, answers to surveys, etc.), and quotes to help illustrate and describe results.
3. Repeat steps 1 and 2 with secondary questions.
4. After research questions have been answered, describe any peripherally related information that you feel may be important.

Research Paper Activity: Under the heading *Results of the Study* (or a similar heading such as *Results, Findings,* or another appropriate heading), write a section that provides answers to your primary and secondary research questions. Use responses to steps 2 through 4 above to complete this section. Include graphical displays, examples, and quotes as applicable. This section should follow the section on increasing validity (Activity 6.1).

5. Refer to the answers to your research questions, and then describe the conclusions you have reached about your study.
6. Conclude with a paragraph about how your results and conclusions will be used to inform your practice (reflective planning).

Research Paper Activity: Under the heading *Conclusions* (or a similar heading), write a section that provides your conclusions and your future goals based on your engagement in reflective planning. Use responses to steps 5 and 6 above to complete this section. This section is the last section of the research paper.

What if triangulation results in data sources that do not corroborate each other? If you find that data sources reveal conflicting information (for example, in the study on cooperative study groups, the teacher finds that student achievement decreases during the intervention but other sources of data, such as observations and conferences, reveal that students interest in and understanding of the content has increased), *collect more data.* As more data are collected, you will be able to determine the reasons that data sources provide conflicting information, you will be able to answer your *why* questions, and you will increase the likelihood that results are valid.

SUMMARY

The purpose of the chapter was to explain the process of analyzing data. The importance of engaging in interim analysis was described and various ways to analyze, report, and display results for quantitative data were provided. The process of thematic analysis of qualitative data—looking for themes and patterns from textual forms of data—was illustrated through a number of educational examples. The method of triangulating data sources to corroborate sources of evidence was explained, and drawing valid conclusions from results was emphasized.

The next stage of the action research process is one of renewing or beginning again. At this point, each step of the process, from reflecting on practice to identify a problem to determining the effectiveness of an intervention to deal with that problem, has been completed. Now the process begins anew as you reflect on what you have learned and use that information for ongoing reflective planning.

The final chapter of this text is a supplemental chapter for individuals interested in writing and disseminating their results. In Chapter 8, methods are described for completing the written report, which involves compiling the research paper activities provided in Chapters 2 through 7. The written report can serve as documentation of your action research experience to be placed in your professional portfolio. It can also be submitted to an educational journal or teaching magazine for publication or for presentation at a conference. In Chapter 8, specific guidelines for writing your report will be provided.

TABLE 7.12   Software for Quantitative and Qualitative Data Analysis

SOFTWARE	USES	INFORMATION AVAILABLE AT:
SPSS	Quantitative data analysis. Descriptive, inferential, and nonparametric statistics.	www.spss.com
SAS		www.sas.com
Minitab		www.minitab.com
NVivo	Coding and analysis of textual data as well as graphical models patterns and relationships.	www.qsr-software.com
QSR N6	Rapid coding of textual data, automatic processing of some types of data (e.g., questionnaires and focus groups).	www.qsr-software.com
ATLAS.ti	Analysis of textual, graphical, audio, and video data. Feature for automatic coding of data.	www.atlasti.de

CHAPTER EIGHT

WRITING AND DISSEMINATING THE ACTION RESEARCH REPORT

CHAPTER GOALS

- Explain how to assemble a written report of an action research study.
- Illustrate ways to properly format the written report using APA (5th Edition) guidelines.
- Describe methods for dissemination of research results through presentation and/or publication.

This chapter is a supplemental chapter for individuals who wish to prepare a written report of their action research studies. The previous chapters of this textbook provided information and activities to help you complete each step of your action research study—from initial reflection on a problem to reaching conclusions about the effectiveness of an intervention for dealing with that problem. You can now take your written responses to the activities in Chapters 2 through 7 (particularly the Research Paper Activities provided with the chapter activities) and assemble them to complete a final written report of your study. This chapter suggests ways to organize the paper, provides examples of how to use proper publication formatting (using APA 5th Edition guidelines), and explains the process of disseminating the paper through presentation or publication.

GUIDELINES FOR WRITING THE FINAL ACTION RESEARCH REPORT

The formatting guidelines presented here are based on those provided in the *Publication Manual of the American Psychological Association* (5th Edition), and the content guidelines presented are based on the suggestions provided in this text for conducting the action research study. A brief explanation is provided about how to format your paper, which is followed by a description the kind of information to include in each section of the final report. A checklist that can be used to evaluate your final paper is also provided.

Paper Format

Your paper should be typed on standard-sized, heavy white bond paper. Use a 12-point Times New Roman or Courier font. Double-space the entire paper, but do not put an extra double space between paragraphs or before or after headings. Margins should be set at one inch on all sides and left justification for line spacing (not justified where all lines are of equal length) should be used. Each page should be numbered, beginning with the title page. All pages of the manuscript should also have the running head in the page header. Each first line of every paragraph must be indented. All headings, the title of the paper, author information, and text should be typed in both uppercase and lowercase letters. Do not use all uppercase letters anywhere in the paper. Use headings to delineate sections and subsections of the paper. For action research studies, two levels of headings are probably sufficient. Center the first level of headings (for major sections of the paper such as the reflection, setting and participants, intervention, etc.) and for the second level of headings, use a flush left, italicized heading. Include in the written report:

- A title page that includes a running head, the title of the paper, the author's (or authors') name(s) and affiliation(s), and the primary author's contact information. The title page is page 1. Figure 8.1 illustrates how the title page should look.
- An abstract, which is included on page 2. Include in the abstract a sentence on the purpose of the study, a brief description of the setting and participants, a short explanation of the intervention or innovation studied, results of the study, and the conclusions made. Abstracts are typically 120 words or less.
- The action research report, which begins on page 3.
- The reference list, which follows the research report and begins on a separate page.
- Any appendices, which should be placed after the references beginning on a separate page.

References must be written in APA format, and some general guidelines and examples are provided here. Consult the APA manual for additional information. References should be arranged in alphabetical order by last name. If two or more works by the same author are in the reference list, the earliest publication should be listed first. If there is more than one publication for an author in the same year, use lowercase italicized letters, beginning with *a* to identify the articles (e.g., Hendricks, 1999a; Hendricks, 1999b). References are arranged using a hanging indent. Examples of ways to cite various reference types are included here. Pay close attention to the use of commas, italics, and capitalizations.

- **Journal Articles** (author, date, article title, journal title, volume number, page numbers):

  Sparks-Langer, G. M., & Colton, A. B. (1991). Synthesis of research on teachers' reflective thinking. *Educational Leadership, 48,* 37–44.

  Stenhouse, L. (1981). What counts as research? *British Journal of Educational Studies, 29,* 103–113.

FIGURE 8.1   Title page example with header.

Teacher Study Groups   1

Running Head: The Effect of Teacher Study Groups

The Effect of Teacher Study Groups
on Integration of Research-Based
Teaching Practices in the Classroom

Pat Jackson
Shady Grove Middle School

Pat Jackson
Shady Grove Middle School
151 Shady Grove Lane
Shady Grove, GA 30117
pjackson@shadygrovems.org

■ **Journal Articles Retrieved from the Internet** (author, date, article title, journal title [electronic version], volume number, page numbers):

Buschman, L. (2001). Using student interviews to guide classroom instruction [Electronic version]. *Teaching Children Mathematics, 8,* 222–227.

Ho, B. S. (2002). Application of participatory action research to family-school intervention [Electronic version]. *School Psychology Review, 31,* 106–121.

■ **Books** (author, date, title of book, location of publication, publisher):

Burns, A. (1999). *Collaborative action research for English language teachers.* Cambridge, England: Cambridge University Press.

Cole, A. L., & Knowles, J. G. (2000). *Researching teaching: Exploring teacher development through reflexive inquiry.* Boston: Allyn and Bacon.

■ **Chapters in Edited Books** (author, date, title of chapter, editor, title of book, page numbers of chapters, location of publication, publisher):

Kemmis, S., & McTaggart, R. (2000). Participatory action research. In N.K. Denzin & Y. S. Lincoln (Eds.), *Handbook of qualitative research* (2nd ed., pp. 567–605). Thousand Oaks, CA: Sage.

Kemmis, S., & Wilkinson, M. (1997). Participatory action research and the study of practice. In B. Atweh, S. Kemmis, & P. Weeks (Eds.), *Action research in practice: Partnerships for social justice in education* (pp. 21–36). London: Routledge.

■ **ERIC Reports** (author, date, report title, report number, location of publication, publisher, ERIC document number):

Anderman, L. H., & Midgley, C. (1998). *Motivation and middle school students* (Report No. EDO-PS-98-5). Washington, DC: Office of Educational Research and Improvement. (ERIC Document Reproduction Service No. ED421281)

Brophy, J. (1998). *Failure syndrome students* (Report No. EDO-PS-98-2). Washington, DC: Office of Educational Research and Improvement. (ERIC Document Reproduction Service No. ED419625)

■ **Article in an Internet-Only Journal** (author, date, article title, journal title, volume number, date of retrieval, Internet address):

Edelstein, S., & Edwards, J. (2001). If you build it they will come: Building learning communities through threaded discussions. *Online Journal of Distance Education Administration, 5*(1). Retrieved June 9, 2002, from http://www.westga.edu/%7Edistance/ojdla/spring51/edelstein51.html

Jordan, L., & Hendricks, C. (2002). Increasing sixth grade students' engagement in literacy learning. *Networks: An On-line Journal for Teacher Research, 5.* Retrieved August 5, 2002, from http://www.oise.utoronto.ca/~ctd/networks/journal/Vol%205(1). 2002march/Jordan.html

■ **Other Internet Sources** (author, date [if known. If no date is given, use "n.d."], title of source, date of retrieval, internet address):

Green, P. (n.d.). *What types of learning activities are most likely to increase the involvement of non-participating students?* Retrieved January 3, 2001, from http://www.enc.org/professional/learn/research/journal/science/document.shtm?input=ENC-002432-2432_ch2

National Council of Teachers of English. (n.d.). *Positions and guidelines: Standards for the assessment of reading and writing.* Retrieved July 25, 2002, from http://www.ncte.org/positions/standards.shtml

Content Format

Your paper should include information on the reflection that led to the identification of your area of focus, your review of the literature, a description of the participants and setting of the study, an explanation of the intervention used, a description of the data collection strategies you used, information related to how you increased validity in your study, a description of the results based on your analysis of the data, and conclusions you made—including your reflective planning—based on those results. The paper needs to logically flow from one section to the next, showing the ways in which the reflection, literature review, research questions, and intervention are connected. The reflection and all sections after the literature review should be written in past tense. This means that you may need to change the verb tense in the research paper activities you completed in Chapters 2 and 4 through 7. The checklist provided in Table 8.1 suggests the information that should be included in each section of the paper.

TABLE 8.1   Checklist for Action Research Report

REFLECTION (See Activity 2.2, Research Paper Activity)

_____ Is the reflection written in first person?

_____ Are reasons clearly stated describing why the issue is important to you?

_____ Are initial actions that you planned to take provided?

_____ Have you provided an explanation of the outcomes that you desired as a result of your study?

_____ Does the reflection contain a brief description of your educational role and your setting (grade level, subject, etc.)?

_____ Does your reflection illustrate the reflective process(es) you used and their relationship to your core educational values?

LITERATURE REVIEW (See Activity 3.1, Research Paper Activity)

_____ Does the literature review relate to the focus of your reflection?

_____ Is your literature review a synthesis of the information you reviewed?

_____ Are reviewed sources clearly relevant to the purpose of your study?

_____ Does a logical transition exist between the reflection section of your paper and the literature review?

PURPOSE (See Activity 4.1, Research Paper Activity)

_____ Have you clearly articulated the purpose of the study, focusing on the intervention used and the outcomes desired?

_____ Is the purpose tied to the reflection?

_____ Does the purpose logically follow the literature review?

_____ Have you clearly articulated the primary and secondary research questions?

_____ Are the research questions aligned with your purpose statement?

(continued)

TABLE 8.1 Continued

SETTING/PARTICIPANTS/COLLABORATION (See Activity 4.2. Research Paper Activities)

_____ Have you described the setting and participants in sufficient detail so that the context of your educational environment can be understood?

_____ If your study involved collaborators, did you explain the nature of the collaboration and the collaborators' roles in the study?

INTERVENTION/INNOVATION (See Activity 4.2, Research Paper Activities)

_____ Is the intervention based on what was learned in the review of literature?

_____ Have you described the intervention or innovation that you used in enough detail so that a colleague could implement the intervention?

METHODS OF DATA COLLECTION (See Activity 5.1, Research Paper Activity)

_____ Did you use multiple forms of data collection to answer your research questions?

_____ Did you provide a justification for the connection between your data collection strategies and research questions?

_____ Did you describe the data collection methods you used in sufficient detail so that they could be replicated by a colleague?

_____ Did you include surveys, questionnaires, interview questions, or other data collection instruments in this section or in an appendix?

_____ If baseline data were used, did you describe how baseline data were collected?

PLAN FOR INCREASING VALIDITY (See Activity 6.1, Research Paper Activity)

_____ Did you describe the types of validity you chose to focus on in your study?

_____ Did you provide a justification for the types of validity chosen and link them to the purpose of the study?

_____ Did you explain the methods used to increase these various types of validity?

RESULTS OF THE STUDY (See Activity 7.3, Research Paper Activity)

_____ Have you provided results, based on multiple sources of data, for each research question?

_____ Have you presented results in appropriate forms (tables, graphs, percentages, examples of work samples, narratives, tally sheets, quotes, etc.)?

_____ Have you given an explanation about how you triangulated data sources?

CONCLUSIONS (See Activity 7.3, Research Paper Activity)

_____ Have you described the conclusions you reached about the effectiveness of the intervention?

_____ Can the conclusions be supported by the results provided in the _Results of the Study_ section?

_____ Have you provided future plans (reflective planning) based on your results and conclusions?

TABLE 8.1 Continued

GENERAL

_____ Is your paper free of spelling and grammatical errors?

_____ Have you used APA format correctly throughout your paper, including in the reference section?

_____ Is your paper typed in 12-point Times New Roman or Courier font?

_____ Did you use margins of 1" on all sides?

_____ Did you double-space your paper?

_____ Have you included a header with page numbers?

_____ Does your paper have a title page that includes a running head, title of your report, and information about you?

_____ Does your paper contain an abstract of no more than 120 words?

_____ Is the abstract a concise account of the purpose and results of your study?

_____ Have you used headings (and subheadings, if appropriate) in your paper?

DISSEMINATING ACTION RESEARCH FINDINGS

Dissemination of your research findings is an important part of the action research process. There are a variety of ways to disseminate your study, and there are a number of audiences with whom to share your findings. First, I urge you to share your results with your participants. Researchers often forget to discuss results with participants, but it is important to let your participants, whether they are students, teachers, parents, or administrators, know what you concluded. Sharing results with participants is a thoughtful way to provide them with a sense of closure to the research project.

After you have shared your findings with participants, consider disseminating the results of your study to a wider audience. You can share results with those in your school community—teachers, administrators, parents—and it may be beneficial to explain your findings to more than one audience. For example, a teacher who finds that increasing students' organizational skills improves their achievement may wish to send a letter home to parents describing the intervention used, the ways it improved students' organization, and the impact it had on students' achievement. The teacher could also share the results of the study, perhaps in a schoolwide or districtwide workshop, with colleagues who might wish to try the intervention in their own classes.

Another way to disseminate the results of your study is in presenting the work at a professional conference. Professional organizations such as the American Association of School Administrators, the Association for Supervision and Curriculum Development, the International Reading Association, the National Council for Social Studies, the National

Council of Teachers of English, the National Council of Teachers of Mathematics, and the National Science Teacher Association are just a few professional organizations that sponsor conferences. Many of these national organizations include affiliated regional groups that sponsor smaller conferences at the state or regional level. You can check an organization's website to find upcoming conferences, conference themes, conference locations, and submission dates and guidelines. Table 8.2 at the end of this chapter provides links to a few selected organizations' conferences. If you present your study at a conference, you will need to take copies of your paper to give to the audience. It is imperative, too, that you plan a presentation that meets the established time limit (usually between 10 and 25 minutes), so before going to the conference you need to practice giving your presentation. Also, if overhead projectors or computers will be available to presenters, you may wish to prepare overheads or a PowerPoint® presentation.

Professional organizations such as the ones mentioned previously also generally support one or more professional journals or magazines, which are other options for disseminating your study. Publishing your work is the best way to disseminate your findings to the largest audience possible. Although it may seem to be an overwhelming project to take on, if you completed the research paper activities provided in this book in Chapters 2 through 7 and if you followed the guidelines presented in the previous section of this chapter for writing the final report, it is likely that your final paper will be of publishable quality. You need only to find a suitable journal or magazine and submit your work for consideration.

To find a place to publish your study, search the websites of the professional organizations that seem best suited to your topic. For example, if your study focused on increasing students' reading achievement, you would focus on the International Reading Association and the National Council of Teachers of English. Once you have found the websites for the professional organization(s), look for a list of journals and magazines that each me publisher. Read the description for each journal or magazine to determine which solicit research by educators or administrators. Make sure to read the guidelines to authors for the journal or magazine that you select so you will know exactly how to submit your study for publication consideration. Table 8.2 at the end of this chapter provides links to journals associated with professional organizations that publish practitioner studies.

Most educational journals require that the paper is written in APA format, but a few journals require writing in other formats, such as MLA. Make sure that your paper is in the format required by the journal to which you will submit your work. Be mindful of other requirements, such as the maximum length of the paper, the number of copies that need to be submitted, whether a disk must be included, and whether your name and the names of any co-authors should appear on the paper. Often, one copy of the paper will include a title page with the author's or authors' names and other copies will include a title page with no authors' names. This is so the papers can be blind reviewed by the journal reviewers, which means that they do not know who wrote the paper. Many of these same guidelines are often followed when papers are reviewed for presentation at a conference.

You should include with your paper a cover letter to the journal editor explaining that you are submitting your paper for publication. The letter should contain the title of the manuscript and a brief description of the study that is no longer than one or two sentences. You must make clear that the study has not been published elsewhere, and if you have presented the paper you need to report where the paper was presented. Finally, include a statement that explains that you followed acceptable ethical standards through gaining approval to conduct the study (either through a university Institutional Review Board, school district review board, or other reviewing agency) and by gaining informed consent from participants and their parents if the participants were minors. Also be sure to include contact information such as mailing address, telephone and fax numbers, and an email address. An example cover letter, which was sent via email to an online journal, is included in Figure 8.2.

Once the journal editor receives your paper, he or she will determine whether its contents are suitable for the journal. The editor will then send the paper out for review, usually to three or so reviewers. At that point, the editor will contact you to let you know that the paper is under review and to tell you approximately how long the review process will take. Once the editor receives comments from the reviewers, a determination will be made based on those comments whether to accept the manuscript as it is, to accept it but require some revisions, or to reject the manuscript. The editor will then send you a letter about the status of the paper with the reviewers' comments. If the article is accepted as it is, which is rare, then you have no more work to do. If the article is accepted with revisions, you must make those revisions in a timely manner and send the revised paper back to the editor. Remember that if editor asks for revisions it means that the journal is interested in publishing the work but that revisions must be made before it can be published. If the article is rejected, a good strategy is to carefully read the reviewers' comments, make the suggested changes, and submit the article to another journal. Though a rejection is painful, a lot can be learned by reading reviewers' comments and working to strengthen the manuscript. From experience I have learned that often, with work and perseverance, a rejected manuscript can be revised and eventually published.

CONCLUDING COMMENTS

Congratulations on completing your action research study. I hope that the experience has impacted your work as an educator and has allowed you to see how you can use the action research process to guide your ongoing professional development and to impact school improvement. I encourage you to disseminate the results of your study to many different audiences so that other teachers, administrators, parents, and academic researchers can learn from the important work you have done. I also encourage you to teach your colleagues to use the action research process. Pass on the knowledge and skills you now have and mentor other educators so that they can benefit from studying their practice.

FIGURE 8.2   Cover letter sent to *Networks: An Online Journal for Teacher Research.*

Gordon Wells, Editor
Networks: An Online Journal for Teacher Research

30 January 2002

Dear Dr. Wells,

Attached to this email message you will find our submission entitled "Increasing Sixth-Grade Students' Engagement in Literacy Learning." The attachment is in Word. We submit this for consideration as a full-length article.

We believe this article fits nicely with the purpose of *Networks*. The study is a result of collaboration between a middle school teacher (Laura Jordan) and an assistant professor at a university (Cher Hendricks). We investigated increasing student engagement in literacy activities by allowing students to choose their own tools for learning.

This article is not under review elsewhere nor has it been previously published. We maintained the highest ethical standards during this study, including seeking institutional and school permission and gaining informed consent from students and parents.

We hope that you find this article suitable for publication in *Networks*. If you have any questions or concerns or if you experience any difficulty opening the attachment, please contact Laura Jordan.

Respectfully submitted,

Laura Jordan
Taylor Street Middle School
ljordan@spalding.k12.ga.us

Cher Hendricks
College of Education
University of West Georgia
Carrollton, GA 30118
cchester@westga.edu

TABLE 8.2 Links to Professional Organizations' Conference and Journal Sites

PROFESSIONAL ORGANIZATION	CONFERENCE AND JOURNAL WEBSITES
American Association of School Administrators	**Conference:** http://www.aasa.org/conferences/ **Journal:** *The School Administrator:* http://www.aasa.org/publications/sa/
Association for Supervision and Curriculum Development	**Conference:** http://www.ascd.org/cms/index.cfm?TheViewID=354&flag=354 **Journals:** *Educational Leadership; Journal of Curriculum & Supervision:* http://www.ascd.org/cms/index.cfm?
National Council for Social Studies	**Conference:** http://www.socialstudies.org/conference/ **Journals:** *Social Education; Middle Level Learning; Social Studies and the Young Learner:* http://www.socialstudies.org/publications/
International Reading Association	**Conference:** http://www.reading.org/meetings/ **Journals:** *The Reading Teacher; Journal of Adolescent and Adult Literacy; Thinking Classroom; Reading Online:* http://www.reading.org/publications/
National Council of Teachers of English	**Conference:** http://www.ncte.org/convention/ **Journals:** *Language Arts; Primary Voices: K-6; Voices from the Middle; English Journal:* http://www.ncte.org/journals/
National Council of Teachers of Mathematics	**Conference:** http://www.nctm.org/meetings/index.htm#annuals **Journals:** *Teaching Children Mathematics; Mathematics Teaching in the Middle School; Mathematics Teacher; Online Journal for School Mathematics; Journal for Research in Mathematics Education:* http://www.nctm.org/publications/index.htm#journals
National Science Teacher Association	**Conference:** http://nsta.org/conventions **Journals:** *Science and Children; Science Scope; The Science Teacher:* http://nsta.org/journals

ACTION RESEARCH ARTICLES

ARTICLE A.1

Conceptual Learning and Creative Problem Solving Using Cooperative Learning Groups in Middle School Science Classes

Michael H. DuBois
Wakulla Middle School
Crawfordville, Florida

Abstract

This research project was initiated to develop a model for middle school science teaching that utilizes carefully selected, heterogeneous, cooperative learning groups to enhance student motivation, conceptual learning, and creative problem-solving. Data collected from observations and student interviews show evidence that conceptual learning and problem-solving strategies were prevalent throughout the study.

I have been teaching seventh grade mathematics and physical science for eight years in a rural middle school (grades six-eight) with a population of approximately 1,000 students. Our school is organized in academic teaching teams consisting of two or three teachers. Each team of teachers is assigned a block of students (usually 34-35 per homeroom) and has the responsibility of scheduling classes for students. Team teachers have a great deal of flexibility in deciding which courses they will teach (depending on certification) and what period of the day they will teach them. Since most teachers teach two or three subjects, they generally see students from their team in their classrooms more than once per day. Student schedules can easily be adjusted within a team in order to meet a variety of individual student needs.

"Action Research: Perspectives from Teachers' Classrooms." Southeast Eisenhower Regional Consortium @ SERVE. Reprinted with permission.

About six years ago, a majority of teachers from my school attended an intensive three-week summer workshop on teaching middle school mathematics. The mathematics content portion was

"I tended to group students by gender and race."

an excellent refresher course, but it also included a cooperative group learning component that was somewhat new to most of us. Since then, many teachers have had more training in designing group work, and virtually every teacher in the school now uses some form of group work in their teaching methods. Furthermore, the philosophy that group work is an effective technique for achieving many kinds of intellectual and social learning goals is shared among many of the teachers at my school.

Middle school science classes lend themselves particularly well to group learning. In our science department our teachers share a common philosophy that science classes should be active, and students should have hands-on experiences to build and reinforce concepts. Obtaining and preparing materials for science classes takes a substantial amount of time and planning, and it nearly always requires planning for group work so materials can be shared. In the past, this has added a significant time-consuming component to my planning. Decisions regarding who would be in each group, how many students per group, and where to locate each group involved many considerations. Also, depending on the activity and the materials to be shared, I frequently found myself rearranging groups. Sometimes I would even allow students to choose their own groups. But my decisions for group compositions were usually based on how well I thought the individuals would work together. I wanted the groups to consist of students who were compatible with one another so that more time might be spent working on the science topics at hand, and less time spent in arguments due to personality conflicts.

Several problems or dilemmas arose from my past methods of grouping students. By concerning myself with the compatibility of group members, I tended to group students by gender and race. My methods also allowed groups of friends or social cliques to form, which tended to amplify the status of those who did not seem to fit into any particular group. The groups of friends would often treat the laboratory or activity as "playtime" and would create classroom disruptions as a result. Finally, students who were in other classes together would tend to form groups, thereby creating extreme differences in abilities between groups.

Another problem I encountered with my former methods of grouping students was the inefficient use of planning time and classroom time. Each time the groups in the classroom were rearranged, the many decisions regarding group compositions, work stations, leadership roles, etc., had to be made. I generally found that at least two or three students would be extremely unhappy with their new group assignments or roles within their new groups, and occasionally I would make adjustments to appease them. All of this took a large amount of time out of our 45- to 50-minute class periods. It often seemed that the students were more concerned about whom they were or were not working with, than the task to which they were assigned. So, in addition to the inefficient use of class time, the focus of attention seemed to be diverted from the instructional objectives.

Although I have listed some problems related to group work that I have experienced in the last seven years, I have also recognized that group work can be a powerful teaching strategy that allows for a wide range of academic abilities. Several researchers have recognized and studied this as well. The ones I found that provided the best blend of theory and practice were Elizabeth Cohen and David and Roger Johnson and E. Holubec. Cohen's book, *Designing Group Work: Strategies for the Heterogeneous Classroom* (1994), has been an invaluable resource that helped guide me through my own research project. The Johnson and Holubec book, *Cooperation in the Classroom* (1988), along with other writings from their extensive research, has also provided me with many ideas and guidelines for implementing a cooperative group learning environment in my classroom.

Among the numerous findings of these researchers that effectively argue in favor of cooperative group learning in heterogeneous classrooms, several key features seem to stand out. One of these key features is the delegation of authority. When teachers give students a group task and allow them to make mistakes and struggle on their own, they have delegated authority. Delegating authority versus direct supervision in an instructional task makes students responsible for specific parts of their own work. Students are free to make their own problem-solving decisions, but they are accountable to the teacher for the final product (Cohen, 1994).

Another key feature of cooperative group learning is the idea that it is a superior technique for conceptual learning, for creative problem solving, and for increasing oral language proficiency (Cohen, 1994). The group situation is ideal for the development of thinking skills. Cooperative groups provide learners with the opportunity to practice generating causes and effects, hypothesizing, categorizing, deciding, inducing, and problem solving (Solomon, Davidson, & Solomon, 1992). When the group work assignment demands thinking and discussion, and when there is no clear, right answer, everyone in the group benefits from the interaction. Frequency of interaction on the task consistently predicts individual group learning when groups are working on discovery problems (Cohen, 1991).

One consistent finding of researchers trying to determine how talking and working together assist conceptual learning has to do with the student who takes the time to explain, step-by-step, how to solve a problem. This seems to be the student who gains the most from the small group experience. Putting concepts into words in the context of explaining to a peer is particularly helpful for conceptual attainment (Durling & Shick, 1976). Students can often address other students' questions more effectively than the teacher. In addition, discussion often captures various students' misconceptions that the teacher may never uncover (Bassarear & Davidson, 1992). They learn from each other; they are stimulated to carry out higher order thinking; and they experience an authentic intellectual pride of craft when the product is more than what any single member could create (Cohen, 1994).

Heterogeneous, cooperative groups can represent a solution to some of the problems associated with having a wide range of academic abilities within a classroom. Lack of

"Action Research: Perspectives from Teachers' Classrooms." Southeast Eisenhower Regional Consortium @ SERVE. Reprinted with permission.

skills in reading, writing, and computation need not bar students from exposure to lessons requiring conceptualization. These students can develop their basic skills with assistance from what is often an unused resource, the knowledge of their classmates (Cohen, 1994). As I planned the types of instructional activities that would challenge my students intellectually and provide opportunities for creative problem solving, the idea to implement a long thematic unit of instruction began to emerge. The purpose for choosing a thematic teaching approach, rather than teaching isolated concepts, was to present problems to be solved as they related to the theme. This would also allow the cooperative groups to work together over a longer period of time than would normally be allotted using the isolated concepts approach.

At this point, it appeared that I had a clear, concise purpose for my research project. I wanted to see if my students' conceptual learning and creative problem-solving skills could be enhanced through the use of heterogeneous, cooperative groups. However, there seemed to be two other factors to consider: student motivation and patterns of student interactions. I felt that these were important behaviors to observe and collect data on because the conceptual learning and problem solving in the cooperative groups depended on a reasonable amount of student motivation and positive interaction.

Method

The qualitative research method I used most closely resembles an emergent design. At the outset my research design was not clearly focused. Instead, the questions I asked were broad and exploratory. These questions, however, did provide a strong beginning focus for my study. The idea of choosing a theme like rockets and using it to drive my physical science curriculum for an extended period of time really appealed to me. Then the idea of studying cooperative group learning in the context of an extended thematic unit enabled me to visualize a setting from which I wanted to make a detailed examination. My intention was to allow the research design to evolve as my questions became more focused and my data collection methods became more defined.

My first step was to carefully select groups for each of my three physical science classes. The cooperative groups were selected so that each group had a mixture of students by gender and race, but the primary consideration for group composition was to mix students by academic abilities. Once the groups were selected, I implemented the thematic unit on rockets. This required lots of creative problem solving and was conceptually challenging. Before the rocket unit actually began, the students were involved in a number of preliminary group activities that prepared them for rocket science. They also completed some cooperative group training exercises that were designed to teach them that their group successes depended on how well they interacted and assisted each other.

I collected data from four primary sources throughout this study. The source I thought would provide the most useful data came from the observations made by Marsha, a university professor of educational research, and one of her doctoral students, Nina. Together, they made eighteen formal observations in which data were collected on eight groups in my

"Action Research: Perspectives from Teachers' Classrooms." Southeast Eisenhower Regional Consortium @ SERVE. Reprinted with permission.

seventh period science class. The second source of data came from videotapes taken by a parent volunteer. The third source of data was in the form of student interviews, when one student from each group in each class was asked questions about how their groups worked together during the rocket science unit. Finally, I recorded many of my own observations and reflections, entered in the form of journal entries.

Assigning Groups

Each new school year, it usually takes about two weeks for our class lists to become stable, due to late enrollments. Since I intended to arrange the students into cooperative learning groups so that each group was heterogeneous in terms of academic abilities, I began analyzing grades and achievement test scores of the students from the previous year.

On a computer spreadsheet, I entered my class lists for my three science classes and the students' 1994 California Achievement Test (CAT) scores for reading, language, math, and science. About 10 percent of the students did not have CAT scores for a variety of reasons. However, I had administered a science and math inventory test to every student. These scores were also entered on the spreadsheet. Not surprisingly, when I ranked the students from highest to lowest in reading, I got a very different arrangement than the ranking of highest to lowest in math. In fact, each set of scores (reading, language, math, and science) showed remarkable differences in rankings from high to low. Since the unit of instruction that I had planned would involve precise measurement skills and mathematical calculations, I decided to use math scores as the basis for the heterogeneous groups.

I then selected the eight highest and the eight lowest math students in each science class. I chose the first highest and first lowest students to make up the first two members of each group, then the second highest and second lowest members for the next group, and so on until the eighth group had the eighth highest and eighth lowest math students. The remaining students were placed in the eight groups so that each group had four students (a few groups had three). The collective average math scores from each group were approximately equal. Also, I carefully mixed the groups by gender and race such that each group was as heterogeneously composed as possible. Then I showed the groupings to my team teachers and asked them for their suggestions. Since they taught the same students, they were able to make a number of useful suggestions.

Preparing for Data Collection

The activities conducted during the first two weeks focused heavily on measurement activities. Although the students were working in groups during these activities, they had not been assigned to their longterm, cooperative groups yet. I found that the majority of my students were quite deficient in measurement skills. Throughout my teaching experiences, I have generally found these deficiencies to be typical for middle school students. My initial strategy was to inundate them with metric measurement activities. I placed a strong emphasis on identifying the differences between measuring length, mass, and volume.

By the third week of school, when the students returned from Labor Day weekend, the desks were rearranged from rows and columns to eight "quads" (four desks arranged so

"Action Research: Perspectives from Teachers' Classrooms." Southeast Eisenhower Regional Consortium @ SERVE. Reprinted with permission.

that students faced each other rather than the white board at the front of the classroom). The lab counters could now be used to relocate four of the eight groups (groups 1, 3, 6, & 8 or groups 2, 4, 5, & 7) to provide the maximum possible distance between the groups.

In the past I have had students arrange desks in groups as needed, but I always returned them to the "face-the-front" positions after class. This time I intended to leave the desks in quads for an indefinite period of time. Each desk had a label on it with students' names designating "who sat where" each class period. When each of my three science classes arrived, and the students found their assigned seats, I announced that these would be permanent groups and I assigned each group a number (Groups 1-8). Many students seemed surprised when they saw who their group members were. I had the distinct feeling that this was a different grouping arrangement than they had experienced in the past.

The first activity for the cooperative groups was a two-day project in which they were to determine the edible portion (by mass) of an average banana. This activity involved the precise measurement of mass, expressing masses as ratios (edible portion/entire banana), converting the ratios to percents, averaging percent calculations from all eight groups, using a calculator, collecting data, graphing results, and stating general conclusions.

> "In the past I have had students arrange desks in groups as needed, but I always returned them to the 'face the front' positions after class."

On the second day of the banana laboratory, Marsha came to my class to observe the students working in their newly formed groups. Marsha and Nina had agreed to visit my classroom two to four times per week for nine to ten weeks. This opportunity drastically changed the scope and breadth of my study since two independent observers, each focusing on just four groups, could collect significantly more data than I could by myself.

Marsha, her husband Robert, Nina, and I met to discuss aspects of my study proposal, my classroom environment, my planned unit of instruction, and the focus for data collection. Robert, a secondary school science teacher, had volunteered countless hours in our school. He is very familiar with our student population and my own teaching style. He agreed to assist me with instructional tasks throughout the data collection period. We also discussed the specific types of behaviors to be observed and the type of data collection instrument we should design. Finally, we agreed to plan one more observation before beginning the formal data collection. I designed a trial data collection instrument for this observation, along with a list of individual student behaviors and group behaviors to be observed, and each behavior was assigned either a letter or a number code.

> "I anticipated much discussion within the groups."

For this observation, I decided to zero in on still another measurement skill weakness I have often observed in middle school students, correctly reading measurement scales. I chose four different sizes (10mL, 100mL, 250mL, and 500mL) of graduated cylinders for this activity. The volumes represented by the smallest increments on each of these cylinders

"Action Research: Perspectives from Teachers' Classrooms." Southeast Eisenhower Regional Consortium @ SERVE. Reprinted with permission.

were different and the numbers were only marked every ten to twenty increments. Since it would be necessary for the students in each group to extrapolate information from the volume marks with numbers to the volume marks without numbers, I anticipated much discussion within the groups as they went about the task of completing a group lab sheet. It was a good activity for Marsha and Nina to observe. They were able to identify all the groups and group members, familiarize themselves with the layout of the room, and let the students adjust to their presence in the classroom.

Marsha, Robert, Nina, and I made some final decisions about the data collection methods after this activity, and planned the first data collection for the next day. The group behaviors I decided to focus on were:

- Working together and taking a systematic approach to the task where each group member was involved in some way.
- Working together and devising a trial and error approach to the task.
- Asking the teacher or assistant to suggest an approach to the task rather than relying on resources within the group.
- No focus on an approach to the task.

The individual student behaviors I wanted them to observe were:

- Explaining directions or concepts to other group members.
- Asking questions of other group members.
- Encouraging other group members to get involved.
- Listening to other group members.
- Writing or recording data on the activity/lab sheet.
- Discouraging off-task behavior or playing.

Training Students in Cooperative Learning

It is a mistake to assume that children (or adults) know how to work with each other in a constructive, collegial fashion. Students must be prepared for cooperation so that they know how to behave in the group work situation without direct supervision (Cohen, 1994). For the purpose of training my students to work cooperatively and to rely on each other as primary resources, I devised some activities.

For the next three data collection days, the groups were engaged in a variety of problem-solving activities that required group decision-making. One activity that served to show aggressive or passive behavior was a vocabulary assignment. I wrote twenty-one physics terms on the board. Some of them were easy, everyday words like "weight" and "pressure," while others were harder terms like "buoyant force" and "center of gravity." The assignment was to pick any three terms and draw pictures representing those terms. However, a rule was imposed that no two students in a group could choose the same terms. This activity definitely stirred some commotion within the groups as the members quickly scanned the list of words and decided which ones they personally wanted.

"Action Research: Perspectives from Teachers' Classrooms." Southeast Eisenhower Regional Consortium @ SERVE. Reprinted with permission.

Since the previous activity was designed to reveal the egocentric characteristics of individuals within the groups, it seemed logical to follow with an activity that required individuals to concern themselves with their group members to ensure their own success. Such an activity is called "Broken Circles" (Cohen, 1994). In Broken Circles, each group member is given an envelope containing pieces of a circle. The goal is for each group member to put together a complete circle. In order for this goal to be reached, there must be some exchange of pieces. Group members are not allowed to talk or to take pieces from someone else's envelope. They are allowed only to give away their pieces (one at a time). If the egocentric student finishes his circle before the others in the group, the "I'm-done-and-you're-on-your-own" attitude works against him. This activity seemed to have a profound effect on many students when they realized that they had to look beyond their own needs and see somebody else's needs in order to achieve the goals of the entire group.

Preparing for Rocket Science

By late September the groups had been working together for nearly four weeks. I was ready to begin the rocket unit, but I realized that there were still many prerequisite skills that had to be taught before I was ready to even mention the word "rockets." Meanwhile, I had announced to the science classes that they should start bringing in 2-liter plastic soda bottles because we would need many of them. They wanted to know what they would be used for, but I told them it was a secret. I like building up suspense and speculation in my science classes.

> ". . . they were going to have to understand what angles and right triangles were."

Since they were going to have to use and understand a trigonometric function (the tangent ratio), they were going to have to understand what angles and right triangles were. The next step, then, was to teach the geometric concept of angles and have the groups use protractors to measure angles. This time I announced that there would be a grade given to the entire group for correctly measuring a page of angles (within 1 degree) and that each group member would receive the group grade. The purpose for this was that the students would realize that their own individual success depended on their group's success. If they did not agree, they would have to go back and remeasure the angle and try to determine where the error was. I observed that most group members were discussing the concept and trying to check each other's measurements.

Once the groups had demonstrated proficiency with their understanding of angles, it was time to introduce the trigonometric tangent ratio. I mentioned my intentions for doing this to some other teachers and non-teachers and I received an overwhelming response of, "Are you crazy? How do you think you can teach trigonometry to a science class where some individual students are operating on a math level well below seventh grade?" I think students who understand the concepts of angles, length, and ratios can also grasp the concepts of trigonometry. For example, students were able to understand that for any right triangle, if one starts at either of the two angles other than the 90 degree angle, the ratio of the opposite side over the adjacent side is always the same. For example, in the right triangle shown in Figure 1, the ratio of BC / AC = DE / AE, for any angleθ.

The groups were required to work under very structured conditions throughout the trigonometry lessons, which lasted for several days. It was time to provide another cooperative group training exercise called "Alligator River" (Cohen, 1994). This exercise required students to make moral judgments about the characters in a story and then rank them from best to worst. The activity required them to produce a group consensus and an explanation for their choices. Since this activity did not involve rigid calculations like the activities of the previous days, there seemed to be more contributions from certain group members than before. Marsha and Nina continued to collect data throughout all of these described activities.

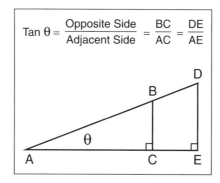

In early October, as I continued to make preparations for the beginning of the rocket unit, it was time for the groups to construct inclinometers (instruments used to measure angles of inclination). I then told the students that we would use inclinometers, right triangles, and the tangent ratio to find the height of tall objects like flagpoles, buildings, pine trees, etc. I still had not mentioned the word "rocket."

After the construction was complete we spent two days practicing on a pine tree that was approximately twenty meters in height. This required a cooperative group effort since one student had to aim the inclinometer, another had to read it, and still another had to operate a calculator. Finally, a group member had to record all of this information on a group data sheet. I had each student practice these tasks several times until they demonstrated proficiency. Then, back in the classroom, we took each group's calculations and found an average for the height of the pine tree. Throughout this activity, Marsha and Nina continued to collect data on group behavior.

Beginning the Rocket Unit

Now the students knew how to use inclinometers to indirectly measure the heights of tall objects. Meanwhile, they had been bringing in 2-liter bottles for the past several weeks, and we had accumulated about 100 of them. Some students asked if the bottles had anything to do with the inclinometers. Finally, I introduced the "Panther Rocket Launcher," named after our four-teacher instructional team, "The Panthers."

The Panther Rocket Launcher is a mechanical device designed to pressurize 2-liter bottles to pressures up to 100 pounds per square inch (psi). We used English system units for pressure (psi) because I couldn't find a pressure gauge that measured Kg per square cm. Since pressurized gasses are potentially dangerous I also designed the unit of instruction so that there would never be more than one group (4 students) near the launcher at any given time on launch days. The remaining seven groups would all be at designated tracking stations, each thirty meters away from the launch site. Figure 2 shows the locations of the tracking stations in relation to the launch site. I spent an entire class period with each science class discussing the potential hazards and safety procedures that must be practiced during rocket launch activities. I was emphatic when I stated that safety goggles must be worn at all times near the rocket launcher.

By the middle of October we had our first two rocket launch days. The students all seemed very excited and fascinated that a 2-liter bottle could climb so high. I limited the air pressures to 60 psi, but I left the decision for the quantity of water in each bottle up to each group. At the tracking stations each group was responsible for recording launch data for every launch on a group data chart. This data included launch numbers, the group launching, quantities of H_2O in milliliters, pressures (psi), the horizontal distance from the tracking station to the launch site (m), the angle of inclination (0), the eye height (distance from a person's eye to the ground) of the inclinometer operator (to be added to final calculation), and the altitude (rounded to the nearest whole number). In addition to recording the data, the group laboratory sheets had questions to answer and predictions to make. Since there was always some "down time" between launches there was ample time for each group to answer the questions.

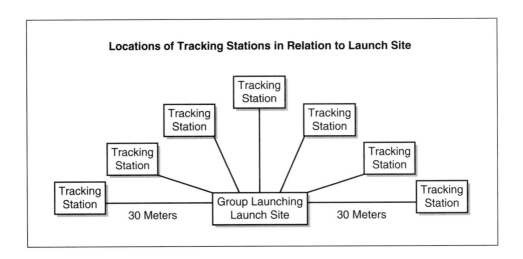

"Action Research: Perspectives from Teachers' Classrooms." Southeast Eisenhower Regional Consortium @ SERVE. Reprinted with permission.

After each launch day we had a data compilation day. Each group recorded the altitude calculations of the other groups and found the average altitude for each launch. They also recorded the group number that performed the launch, the date, the quantity of water, and the pressure. Unlike the group data sheet, the data compilation was an individual data sheet. After the average altitude for each launch was calculated and confirmed throughout the class, that altitude would become the official altitude for that launch. Each student was then given a blank sheet of paper, a ruler, and a set of colored pencils which they used to construct a bar graph from the data. Using the bar graphs as references, several students commented on what they thought was the best quantity of water and the best pressure to achieve the highest altitudes. I did not tell them at the time that they were forming a hypothesis when they made those comments. I wanted to wait until the aerodynamic variables were introduced.

Assigning Roles Within the Groups

The data collection period still had about four weeks to go. It was time to assign each student a specific role or job to play in the cooperative groups (Cohen, 1994). The job titles I decided to use were: Principal Investigator (PI), Materials Manager (MM), Data Specialist (DS), and Safety Director (SD). Marsha, Nina, and I each assigned the students in each group a title and then met to compare notes. After some discussion about our decisions, we came to a consensus. We made many of our choices based on observed behaviors of the members of each group. For example, we gave the leadership roles to students who were displaying passive behavior and data specialist roles to students who resisted writing or displayed careless habits of writing. When I announced the job titles and their descriptions, I also presented the students with a badge that indicated their name and title. Some students seemed shocked and even upset at their role assignment, while others seemed genuinely pleased.

Designing Controlled Experiments

I asked students what factors or variables were the most important to achieving maximum altitude. We seemed to agree that the air pressure should be as high as allowable, but there was a wide range of opinions about the quantity of water, ranging from no water at all to more than one thousand milliliters. When several students said they thought the rockets would climb higher if they did not start tumbling at about 20 meters, we began discussing the aerodynamic shape of rockets. I then had them draw a 2-liter bottle upside down, and add components to it that they might like to build. For the next three days, we built many kinds of rockets with several different methods for attaching fins and nose cones.

Once the rockets were completed (including creative spray-painted designs), we set up a controlled experiment to test two variables: the quantity of water and the aerodynamic design. My fifth-period class did the experiment to find the best quantity of water and

"She then volunteered to write the questions and conduct the interviews for me !"

"Action Research: Perspectives from Teachers' Classrooms." Southeast Eisenhower Regional Consortium @ SERVE. Reprinted with permission.

found it to be between 400mL and 600mL. From fifth-period's results, my sixth- and seventh-period classes decided on 500mL of water for every launch in their aerodynamic experiments. Unfortunately, we had an uncontrolled variable that adversely affected our experiments, Tropical Storm Gordon. The wind was blowing so hard on our launch days that our data was seriously skewed. Since we needed some data for our school science fair and we were running out of time, we had to launch our rockets anyway. I explained to my students that things like this probably happened to scientists all the time.

Completing the Rocket Unit

The last rocket launch day was also the last day that Marsha and Nina came to collect data. Although the experimental portion of our rocket science had ended, several students started exploring better ways to build new designs. The enthusiasm some students was so lingering that I continued to encourage them to try building new designs at home and bring them to school for testing.

An Additional Data Source

By the end of the first semester and before the Christmas holidays, I decided that I was through with the data collection phase of my study. I was fairly certain that the data collected by Marsha and Nina, my own reflections and observations, and the videotapes produced by my parent volunteer, Susan, during the unit would be enough to answer my questions. However, I soon realized that I was missing an important piece of the puzzle. That was, thoughts and reflections of the whole process from the students' perspective. I talked about this with one of my more outgoing students and she suggested I interview some of the students about their reflections of the rocket science unit. She then volunteered to write the questions and conduct the interviews for me!

The next day she presented me with an interview form she composed on her word processor called, "The Panther Group Efficiency Survey." The questionnaire consisted of eleven questions designed to elicit students' perceptions of how well their groups worked together from the beginning of the rocket science unit to the end. She then volunteered to randomly select one student from each group and conduct the interviews. She finished the task in two hours and presented me with twenty-four completed survey forms in which she carefully wrote down each interviewee's response to each question.

Results

Marsha and Nina made eighteen formal observations in which data were collected. The data collection instruments were designed so that each observer could focus on four groups. However, on six of the observation days, only one observer could be present, so data were not collected for some of the groups on those days. As Marsha and Nina observed the students, they added behaviors to the list which they thought were related to the questions being asked in the study. These additions were usually in written rather than coded form, so they were not added to the original list of behaviors.

Throughout the period of time in which data were being collected, I frequently wrote in a journal. My entries generally included my thoughts about student motivation and what activities were taking place in my classroom. My perceptions were that I had never seen such high level student motivation in my entire teaching career as I had throughout the rocket unit. I observed students talking about the rocket unit between classes, and many students asked to come into my classroom during lunch to work on their rocket designs. I was certain that the cooperative groups had much to do with individual student interest.

Without initially having a clear plan as to how I might transcribe and condense thirty-four pages of coded and written data that covered a period of two months, I decided to select just four of the eight groups and track individual and group behaviors across the entire period of time. I selected two of the groups Marsha observed (Groups 1 & 8) and two that Nina observed (Groups 4 & 7). The method I used to transcribe and condense the data was to take one group at a time, list all of the activities for which data were collected on a computer spreadsheet, and write a brief description of individual and group behaviors for each activity. This allowed me to reduce the information to eight manageable pages so that I could easily read and compare the descriptions of behaviors for individuals and groups.

Group 1

Group 1 consisted of three boys and one girl. Initially, the members of this group accepted directions to work cooperatively with one another but often worked independently to complete tasks. For example, when I felt that the method for using the tangent function to calculate altitude had to be retaught and reinforced, I assigned each group to make calculations for the angles of 20 degrees through 89 degrees for a horizontal distance of 30 meters. When the papers were turned in, two of the group members had completed all 70 calculations, another had completed about half of them, and the fourth had completed less than one-fourth of the page with inaccurate calculations. This indicated a lack of sharing of information among the members of this group, as well as individuals working independently to complete tasks.

Most of the data sheets portrayed one of the students as being passive and unsmiling. She stated to one of the observers that she did not like group work. When asked why, she indicated the reason was because of her particular group assignment. When Group 1 was allowed to make decisions about who would do which jobs to complete an assignment, she always chose to fill out the lab sheet or record the data. However, when she was assigned the role of Principal Investigator, another of the students was very unhappy, as indicated in his journal.

Another group member was very outgoing and talkative. He raised his hand often and liked to participate in class discussions. During several of the group activities he was observed explaining directions to his group and initiating action plans. For example, when the task was to measure both the mass and the volume of a variety of solid objects, he attempted to explain his ideas of how the task could best be completed by the group. During other group activities, like the inclinometer construction activity, he sought feedback and approval from the teacher and assistant rather than from his group members. He also had a propensity for playing and being off-task.

The third member of the group was considered to be the main instigator of off-task behavior in the group. According to his CAT scores his academic skills were extremely low for his age and grade level. On some of the earlier group activities he was observed recording data on the lab sheets, but on almost every subsequent activity he was observed being disruptive to the other group members.

The final group member really became enthusiastic about the rocket unit. After the first launch day in which unmodified 2-liter bottles were launched, he began designing rockets at home and bringing them into class. He took advantage of an opportunity to attend a rocket demonstration day sponsored by Tallahassee's Science Odyssey Center. He built his own rocket launcher and began testing new designs on his own. Eventually he entered his own research in our school science fair.

Group 4

Like Group 1, Group 4 consisted of three boys and one girl. An early observation I made was that one student either would not turn in written work or would turn in very carelessly done, incomplete work. However, when his group was required to investigate something that involved a hands-on approach, he would become more involved. He demonstrated his mechanical abilities by volunteering to be the person who would transport and operate the rocket launcher, and after observing his techniques and safety practices near the launcher, I developed a trust and dependence on him.

The second group member was observed to be extremely passive, frequently off-task, and engaged in extraneous conversations that had nothing to do with the topic of study on at least six of the data collection days. Approximately one-third of the way through the study, she became very aggressive toward another group member, and pushed him out of his chair. On this same day, she became more involved with the group than was observed on the other days, she assisted in building the inclinometer. After that, she was absent from school during three of the rocket construction days and the last three launch days when the groups flew their new designs.

The third student started out to be competitive within the group, but on at least six observed activities he would appear to lose interest in the task at hand and would resort to playing. He showed more interest in the rocket unit later in the data collection period when he was recognized as having a creative idea for a method of attaching fins to the rockets.

Finally, the fourth student was slow to become interested in the rocket unit and was observed demonstrating passive or off-task behavior. He was absent (caught skipping) for three days during the instruction on how to calculate altitudes using the tangent ratio. Since his skills in math were already very low, when he returned and did not understand what we were doing, his motivation continued to drop. However, when he was appointed to the role of Principal Investigator his motivation took a major turn. He was observed asking questions, leading discussions, and offering ideas for improved rocket designs.

"Action Research: Perspectives from Teachers' Classrooms." Southeast Eisenhower Regional Consortium @ SERVE. Reprinted with permission.

Group 4 showed evidence of improvement in their cooperative behaviors over the twelve-week period of time. Initially, the group members demonstrated a lack of focus in terms of how they completed tasks as a group. However, near the end, the group could be described as much more cohesive. They clearly demonstrated systematic approaches to their problem solving and they divided up tasks for completion.

Group 7

Group 7 consisted of two boys and two girls. The females seemed uninvolved during the first several weeks of the rocket unit as they were observed being passive and noncommunicative with their group members. The males, on the other hand, were extremely participatory. Both the observation records and the videotape records of classroom activities show them raising their hands to respond to almost every question. In addition, they were extremely engaged in the group activities and investigations throughout the entire rocket unit.

About the time when the cooperative group training exercises took place, the girls both took more active roles in the group. Both participated in filling out lab sheets and checking on each other's calculations, as well as making decisions about who would do each job. By the time the rocket construction and rocket launch activities began, this group had developed their own systems for sharing and rotating duties, and checking on each other for accuracy and completeness.

Group 8

Group 8 was another three-boy-and-one-girl group. The dominant member of this group was clearly the female. She was constantly observed leading discussions, initiating activity with data collection sheets, explaining directions to her group members, and keeping everyone focused. She always seemed to be aware of what was going on in the classroom. Generally, she was the first member of her group to understand a direction and was quick to convey what was expected to her group members. I observed her nudging her group members and cueing them as to what they should be doing.

One of the males was a relatively quiet group member but was observed working cooperatively with the group on most tasks. The group had a system for sharing the tasks to be completed and usually turned in lab sheets that were thoroughly completed. Although I encouraged groups to keep tabs on each other in this respect, the student still came up deficient when it came time to turn in individual work. He would neglect individual assignments like journal entries and his log of daily activities and assignments.

According to the CAT scores, the third group member was certainly the lowest of the group. He was extremely quiet, and when he spoke it was noticeable that he had a speech problem. He never raised his hand and volunteered information but would turn in his share of the work completed by the group. I asked if he liked the group work and his assigned group. He responded very positively. However, he also told me that he did not like being the Principal Investigator, the role to which he was assigned.

The fourth group member was also fairly quiet in the classroom. He had the highest CAT math scores of any of his group members and shared his skills with the whole group.

"Action Research: Perspectives from Teachers' Classrooms." Southeast Eisenhower Regional Consortium @ SERVE. Reprinted with permission.

He was observed during several of the activities taking charge of the lab sheet and trying to keep the group focused.

Another observation of Group 8 was that there seemed to be a lot of giggling going on during many of the group activities. However, the giggling never seemed to interfere with their efficiency in completing their tasks. As a group, they were very successful at completing all group assignments, developing systems for problem solving, and sharing information with each other.

> ". . . data consistently indicated that the students were working together in their groups to overcome some of the obstacles to understanding."

Discussion

Marsha and Nina systematically TV 1 recorded data on eight cooperative learning groups in my seventh-period physical science class for twelve weeks. They were looking for specific behaviors that might indicate that conceptual learning and creative problem-solving skills were enhanced through the use of cooperative learning groups. Their data consistently indicated that the students were working together in their groups to overcome some of the obstacles to understanding and using the difficult conceptual material involved in the rocket science unit. Their data also indicated that sometimes there were strong disagreements among some group members, especially in Group 1 and Group 4. Interestingly, I observed many more instances of disagreement about concepts and approaches to problem solving in my fifth- and sixth-period classes than I did in my seventh period. This was not necessarily negative as I surmised from the results of Kathy's survey.

Although the results of Kathy's survey cannot be used directly to support the argument that conceptual learning and creative problem solving took place through the use of cooperative learning groups, it can definitely be used to argue that a significant amount of conflict and conflict resolution took place. According to some researchers, conceptual conflict, resulting from controversy in the group, forces individuals to consider new information and to gain cognitive understanding in a way that will transfer to new settings (Johnson & Johnson, 1990).

When queried as to whether or not there were any "fights" during the group work, 42% of the respondents, representing 10 out of the 24 groups answered "yes." Meanwhile, 71% of the respondents rated their group performance as "good," and 88% reported it was "better" at the end of a semester of working together. This indicated to me that a certain amount of controversy took place during the semester of group work, but the large number of positive responses to the question of how they perceived themselves now in terms of working together indicated that many conflicts were resolved.

Another interesting result of Kathy's survey was that when asked which type of work they preferred, 25% said they preferred group work 12% said individual, and 63% said they preferred a mixture. This information did not help me with my study questions, but it did inform me that I should provide a balance of types of work when planning for instruction.

"Action Research: Perspectives from Teachers' Classrooms." Southeast Eisenhower Regional Consortium @ SERVE. Reprinted with permission.

One of my primary focuses for this study was to carefully choose my groups so that they were clearly heterogeneous from both an academic and cultural standpoint. Another main focus was to assign specific roles or jobs within the groups so that each member would be perceived as a valued player. The roles were also designed to make the group members more dependent on each other and less dependent on the teacher. However, according to the respondents of Kathy's survey, 92% indicated that they would have changed their jobs if they could. When the jobs were assigned, the intent was to "bring out" the very behaviors that were not being observed. For example, when one student was observed as being passive and unsmiling, we assigned her the job of Principal Investigator to bring out more assertive behavior in her. All of the roles were assigned to all of the students with similar objectives in mind. Perhaps allowing the students a part in the decision making for jobs would be a good idea next time.

Cooperative group learning is much more than just putting students in groups and giving them assignments to complete. In doing this study, I set higher expectations of my students than I ever had before. The conceptual learning and creative problem solving that took place was clearly indicated from the data sources. The rocket science unit of instruction challenged all of the students, especially in terms of the difficult mathematics concepts. However, all of the other aspects of the unit were equally challenging, and the sharing of ideas and group problem-solving strategies were prevalent throughout the unit. Student motivation was higher than I had ever seen when we were in the midst of rocket science. In fact, one student became so motivated about rocket science that he won third place in the 1995 State Science Fair and an overall "Best of Show." If anyone else can benefit from the model of middle school teaching that I developed, I would be ecstatic, but the model was truly for myself and the students that I teach. I certainly intend to keep improving the model in the years to come.

REFERENCES

Bassarear, T., & Davidson, N. (1992). The use of small group learning situations in mathematics instruction as a tool to develop thinking. In N. Davidson & T. Worsham (Eds.), *Enhancing thinking through cooperative learning* (pp. 236–250). New York: Teachers College Press.

Cohen, E. G. (1991). Teaching in multiculturally heterogeneous classrooms: Findings from a model program. *McGill Journal of Education, 26,* 7–23.

Cohen, E. G. (1994). *Designing group work: Strategies for the heterogeneous classroom* (2nd ed.). New York: Teachers College Press.

Durling, R., & Shick, C. (1976). Concept attainment by pairs and individuals as a function of vocalization. *Journal of Educational Psychology, 68,* 83-91.

Johnson, D., Johnson, R., & Holubec, E. (1988). *Cooperation in the classroom* (Rev. ed.). Edina, MN: Interaction Book Company.

Solomon, R. D., Davidson, N., & Solomon, E.C.L. (1992). Some thinking skills and social skills that facilitate cooperative learning. In N. Davidson & T. Worsham (Eds.), *Enhancing thinking through cooperative learning* (pp.101-119). New York: Teachers College Press.

"Action Research: Perspectives from Teachers' Classrooms." Southeast Eisenhower Regional Consortium @ SERVE. Reprinted with permission.

ARTICLE A.2

The Influence of a Peer-Tutoring Training Model for Implementing Cooperative Groupings with Elementary Students

Leslie R. Nath
Steven M. Ross

This study examined the effects of peer-tutoring training on elementary school student communication and collaboration skills when used in conjunction with cooperative learning. Within six classes (grades 2–6) in an inner-city school, cooperative learning pairs were randomly assigned to two groups (control and training). Multivariate analyses of variance (MANOVA) of quantitative data from a systematic observation instrument used over an entire year showed that, in general, the training group surpassed the control group in both communication and collaborative skills. Students in grades 2–3 showed substantially more improvement than students in grades 4–6; also, students with average or below-average reading levels required more time to acquire these skills than did above-average students. The qualitative data further substantiated these findings while revealing a large variation among teachers in implementing cooperative learning.

Cooperative learning and peer tutoring are teaching approaches with a long history of use that have made powerful comebacks to the academic arena (Johnson & Johnson, 1992). Both are based on social psychological theories, and both are considered successful strategies for promoting student social skills and increasing student academic achievement (Cohen, Kulik, & Kulik, 1982; Jenkins & Jenkins, 1985; Johnson & Johnson, 1985; Miller, Kohler, Ezell, Hoel, & Strain, 1993; Slavin, 1988). Teachers may profit by maximizing their instructional influence and increasing their pool of available resources (Brandt, 1987; Miller et al., 1993; Webb & Schwartz, 1988). Administrators also profit through cost effectiveness in a time of limited funding. Instead of securing outside sources of academic assistance, a school employs its most bountiful resource "students" (Levin, Glass, & Meister, 1984; Slavin, 1987). In addition, as integration of technology with school curricula and teacher-led instruction increases, cooperative learning and peer tutoring are becoming popular ways of facilitating computer-based learning activities, especially when the number of computers in a classroom may be limited (see, e.g., Brush, 1998; Mevarech, 1994). Although the present study dealt with learning activities involving print material rather than computers, its findings were expected to have implications for peer-tutoring training in a variety of contexts, both traditional and technology-rich.

Both cooperative learning and peer tutoring are believed to facilitate learning through the powerful influence of peers not only sharing answers but also engaging in the process of finding those answers (Johnson & Johnson, 1984; 1990; 1992; Slavin, 1991; Webb, 1988; Webb & Schwartz, 1988). Further, cooperative groupings offer social advantages as students learn and exercise collaborative skills such as expressing appreciation and encouragement, learning to disagree constructively, decision making, communicating, and managing conflicts (Johnson & Johnson, 1992; Warger, 1991).

A key difference between the two approaches is that in the most widely used forms of cooperative learning, students are expected to help each other but usually do not receive formal training in tutoring skills, whereas in peer tutoring, students typically are trained on how to teach (Jenkins & Jenkins, 1987), although other elements of cooperative learning may not be in place. If elementary students are taught tutoring skills as part of their involvement in cooperative learning, they may further enhance their academic achievement while refining their collaborative and social skills. In this research, usage of a peer-tutoring training model to augment cooperative learning methods was examined. Among our specific interests were whether students who received tutoring-skills training communicated more effectively, collaborated better with one another, and provided more and richer explanations to teammates than students without training. The specific cooperative learning strategy employed was CIRC (Cooperative Integrated Reading and Composition), which will be discussed in detail later. CIRC, however, is not the only cooperative learning method that is used for the development of literacy. Reciprocal teaching, for example, is an instructional procedure employed to teach four comprehension monitoring strategies (Palincsar & Brown, 1984). A further objective of this research was to assess the effects of tutoring-skills training on student academic performance.

Key Elements in Cooperative Learning and Peer Tutoring

According to Johnson and Johnson (1984), the basic elements required for building functional and effective cooperative groupings include individual accountability, face-to-face interaction, positive interdependence, and acquisition and usage of collaborative skills. Positive interdependence includes establishing common goals, dividing labor and resources, and assigning roles to group members. Achieving positive interdependence in practice requires students to use collaborative skills appropriately (see Baris-Senders, 1997; Johnson & Johnson, 1984; Slavin, 1995). To collaborate, in turn, requires adequate training in and practice at disagreeing constructively, encouraging and coaching one another, using appropriate voice levels, and taking turns (Johnson & Johnson, 1990; 1992). Unfortunately, teachers rarely train students in these skills, and when they do, the training is generally short term and inconsistent (Nath, Ross, & Smith, 1996).

Tutorial training sessions may vary in duration depending upon the tutor's skill and age, and the complexity of the material being taught (Miller et al., 1993). Training involves an explanation of the tutoring role and specification of those things a tutor should and should not do. For example, a tutor should not complete the tutee's work or exercise discipline to a student (Candler, Blackburn, & Sowell, 1981). Training further entails teaching tutors when and how to give positive feedback, encouragement, directions, and corrective feedback (Levirte, 1986). Tutors also receive information on positive regard for the learner, confidentiality, lesson structure-teaching procedures, and interpersonal skills such as active listening and patience (Jenkins & Jenkins, 1985). According to Candler et al. (1981), tutors should not be allowed to tutor until they have demonstrated their ability to be effective.

Once tutors have had several solo tutoring sessions, teachers should have a conference with them to provide evaluative feedback. As tutors become more familiar with their roles, supervision may be decreased but not completely dropped (Jenkins & Jenkins, 1985) as it is associated with sustained interest and participation by the tutor. Interest may also be preserved through drawing attention to tutee accomplishments or providing reinforcing events such as awards, parties, and letters of thanks from teachers and tutees (Jenkins & Jenkins, 1985).

Cooperative Integrated Reading and Composition

The present focus was on a form of tutoring based on the CIRC design (Slavin, 1995; Slavin, Stevens, & Madden, 1988). CIRC uniquely combines the use of mixed-ability groupings with teacher instruction to same-ability groupings. Students are initially assigned to pairs (or triads) within their reading group and then assigned to teams. Each team or "cooperative grouping" is made up of two pairs of students, where each pair is from a different reading group.

There are three fundamental elements in the CIRC program: (a) activities related to basal readers, (b) direct instruction in reading comprehension, and (c) integrated language arts-writing. In all of these activities, students work in mixed-ability groupings. After the teacher introduces new vocabulary and discusses the story with the various reading groups, students are asked to complete a series of activities with their partners, teams, or both. A brief description of these activities is as follows (Slavin, 1995):

- *Partner reading* consists of pairs of students from the same ability reading group working together. All students read a story silently and then read the same story aloud with their partners. This practice provides students an opportunity to work on decoding skills, comprehension, and oral reading skills.
- *Treasure hunts* relate to story structure and story-related writing. This activity provides students with an opportunity to focus on the structure of a specific story. Pairs of students are instructed to stop halfway through a story and identify the characters, setting problem in the story, and how the problem might be solved. They are also asked to predict an ending to the story based on partial information.
- *Words out loud* is a list of new and difficult words that students are asked to practice reading until they can recognize them without hesitation.
- *Word meaning* consists of a list of new vocabulary words that students are expected to define and use in meaningful sentences that help to describe the word. Dictionaries are used in this practice activity.
- *Story retell* requires individuals to summarize the main points of the story in their own words to their partners.
- *Spelling* allows students to pretest one another on their weekly spelling words for mastery.

As students work through the series of activities, their partners keep track of their progress. Students advance at their own rate, and those who finish early use the extra time for independent reading. Toward the end of the week students are given a comprehension test that they take independently on a story they have previously read. Each student's individual growth score contributes to the team's weekly team score (Slavin et al., 1988); teams earn recognition when their members' growth scores reach certain levels.

CIRC was employed by the site school in the present study in conjunction with Success for All (SFA), a comprehensive program, designed to improve the reading achievement of disadvantaged youths in grades pre-K through 5 (Slavin et al., 1994). In SFA, students are regrouped by reading level across age lines, and attend a daily 90-min reading class. For grades 2 through 5 the emphasis is on reading, which encompasses partner reading, identifying characters, settings, summarizing stories, problem resolution and prediction, and writing using cooperative learning to develop student reading skills (Balkcom & Himmelfarb, 1993). Students requiring additional assistance in grades 1 through 3 are provided with specially trained, teacher-certified tutors. In addition, a Family Support Team is organized to promote parent involvement and help ensure children's success. Extensive evaluations of SFA, compared to alternative school programs, consistently show that it improves student performance in reading (Slavin et al., 1994; Slavin & Madden, 2001) and reduces retention and special education placements (Balkcom & Himmelfarb, 1993; Slavin et al., 1994). (For more detailed descriptions of SFA, see Slavin & Madden).

Purpose of the Present Study

Prior research indicates that teachers frequently fail to demonstrate or model collaborative interaction skills effectively in the classroom (Johnson & Johnson, 1984; Keyton & Dodson, 1996; Nath et al., 1996). Therefore, alternative means of providing students with such skills need to be identified, especially in light of the current expansion of cooperative learning methods as part of educational reform efforts (Stringfield, Ross, & Smith, 1996), technology usage (Brush, 1998), and in connection with specific restructuring models such as SFA (Slavin et al., 1994).

The primary objective of this research was to design, using practices and concepts advocated in the literature (e.g., Blumenfeld, 1978; Jenkins & Jenkins, 1985; 1987; Miller et al, 1993; Shapiro, 1988; Warger, 1991), a practical, comprehensive model for tutoring-skills training and to investigate its impact on student behaviors and achievement. Specifically, the following research questions were addressed:

- To what extent do the collaborative and communication skills of students receiving tutoring training differ from those not receiving training?
- Does the training affect students in cooperative groups differently according to their reading level?
- Are there differences in reading comprehension test scores between those receiving tutoring-skills training and those not receiving training?

Method

Participants

The research was conducted in an inner-city school, located in a large urban district that serves a 100% African American student population from low-income families. This school had been using the SFA program for the prior two years. The school administration and six out of eight teachers from grades 2 through 6 agreed to participate in the proposed research. The two teachers who declined were from grades 5 and 6. There was a total of six ability-grouped classes (*high, average,* and *low*): three containing a mixture of second- and third-grade students and three containing a mixture of fourth- through sixth-grade students. In all, six teachers and 124 students participated in the study.

CIRC in SFA

Student placement in reading groups was determined by their scores on reading placement tests administered at the beginning of the first semester. Consistent with SFA's regrouping component, the school chose to set up three fairly homogeneous reading groups during a 90-min reading block. These three groups were formed for each of the lower and upper grades, and consisted of below-average, average, and above-average reading ability students. Within each reading class, the teacher placed students in three- to six-member groupings and then formed partnerships within each grouping. For example, a six-member grouping could have been split into three pairs or two triads. Students with higher reading assessment scores were coupled with students having lower reading assessment scores. A further consideration in forming groupings and partnerships was the ability of students to get along with one another.

All reading classes began with a short teacher presentation reviewing previous material and introducing the lesson for the day. The teacher introduction was generally followed by 20 minutes of listening comprehension where students were instructed on the various elements of story structure using children's literature. Students then separated into their paired groupings or triads for silent reading, partner reading, and subsequent activities for approximately one hour. For subsequent activities, second- through third-graders often remained in their assigned partnerships whereas fourth- through sixth-grade students regrouped into their larger grouping to work as a team.

Treatments and Design

Half of the cooperative groupings within each class were randomly assigned to the control group and the remaining groupings were assigned to the training group. The number of students in each group (control $n = 63$ and training $n = 62$) was approximately the same.

Training group.   Based upon a review of the literature (e.g., Blumenfeld, 1978; Candler et al., 1981; Cotton, 1988; Jenkins & Jenkins, 1985, 1987; Miller et al., 1993; Shapiro, 1988; Warger, 1991), the first author developed a seven-step framework for peer-tutoring skills training as described below. A ½-hour tutoring-skills training session was developed corresponding to each step described in the model.

Session 1.   The concept and definition of tutoring were discussed and examples provided on how tutoring is a daily occurrence in students' lives. Examples included anecdotes on children teaching one another how to play various games. Students were asked to provide examples of tutoring experiences they could recall. In addition, the instructor reviewed and demonstrated effective and ineffective collaborative skills with students. In turn, students formed groups and demonstrated and identified effective and ineffective collaborative skills.

Session 2.   The instructor introduced the term *immediate feedback* and explained its importance and demonstrated its effectiveness using student volunteers from the class. Students observed corrective feedback being administered properly and improperly. Students in groups were asked to brainstorm and come up with 10 ways of praising or encouraging their teammates and to explain why they felt their remarks would compel a teammate to continue working as part of the team. Students also provided examples of sarcastic remarks and put-downs that would discourage teammates from working together.

Session 3.   The instructor explained and demonstrated prompting techniques using verbal remarks and body language. Overprompting was discouraged. Students modeled the instructor in groups by using prompting techniques with one another.

Session 4.   Students were presented with unclear instructions and were purposely left to wonder about them for a short period of time. The instructor used this as an example to explain the importance of good communication skills. Once the instructor defined and explained the difference between effective and ineffective communication, students were given exercises in which each teammate was expected to give group members directions to a specified location within the school. A discussion between teammates followed this exercise on the effectiveness of each member's ability to give directions.

Session 5.   This session was a continuation of effective communication skills and focused on the aspects of listening and taking turns. Students were asked jointly to devise justifications for the importance of listening and taking turns in the art of communication.

Session 6.   Because all students had the opportunity to function as tutors and tutees, the issue of confidentiality and respect for one another was examined and discussed. In addition, students were reminded that they functioned as team players and as such were to assist one another whenever possible. However, other situations, such as disciplinary problems, that did not fall under the scope of the group were to be handled separately by the teacher.

Session 7. In addition to using the skills above, students were given group assignments and asked to practice staying on task. The purpose of this exercise was to increase their awareness of time constraints. At the end of the session, they were notified that they would have 30-min, monthly meetings with the instructor to review the above skills and to identify and address any existing problems and concerns having to do with cooperative groupings. Students would also be given opportunities to discuss how effective they thought the cooperative process was.

The first author developed these seven sessions and implemented the training program. The training began in early October and lasted for seven consecutive weeks. One step was covered each week. Monthly follow-up sessions were conducted at the conclusion of the initial training to review peer-tutoring skills and to address any problems students experienced in their role as tutor or tutee.

Control group. To ensure that control students did not feel left out, they participated in a placebo treatment consisting of the presentation of short stories and slides whose contents were completely unrelated to tutoring-skills training. The number and duration of the placebo sessions were the same as those in the training group.

Outcome Measures

Triangulation was achieved by combining quantitative and qualitative measures of the effectiveness of tutoring training (Denzin, 1970; Patton, 1990).

Quantitative measures. Quantitative measures of group dynamics and achievement were reading test scores, observers' ratings on 16 collaborative skills, and teachers' end-of-year ratings of individual student's group skills. Students' basal reading test score averages were recorded for each of five six-week grading periods as students moved through the basal reading series.

To capture group dynamic properties such as collaborative and communication skills, two instruments were developed for this study. The first instrument (Collaborative Skills Group Observation Instrument or CSGOI) was completed by the observers (see later section) and consisted of two parts. Part I contained 16 items designed to gauge different aspects of collaborative-communication skills demonstrated by the reading groups, such as the frequency with which students communicated effectively, asked questions, stayed on task, respected teammates, encouraged and praised one another, provided corrective feedback, and accepted and offered help within the group. These items were developed by carefully synthesizing the research in the areas of cooperative learning and peer tutoring. Each item was worded so it could be rated using a 5-point Likert scale (1 = *never,* 2 = *seldom,* 3 = *sometimes,* 4 = *often,* and 5 = *always*). Based on a review by several cooperative learning experts and a pilot test by the researchers, minor modifications were made to the CSGOI. Table 1 shows the 16 items used.

For the final 16-item instrument, Cronbach's alpha coefficient was 0.94, indicating a very high level of internal consistency. However, even though individual items overall were strongly interrelated, it was still decided to examine results for each (using appropriate multivariate techniques) to determine possible behaviors that would need more or less attention in future training rather than to restrict analyses to one global measure. Part II of the CSGOI was designed to collect qualitative data concerning observer impressions on how effectively students within groupings explained their answers and praised and encouraged one another (see later section).

To increase interrater reliability, we first trained observers so that they understood the concepts, definitions, and rating scales employed in the CSGOI. Second, observers completed a CSGOI on the same groups. At the conclusion of each observation, the two observers conferred and determined the level of agreement on the ratings of the items. To check for interrater reliability, approximately 10% of the total observations were taken by multiple observers. Of the 30 resultant interrater correlations, 24 were above .90; 5 were between .80 and .90; 1 was between .70 and .80. All correlations thus exceeded Morris and Fitz-Gibbon's (1978, p. 136) benchmark criterion of .70.

The second instrument (Student Collaborative-Communication Skills Instrument or SC-CS) was completed by the teachers at the end of the academic year. The objective of the SC-CS instrument was to provide supplementary information about student collaborative and communication skills based on teacher retrospective impressions of such behaviors. Each student was given one global rating using a four-point Likert-type scale (1 = *poor,* 2 = *average,* 3 = *above average,* 4 = *excellent*). The global rating dealt with the degree to which an individual student respects, communicates with, and accepts help from teammates; works in a group setting; enjoys working in groups; and exhibits desirable collaborative skills such as praising and encouraging others in the group.

Qualitative measures. Qualitative data were collected from two sources, field notes and teacher references. The field notes were recorded by observers in the narrative section of the CSGOI (Part II). Prompts asked the observers to: (a) provide samples of explanations students give one another when explaining an answer or resolving a problem; (b) provide examples where students encouraged teammates to behave, stay on task, try the problem again, and so forth; (c) provide examples where students praised their teammates; and (d) describe how the students cooperated with one another in their groups.

At the conclusion of the academic year, all teachers participating in the study (except for one because of prolonged illness) were interviewed by the first author using a "standardized open-ended" interview approach (Patton, 1990, p. 284). Although all interviewees were asked the same questions in the same order, the interviewer could deviate from this sequence to explore, probe, and ask questions that elucidated the issues being discussed. The main objective of these interviews was to capture teacher perceptions and views regarding the usefulness of tutoring training in conjunction with cooperative learning. Each interview session lasted approximately one hour and was tape-recorded with the teacher's permission. Tapes were transcribed in their entirety for analysis.

Additional measures. Because it was anticipated that all six teachers would vary in their implementation of CIRC, the first author recorded impressions in a journal of each

TABLE 1   Collaborative Skills Group Observation Instrument

ITEM

STUDENTS:

1. Use group voices so as not to disturb other groups
2. Disagree constructively
3. Ask questions of one another
4. Move into their groups quickly and quietly
5. Encourage one another verbally, with gestures, or with both
6. Praise one another
7. Explain the process used in finding an answer
8. Listen to one another while making eye contact
9. Provide one another with immediate corrective feedback
10. Take turns speaking
11. "Prompt" one another for answers
12. Ignore questions asked by teammates
13. Show respect for one another and avoid put-downs, sarcastic remarks, and unkind gestures
14. Exhibit behavioral problems (hitting, playing, etc.)
15. Stay on task
16. Accept help from their teammates

teacher's implementation of CIRC and of cooperative learning. Also, she visited each teacher's class at least once monthly for one hour during which time journal entries were made. The areas observed included teacher roles in team building, rewarding group performance, and reviewing collaborative skills.

Data Collection Procedures

Observers. Five graduate students working as educational research assistants at a local university served as classroom observers. All had prior experience with classroom observations and qualitative research methods. As suggested by Morris and Fitz-Gibbon (1978), the observers were trained in the definitions being used in this study (e.g., cooperative learning) and data collection procedures.

Observation procedures. In order to establish a baseline of how students collaborate and communicate within their cooperative groupings, all six classes were observed by the researcher one week prior to the first week of training, and a CSGOI was completed on each cooperative grouping in each class. During the remaining eight observations, a CSGOI was completed for the control and training groups in each class. The first observation was taken the week following the third training session. All control and training groupings in all six classes were observed. Subsequently, every third week another observation was taken, resulting in a total of eight 45- to 60-min observations. Two observations were taken during the first semester; the remainder were taken in the second semester. Each student was assigned a code number which was attached to his or her desk and easily visible. The observer noted these numbers on the CSGOI, thus allowing the groupings to be identified subsequently for analysis. In each session, all groupings in each class were observed by one or more of the observers. To avoid a situation in which an individual observer would observe the same class repeatedly, observers were rotated among the six classes.

Across all eight observations, 60 training groups and 76 control groups were observed. Within each observation the number of training or control groups varied from 2 to 4. To minimize contamination effects, all students were given blue or red nameplates which were displayed during the observations. Students were to be seated only with other students having the same color name plates. Only the researcher knew that blue signified the training group and red signified the control group.

Results

Quantitative Outcomes

Baseline reading and cooperative learning. To determine the similarity between the control and training groupings in basal reading abilities, separate *t* tests were conducted on the scores for each of the six classes. None was significant. Before the first of the eight CSGOI observations, a baseline observation was taken on each group to determine the comparability of the control and training groupings on cooperative learning skills. Using *t* tests, no significant differences on any of the 16 items were found.

Tutoring-skills training and collaborative-communication skills. To determine the effect of tutoring-skills training on student collaborative and communication skills, we compared the control and the training groupings on each of the 16 items and on an aggregate (16-item mean) measure across each of the eight observations. Table 2 shows the means and standard deviations on the aggregate measure for the baseline and the eight observations.

To determine if there was a grade-by-treatment interaction, a two-way multivariate analysis of variance (MANOVA) was performed. It was not significant ($p > .10$). Therefore, in all subsequent analyses, scores were collapsed across grades.

Figure 1 depicts the mean of the aggregate measure for both the control and training groups for all eight observations. Note that the mean of the training group is consistently higher than that of the control group across all observations. For each observation, an analysis of variance (ANOVA) was performed to determine if the training group mean differed from the control group mean. Separate ANOVAs were used because students were frequently regrouped (within treatments) over time, thus changing the specific units of observation each observation period. To reduce the chances of a Type I error across the eight tests, a .01 rather than a .05 significance level was used. The comparisons were statistically significantly different for Observations 6 ($F = 15.58$; $MSE = 0.406$; $p = 0.001$) and 7 ($F = 8.43$; MSE = 0.237; $p = 0.007$) and approached significance for Observation 2 ($F = 5.18$; $MSE = 0.290$; $p = 0.031$). Training and control group means on these trials were, respectively, 3.74 versus 3.28 (Trial 2), 3.70 versus 2.69 (Trial 6), and 3.10 versus 2.58 (Trial 7).

TABLE 2   Aggregate score across observations

OBSERVATION NO.:		BASE	1	2	3	4	5	6	7	8
Control:	M	2.39	2.81	3.28	3.48	3.12	2.92	2.69	2.58	2.62
	(SD)	(0.34)	(0.62)	(0.54)	(0.53)	(0.61)	(0.51)	(0.53)	(0.44)	(0.44)
Training:	M	2.66	3.08	3.74	3.53	3.19	3.13	3.70	3.10	2.81
	(SD)	(0.40)	(0.36)	(0.54)	(0.62)	(0.60)	(0.65)	(0.78)	(0.55)	(0.41)

Note: Each item is rated on a 5-point Likert scale (1 = *never;* 2 = *seldom,* 3 = *sometimes;* 4 = *often;* 5 = *always*).

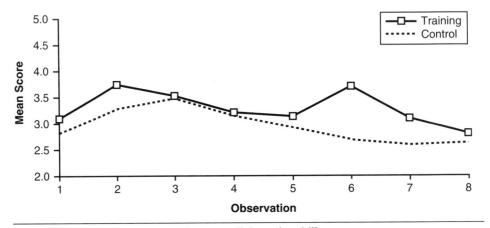

FIGURE 1   Aggregate measure of group collaborative skills

A MANOVA was conducted on the 16 items for each observation. A significance level of .01 was used to reduce the overall Type I error rate. Again, the control and training groups differed significantly on Observations 6 and 7 ($p < 0.01$), thus corroborating the ANOVA results for the aggregate measure. Follow-up *t* tests were performed for Observations 6 and 7 to identify those items on which students in experimental groupings performed better than students in the control groupings. Table 3 shows the means and standard deviations of the control and experimental students on significant items ($p < .05$) on Trials 6 and 7.

Observation 2 approached significance in the aggregate analysis ($p < .06$). Follow-up *t* tests, run for exploratory purposes, showed significant differences favoring the training groups ($p < .05$) on items 3, 5, 8, 10, 11, and 16 (see Table 1 for item descriptors).

Grade level.   To determine grade-level effects, we analyzed the 16 CSGOI item scores, collapsed across observations, using a two-way MANOVA. We could not perform MANOVA for individual observations because of small sample size (fewer than 10) in each

TABLE 3   Treatment mean and standard deviations on significant observation items for Trials 6 and 7

TRIAL 6 ITEM	CONTROL M(SD)	TRAINING M(SD)	P
Students:			
1. Use group voices so as not to disturb other groups	3.72 (1.23)	4.64 (0.67)	.016
2. Disagree constructively	1.67 (0.78)	3.43 (1.27)	.001
3. Ask questions of one another	2.50 (0.73)	3.67 (1.23)	.003
4. Move into their groups quickly and quietly	2.83 (0.75)	4.16 (1.17)	.020
5. Encourage one another verbally, with gestures, or both	1.69 (0.79)	3.40 (1.35)	.001
6. Praise one another	1.19 (0.54)	2.80 (0.79)	.001
7. Explain the process used in finding an answer	1.44 (0.81)	2.30 (1.16)	.018
8. Listen to one another while making eye contact	2.81 (0.98)	3.80 (0.92)	.009
9. Provide one another with immediate corrective feedback	1.75 (1.13)	3.10 (1.45)	.007
11. "Prompt" one another for answers	1.88 (0.81)	2.70 (0.95)	.013
12. Ignore questions asked by teammates	3.75 (0.93)	4.44 (0.88)	.041
13. Show respect for one another and avoid put downs, sarcastic remarks, and unkind gestures	3.56 (1.15)	4.64 (0.67)	.005
15. Stay on task	3.33 (0.97)	4.18 (1.08)	.019
16. Accept help from their teammates	2.88 (1.03)	4.00 (1.05)	.007
TRIAL 7 ITEM	CONTROL M(SD)	TRAINING M(SD)	P
Students:			
2. Disagree constructively	1.75 (1.04)	3.29 (1.11)	.008
3. Ask questions of one another	2.50 (0.86)	3.08 (0.76)	.032
5. Encourage one another verbally, with gestures, or both	1.06 (0.24)	1.38 (0.51)	.011
7. Explain the process used in finding an answer	1.43 (0.85)	2.27 (0.91)	.013
8. Listen to one another while making eye contact	2.33 (0.77)	2.92 (0.28)	.007
10. Take turns speaking	2.50 (0.86)	3.46 (0.66)	.001
12. Ignore questions asked by teammates	3.76 (0.97)	4.46 (0.78)	.022

of the four cells. The two MANOVA factors were (a) treatment (Control and Training) and (b) grade level (2 and 3 Combined and 4–6). Both the treatment and grade effects were significant ($p < .001$). Treatment effects were comparable to those reported for the primary analysis. Follow-up univariate ANOVAs comparing grade levels significantly ($p < .01$) favored grades 2 and 3 on items 1, 13, 14, 15, and 16 (see Table 1 for descriptions).

Reading level. To examine the possible influences of reading skills, we conducted a 2 (Treatment) $\times 3$ (Reading Level: *below average, average,* and *above average*) MANOVA. Data for all 8 trials were combined for each of the 16 items because of small n's on individual trials. Both the treatment and reading level effects were significant ($p < .01$). The treatment-by-reading level interaction, however, was not significant. For the reading-level effect, follow-up univariate F tests showed statistically significant differences for Item 7 only, (students explain the process used in finding an answer), $F = 5.19$; $MSE = 0.352$; $p = .006$. The mean for the average-level group ($M = 2.44$) was significantly higher than the means for the below-average ($M = 1.92$) and above-average ($M = 2.06$) groups.

Comparison of baseline observation with other observations. To assess student progression in developing collaborative skills, we compared the aggregate score on each of the eight observations with the baseline score. In no case did the scores drop below the baseline score. To determine if a significant improvement occurred, each observation was compared with the baseline using independent-sample t tests. Results showed significant improvement (all p's $< .01$) over the baseline by the control group for Observations 2, 3, 4, and 5, and by the training groupings for Observations 1, 2, 3, 4, and 6.

Reading test scores. A repeated-measures ANOVA comparing the training and control group was performed on the five reading comprehension test scores representing final grades for respective six-week periods. Results showed that neither the treatment effect nor the Treatment Test interaction was significant (both p's $< .10$).

Teacher assessment of individual student's collaborative skills. At the end of the academic year, each of the six teachers was asked to provide an overall rating (1–4, where 1 = *poor;* 2 = *average;* 3 = *above average;* 4 − *excellent*) on the cooperative and communication skills of each student. In separate t-test comparisons of treatment groups for each teacher, significant differences were found for Teachers 1 and 3 only: Teacher 1 rated students in groups that had received training higher ($M = 3.50$) than control ($M = 1.67$), $t(16) = 5.22$, $p < .01$), whereas for Teacher 3, the opposite was true (control $M = 3.71$; training $M = 2.60$), $t(15) = -2.55$, $p = .022$.

Qualitative Outcomes

Qualitative data in the form of narratives and teacher interview transcripts were analyzed and reported using inductive analysis (Patton, 1990, p. 390). In addition, teachers were asked to review the summary of teacher interviews to confirm the results (member checking), as recommended by Goetz and Le Compte (1984) and Lincoln and Cuba (1985), to enhance internal validity.

CSGOI comments and journal entries.[1] Part II of the CSGOI required observers to describe how students in groups cooperated with one another. Questions asked for samples of

[1]Only summaries are presented here. Detailed explanations and descriptions of each class can be obtained from the first author on request.

explanations students gave one another when explaining an answer or resolving a problem; how students encouraged teammates in behave, stay on task, or try the problem again; how students praised their teammates, and descriptions of how students cooperated with one another. In addition, the researcher also kept a journal describing monthly visits to each of the six classrooms. Each entry described the teacher's and students' assimilation of CIRC and cooperative learning.

Teacher observations.   According to the observer reports, the weakness with cooperative learning for all but one teacher was inconsistency in reviewing collaborative skills, assigning tasks conducive to cooperative learning, and monitoring CIRC activities. Only one teacher was concordant when it came to encouraging team spirit and awarding deserving groups team points.

Observers in the blind-to-group-identity reported that students who received training exhibited better cooperative skills than students who did not receive training throughout the study. They consistently identified the training groups as being more verbal in terms of discussing, explaining, and encouraging one another. For example, explanations included verbal responses both in their own words and reading from their text. Role modeling was also used but to a lesser extent. Praise was also noted frequently in terms of body language, smiling, and making eye contact. Students occasionally responded to one another verbally using words such as *good, yeah,* and *yes.* Students were observed praising their teammates more often than encouraging them. The most noted form of encouragement was keeping their partners on task by saying things such as, "c'mon get going," "help me find the answer," or "you find this answer and I will look for this one." Observers noted that despite the students' overall success at collaborating with one another, lack of cooperation was often attributed to the nature of the task or to the teacher. For example, tasks were not well suited for cooperative learning, or the teacher discouraged students from discussing and resolving problems by providing clues and answers to their questions, or by insisting that they be quiet.

Control groupings were not as effective in cooperating as the training groups. They were more likely to share their answers than to provide an explanation. Explanations given generally consisted of sounding out or spelling a word. Praise was typically displayed in the form of a smile, and encouragement was most often recorded as being somewhat antagonistic. For example, students were observed hiding their work or saying things such as "do your own work." Observers often identified students in the control groupings as being competitive and working independently.

Teacher Interviews

At the end of this study, all participating teachers (except the one who was ill) were interviewed by the researcher. At that time, teachers were told which students were in the training and which in the control groupings.

Collaborative skills.   Three of the teachers thought that their students had good collaboration skills. They said their students generally tried to work together, some performing better than others, and that students used quiet voices and showed respect for one another. They also indicated that students attempted to praise one another, but mostly in the form of body language. There was further agreement that students sometimes had difficulty explaining answers to students and would resort to pointing out answers in the book.

The two remaining teachers believed that the majority of their students were unsuccessful in cooperating with one another. They both thought that while some students used the time to cooperate and learn, others used it as free time. They also expressed concern that some students showed little regard for one another and preferred to work alone. They described some students as fairly aggressive, making it difficult for those students to cooperate with others.

Training skills.   All teachers agreed that they would like additional training for their students in peer-tutoring skills. In fact, two teachers claimed to have stressed these skills (explaining answers and praising correct answers) when reviewing collaborative skills. They both indicated that they selected certain students, whom they felt have these skills, to help students who were absent.

Academic improvement.   None of the teachers believed that students showed significant improvement academically as a result of receiving tutoring training. On the other hand, they acknowledged that students receiving training were more willing to accept and offer help. One teacher indicated that students in the training groupings in her class were much more amicable and accepting of one another.

Cooperative learning effectiveness.   When teachers were asked how effective they thought cooperative learning was as a methodology, three teachers indicated that their students benefited socially. They also believed that students became more responsible and accountable in the process of helping one another. The remaining teachers indicated that they liked the concept of students working together but that it was not an effective methodology for all students.

The major disadvantage noted by teachers was that some students are prone to working alone and cause disruptions when placed in a group. Teachers also indicated that the higher-achieving students were more likely to become impatient with their teammates for working too slowly. Furthermore, the more capable students generally wanted the leadership role, and that became problematic when there was more than one high-ability student in a grouping. Only one teacher indicated that if the task was interesting and conductive to cooperative learning, the students did fine; otherwise, they were more prone to work alone.

Teacher skills in cooperative learning.   All five teachers indicated that they felt comfortable with their knowledge of cooperative learning and CIRC. All commented that they had support from other teachers and were given opportunities to attend workshops and visit different classrooms to observe teachers using cooperative learning.

Impediments to cooperation.   The main reason given by all five teachers for students not acclimating well in a cooperative learning environment was the students' prior experiences. Teachers indicated that students were not used to sharing with other children or working problems out quietly and calmly. They further indicated that many of the students have to be taught how to behave socially in cooperative groups and elsewhere.

Discussion

Both quantitative and qualitative analyses suggested that peer-tutoring training generally but not consistently enhanced student communication and collaborative skills. In particular, students receiving training were more likely to disagree constructively, ask questions of one another, encourage one another verbally, praise one another, explain the process used in finding an answer, listen, provide one another with immediate corrective feedback, prompt one another, respond to questions asked by teammates, show respect to one another, stay on task, and accept help from their teammates. While these skills are imperative to successful group work, they are equally important in terms of life-long skills. These findings support Jenkins and Jenkins' (1985) assumption that students who do not receive specific tutoring training are much less likely to demonstrate these skills. In addition, some students who received training worked or attempted to work with teammates even when the tasks were not conducive to cooperative learning.

It was further observed that unless tutoring-skills training was reinforced on a continual basis, students tended to revert to typical ways of interacting in group settings. When they initially received such training, their collaborative and communication skills improved substantially, compared with those not receiving training. However, there was a drop in performance when they returned from winter break in early January. Students showed improvement once again after receiving reinforcement in tutoring-skills training via two review sessions.

Grade Level

An unexpected finding was that the grade 1 and 3 students performed better in cooperative groupings than did the grade 4–6 students. Generally, fifth- and sixth-graders are easier to train in tutoring because they have fewer discipline problems and require less supervision (Jenkins & Jenkins, 1987). In this study, however, just the opposite occurred. In addition to positive behavior, younger students outperformed older students in the following areas: showing respect for one another, using quiet voices, staying on task, and accepting help from their teammates. According to Fuchs, Fuchs, Bentz, Phillips, and Hamlett (1994), relatively young children (early elementary school age) can be trained to enhance their interactional style in peer-mediated instruction. Furthermore, they can be guided in the process of providing more elaborate explanations in group settings. Performance by second- and third-grade students may also have been enhanced because their teachers adhered more closely to CIRC guidelines for cooperative learning, suggesting that the younger students were more prepared to work in groups.

There are several possible explanations as to why the upper-grade students did not perform as well as the lower-grade students. First, students in the upper grades have been conditioned to work independently for a longer period of time, suggesting that they need more practice working interdependently. Second, in-class disruptive behavior (e.g., playing, arguing, and chatting) at times hindered student ability to work cooperatively. Third, the upper-grade teachers did not seem to fully buy into cooperative learning and were clearly less supportive than the lower-grade teachers.

Student Ability

Students with above-average reading ability showed marked improvement in their communication and collaborative skills early on, whereas below-average and average students did not show improvement until more than half way through the study. On the other hand, average students outperformed the other two groups in explaining the process used in finding an answer. While students receiving tutoring-skills training outperformed control students in collaborative and communication skills, their reading achievement scores were not found to be significantly different. This outcome does not seem surprising given that cooperative learning tasks were only one part of various exercises, assignments, and activities that contributed to achievement on those exams.

Peer-Tutoring Implications for Cooperative Learning

The results of this study have important implications for cooperative learning. To enhance interaction within cooperative groupings, it appears that students need to receive tutoring-skills training specifically designed for small group work. Because all students working eventually assume the roll of tutor or tutee, knowing how to provide and accept help within the confines of their group without altercation would be beneficial. This, of course, requires preparation and practice communicating (Keyton & Dodson, 1996) and development in the areas of providing corrective feedback, confirming accurate responses, demonstrating patience, offering constructive criticism, maintaining confidentiality, maintaining high quality work, staying on task, being sensitive to the frustrations of others, and praising and encouraging fellow students (Jenkins & Jenkins, 1985, 1987; Miller et al., 1993; Niedermeyer, 1970; Warger, 1991).

The effect of peer-tutoring training in a cooperative learning environment cannot be fully realized unless teachers buy into the concept of cooperative learning (e.g., CIRC) and implement the methodology effectively. The correct implementation of a cooperative learning methodology would only serve to enhance the effectiveness of peer tutoring as far as student communication and collaborative skills are concerned. Therefore, every effort should be made to ensure that teachers accept, understand, integrate, and practice cooperative learning in the classroom.

What is the best vehicle to use in delivering tutoring-skills training to students in cooperative groupings? Based on experiences and findings in the present study, we propose several options. One is to let teachers train their own students on tutoring skills in conjunction with cooperative learning skills. While this would be cost effective, it would require additional time, commitment, training, and effort on the part of the teachers. Therefore, it is imperative that teachers recognize the value of peer tutoring and cooperative learning and that they buy into these concepts. This, of course, would result in a more effective implementation of the strategies benefiting both teachers and students.

A second option is to assign an individual (teacher or administrator) within the school the responsibility of training all students on tutoring skills. This seems to be a more viable strategy provided the assigned person is properly trained and is given ample time to train all students and reinforce tutoring training skills on a continual basis. In addition, this individual or facilitator would also have to train teachers so that they would recognize and reinforce the positive tutoring skills of students in the classroom. The need for this peer support was demonstrated by the teachers in this study who showed an inability to implement cooperative learning consistently across classrooms.

A third option is to use a cooperative learning or tutoring expert to train all teachers and students on tutoring skills and become a resource person to all involved. This method would be quicker and more efficient than developing internal training support but would likely be more costly. According to Nath et al., 1996, cooperative learning is challenging for teachers and raises demands for ongoing professional development and training. It, therefore, seems that the most effective strategy for training might be some combination of all three strategies. That is, an external expert to train an internal "coordinator" and teachers on all skills, while training students intermittently on basic and selected skills.

As technology usage increases in schools, strategies for collaborative skills training may rely more heavily on on-line tutorials and prompting engaged learners in effective group processing activities (e.g., see Brush, 1998). However, based on the challenges revealed in the present study in involving at-risk students with limited experience in cooperating with peers in both social and school activities, a substantive independent training program with continual teacher (or expert) reinforcement of skills appears to be needed.

Because this research was conducted at only one inner-city school, having many students placed at risk, caution is warranted in generalizing its results to schools in other settings. Replication in different settings is needed. Also, in reduce contamination of research, future research might assign entire classes to the control or training groups. However, unless there were a large number of classes involved, this approach would carry the disadvantage of confounding teacher ability with the training variable.

Although proper implementation of cooperative learning practices is challenging, it is a methodology that offers many benefits to students. The most obvious is improved socialization skills. The results of this study suggest the potential of peer-tutoring skills training, when used in conjunction with cooperative learning (CIRC), to enhance student collaborative and communication skills and thereby, in turn, give cooperative learning greater potential to work successfully.

Leslie R. Nath is a consultant based in Omaha, NE, and may be reached at LRNATH @home.com.

Steven M. Ross is with the Center for Research in Educational Policy at The University of Memphis, and is Editor of the Research section of this journal. He may be reached at amross@memphis.edu.

REFERENCES

Balkcom, S., & Himmelfarb, H. (1993). *Success for all. Education research consumer guide, number 5* (Report No. 93–3011). Washington, DC: Office of Research.

Baris-Sanders, M. (1997). Cooperative education: Lessons from Japan. *Phi Delta Kappa, 20,* 619–624.

Blumenfeld, S.L. (1978). *How to tutor* (pp. 15–27), Boise, ID: Arlington House.

Brandt, R. (1987). On cooperation in schools: A conversation with David and Roger Johnson. *Educational Leadership, 45*(3), 14–19.

Brush, T.A. (1998). Embedding cooperative learning into the design of the integrated learning systems: Rationale and guidelines. *Educational Technology Research and Development, 46(3),* 5–18.

Candler, A.C., Blackburn, G.M., & Sowell, V. (1981). Peer tutoring as a strategy individualizing instruction. *Education, 101(4),* 380–383.

Cohen, P., Kulik, J.A., & Kulik, C. (1982). Educational outcomes of tutoring: A meta-analysis of findings. *American Educational Research Journal, 19,* 237–248.

Cotton, K. (1988). *Peer tutoring: Lake Washington High School, Benjamin Rush Elementary School.* Effective practices in place: Snapshot no. 5, School Improvement Research Series II. Northwest Regional Educational Lab. (ERIC Document: Reproduction Service No. ED 296 413)

Denzin, N.K. (1970). *The research act: A theoretical introduction to sociological methods.* New York: McGraw-Hill.

Fuchs, L., Fuchs, D., Bentz, J., Phillips, N., & Hamlett, C. (1994). The nature of student interactions during peer tutoring with and without prior training and experience. *American Educational Research Journal, 31,* 75–103.

Goetz, J.P., & Le Compte, M.O. (1984). *Ethnography and qualitative design in educational research.* Orlando, FL: Academic Press.

Jenkins, J.R., & Jenkins, L.M. (1985). Peer tutoring in elementary and secondary programs. *Focus on Exceptional Children, 17*(6), 1–12.

Jenkins, J.R., & Jenkins, L.M. (1987). Making peer tutoring work. *Educational Leadership, 44*(6), 64–68.

Johnson, D.W., & Johnson, R.T. (1984). Cooperative small group learning. *Curriculum Report, 14*(1), 2–7.

Johnson, D.W., & Johnson, R.T. (1990). Social skills for successful group work. *Educational Leadership, 47*(4), 29–33.

Johnson, D.W., & Johnson, R.T. (1992). Implementing cooperative learning. *Contemporary Education, 63*(3), 173–180.

Johnson, R.T., & Johnson, D.W. (1985). Student-student interaction: Ignored but powerful. *Journal of Teacher Education. 36*(4), 22–26.

Keyton, J., & Dodson, N. (1996). *Exploratory study of children's task groups: Instructional implications.* Paper submitted to the Instructional Development Division, Southern States Communication Association.

Lincoln, Y., & Guba, E. (1985). *Naturalistic inquiry.* Thousand Oaks, CA: Sage Publications.

Levin, H., Glass, G., & Meister, C. (1984). *Cost-effectiveness of four educational interventions.* Stanford, CA: Institute for Research on Educational Finance and Governance, Stanford University.

Levine, M. (1986). Docemur docendo (He who teaches, learns). *American Educator, 10*(3), 22–25, 48.

Mevarech, Z.R. (1994). The effectiveness of individualized versus cooperative computer-based integrated learning systems. *International Journal of Educational Research, 27*(1), 39–52.

Miller, L.J., Kohler, F.W., Ezell, IL, Hoel, K., & Strain, P.S. (1993). Winning with peer tutoring: A teacher's guide. *Preventing School Failure, 37*(3), 14–18.

Morris, L.L., & Fitz-Gibbon, C.T. (1978). *How to measure program implementation* (1st ed.). Beverly Hills, CA: Sage Publications.

Nath, L.R., Ross, S., & Smith, I., (1996). A case study of cooperative learning in elementary classrooms. *The Journal of Experimental Education, 64*(2), 116–136.

Niedermeyer, F.C. (1970). Effects of training on the instructional behaviors of student tutors. *The Journal of Educational Research, 64,* 119–123.

Palinesar, A.S., & Brown, A.L. (1984). Reciprocal teaching of comprehension fostering and Comprehension monitoring activities. *Cognition and Instruction, 1,* 117–175.

Patton, M.Q. (1990). *Qualitative evaluation and research methods* (2nd ed.). Newbury Park, CA: Sage Publications.

Shapiro, E.S. (1988). Preventing academic failure. *School Psychology Review, 17*(4), 601–13.

Slavin, R.E. (1987). Cooperative learning: Can students help students learn? *Instructor, 96*(7), 74–78.

Slavin, R.E. (1988). Cooperative learning and student achievement. *Educational Leadership, 46*(2), 31–33.

Slavin, R.E. (1991). Synthesis of research on cooperative learning. *Educational Leadership, 48*(5), 71–82.

Slavin, R.E. (1995). *Cooperative learning: Theory, research, and practice.* Boston: Allyn and Bacon.

Slavin, R.E., & Madden, N.A. (2001). Summary of research on Success For All and Roots and Wings. In R.E. Slavin & N.A. Madden (Eds.), *Success for all: Research and reform in elementary education* (pp 12–48), Mahwah, NJ: Lawrence Erlbaum Associates.

Slavin, R.E., Madden, N.A., Dolan, L.J., Wasik, B.A., Ross, S.M., & Smith, I.J. (1994). Whenever and wherever we choose: The replication of success for all. *Phi Delta Kappan, 75*(8), 639–640, 642–647.

Slavin, R.E., Stevens, R.J., & Madden, N.A. (1988). Accommodating student diversity in reading and writing instruction: A cooperative learning approach. *Remedial and Special Education, 9*(1), 60–66.

Stringfield, S., Ross, S., & Smith, I. (Eds.). (1996). *Bold plans fur school restructuring.* Mahwah, NJ: Lawrence Erlbaum Associates.

Warger, C.L. (1991). *Peer tutoring: When working together is better them working alone.* Research & Resources on Special Education, Number 30. Council for Exceptional Children, Reston, VA. (Eric Document Reproduction Service No. ED 345 459)

Webb, M. (1988). Peer helping relationships in urban schools. *Equity end Choice, 4*(3), 35–38.

Webb, M., & Schwartz, W. (1988). Children teaching children: A good way to learn. *PTA Today, 14*(1), 16–17.

REFERENCES

Adelman, C. (1997). Action research: The problem of participation. In R. McTaggart (Ed.), *Participatory action research* (pp. 79–112). New York: State University of New York Press.

Airasian, P. W. (2000). *Assessment in the classroom: A concise approach* (2nd ed.). Boston: Mc-Graw-Hill.

Allen, L., & Calhoun, E. F. (1998). Schoolwide action research: Findings from six years of study. *Phi Delta Kappan, 79*(9), 706–710.

Anderson, G. L., Herr, K., & Nihlen, A. S. (1994). *Studying your own school: An educator's guide to qualitative practitioner research*. Thousand Oaks, CA: Corwin Press.

Berg, B. L. (2001). *Qualitative research methods for the social sciences* (4th ed.). Boston: Allyn and Bacon.

Blum, H. T., Lipsett, L. R., & Yocum, D. J. (2002). Literature circles: A tool for self-determination in one middle school inclusive classroom. *Remedial and Special Education, 23*, 99–108.

Bottomley, D. M., Henk, W. A., & Melnick, S. A. (1998). Assessing children's views about themselves as writers using the Writer Self-Perception Scale. *The Reading Teacher, 51*, 286–296.

Bullough, R. V., & Gitlin, A. D. (2001). *Becoming a student: Linking knowledge production and practice of teaching* (2nd ed.). New York: Routledge.

Burns, A. (1999). *Collaborative action research for English language teachers*. Cambridge, England: Cambridge University Press.

Buysse, V., Sparkman, K. L., & Wesley, P. W. (2003). Communities of practice: Connecting what we know with what we do. *Exceptional Children, 69*, 263–277.

Calhoun, E. F. (2002). Action research for school improvement. *Educational Leadership, 59*(6), 18–24.

Chiu, L. (1997). Development and validation of the school achievement motivation rating scale. *Educational and Psychological Measurement, 57*, 292–305.

Clancy, D. (2001). *Studying children and schools. Qualitative research traditions*. Prospect Heights, IL: Waveland Press.

Cochran-Smith, M., & Lytle, S. L. (1993). *Inside outside: Teacher research and knowledge*. New York: Teachers College Press.

Cole, A. L., & Knowles, J. G. (2000). *Researching teaching: Exploring teacher development through reflexive inquiry*. Boston: Allyn and Bacon.

Daniels, H. (2002). *Literature circles: Voice and choice in book clubs and reading groups* (2nd ed.). Portland, ME: Stenhouse Publishers.

Day, J. P., Spiegel, D. L., McLellan, J., & Brown, V.B. (2002). *Moving forward with literature circles: How to plan, manage, and evaluated literature circles that deepen understanding and foster a love of reading*. New York: Scholastic.

Denzin, N. K., & Lincoln, Y. S. (2000). The discipline and practice of qualitative research. In N.K. Denzin & Y.S. Lincoln (Eds.), *Handbook of qualitative research* (2nd ed., pp. 1–28). Thousand Oaks, CA: Sage.

Dewey, J. (1933). *How we think. A restatement of the relation of reflective thinking to the educative process*. Boston: D.C. Heath and Company.

Dinkelman, T. (2003). Self-study in teacher education: A means and ends tool for promoting reflective teaching. *Journal of Teacher Education, 54,* 6–18.

DuBois, D. L., Felner, R. D., Brand, S., Phillips, R. S. C., & Lease, A. M. (1996). Early adolescent self-esteem: A developmental-ecological framework and assessment strategy. *Journal of Research on Adolescence, 6,* 543–579.

Eisner, E. (1991). *The enlightened eye. Qualitative inquiry and the enhancement of educational practice*. New York: Macmillan.

Fecho, R. (1992). Reading as a teacher. In M. Cochran-Smith & Susan L. Lytle (Eds.), *Inside outside: Teacher research and knowledge* (pp. 265–272). New York: Teachers College Press.

Fishman, S. M., & McCarthy, L. (2000). *Unplayed tapes. A personal history of collaborative teacher research*. New York: Teachers College Press.

Fontana, A., & Frey, J. H. (1998). Interviewing: The art of science. In N.K. Denzin & Y. S. Lincoln (Eds.), *Collecting and interpreting qualitative materials* (pp. 47–78). Thousand Oaks, CA: Sage.

Friedman, I. A. (1994). Conceptualizing and measuring: Teacher-perceived student behaviors: Disrespect, sociability, and attentiveness. *Educational and Psychological Measurement, 54,* 949–958.

Fullan, M. (2002). The change leader. *Educational Leadership, 59*(8), 16–20.

Geertz, C. (1973). Thick description: Toward an interpretive theory of culture. In C. Geertz (Ed.), *The interpretation of cultures: Selected essays* (pp. 3–30). New York: Basic Books.

Halpern, E. S. (1983). *Auditing naturalistic inquiries: The development and application of a model*. Unpublished doctoral dissertation, Indiana University.

Henk, W. A., & Melnick, S. A. (1995). The reader self-perception scale (RSPS): A new tool for measuring how children feel about themselves as readers. *The Reading Teacher, 48,* 470–479.

Hitchcock, G., & Hughes, D. (1995). *Research and the teacher: A qualitative introduction to school-based research* (2nd ed.). London: Routledge.

Hobson, D. (1996). Learning with each other: Collaboration in teacher research. In G. Burnaford, J. Fischer, & D. Hobson (Eds.), *Teachers doing research: Practical possibilities*. Mahwah, NJ: Lawrence Erlbaum Associates.

Hobson, D. (2001). Action and reflection: Narrative and journaling in teacher research. In G. E. Burnaford, J. Fischer, & D. Hobson (Eds.), *Teachers doing research: The power of action through inquiry* (pp. 7–27). Mahwah, NJ: Lawrence Erlbaum Associates.

Huberman, A. M., & Miles, M. B. (1998). Data management and analysis methods. In N.K. Denzin & Y. S. Lincoln (Eds.), *Collecting and interpreting qualitative materials* (pp. 179–210). Thousand Oaks, CA: Sage.

Kemmis, S., & McTaggart, R. (2000). Participatory action research. In N. K. Denzin & Y.S. Lincoln (Eds.), *Handbook of qualitative research* (2nd ed., pp. 567–605). Thousand Oaks, CA: Sage.

Kemmis, S., & Wilkinson, M. (1997). Participatory action research and the study of practice. In B. Atweh, S. Kemmis, & P. Weeks (Eds.), *Action research in practice. Partnerships for social justice in education* (pp. 21–36). London: Routledge.

Killion, J. P., & Todnem, G. R. (1991). A process for building personal theory. *Educational Leadership, 48,* 14–16.

Lather, P. (1991). *Getting smart: Feminist research and pedagogy with/in the postmodern*. New York: Routledge.

Lather, P. (1993). Fertile obsession: Validity after poststructuralism. *Sociological Quarterly, 34,* 673–693.

LeCompte, M. D., & Goetz, J. P. (1982). Problems of reliability and validity in ethnographic research. *Review of Educational Research, 51,* 31–60.

Lincoln, Y. S., & Guba, E. G. (1985). *Naturalistic inquiry*. Newbury Park, CA: Sage.

Maxwell, J. A. (1992). Understanding and validity in qualitative research. *Harvard Educational Review, 62,* 279–300.

McNiff, J. (2002). *Action research: Principals and practice* (2nd ed.). London: RoutledgeFalmer.

Mcpherson, I., Aspland, T., Elliott, B., Proudford, C., Shaw, L., & Thurlow, G. (1998). A journey into a learning partnership: A university and state system working together for curriculum change. In B. Atweh, S. Kemmis, & P. Weeks (Eds.), *Action research in practice: Partnerships for social justice* (pp. 141–162). London: Routledge.

Merriam, S. B. (1998). *Qualitative research and case study applications in education*. San Francisco: Jossey-Bass.

National Academy of Education (NAE). (1999). *Recommendations regarding research priorities: An advisory report to the National Educational Research Policy and Priorities Board*. Washington, DC: Author.

National Board for Professional Teaching Standards (NBPTS). (2001). *NBPTS standards for early childhood generalist* (2nd ed.). Arlington, VA: Author.

National Research Council. (1999). *Improving student learning: A strategic plan for educational research and it usability*. Washington, DC: National Academy Press.

Norlander-Case, K. A., Reagan, T. G., & Case, C. W. (1999). *The professional teacher: The preparation and nurturance of the reflective practitioner*. San Francisco: Jossey-Bass.

O'Hanlon, C. (1997). The professional journal, genres and personal development in higher education. In S. Hollingsworth (Ed.), *International action research: A casebook for educational reform* (pp. 168–178). London: Falmer Press.

Palinscar, A. S., Magnusson, S. J., Marano, N., Ford, D., & Brown, N. (1998). Designing a community of practice: Principles and practices of the GIsML community. *Teaching and Teacher Education, 14*, 5–19.

Rearick, M. L., & Feldman, A. (1999). Orientations, purposes, and reflection: A framework for understanding action research. *Teaching and Teacher Education, 15*, 333–349.

Rossman, G. B., & Rallis, S. F. (2003). *Learning in the field: An introduction to qualitative research* (2nd ed.). Thousand Oaks, CA: Sage.

Rudduck, J. (1988). Changing the world of the classroom by understanding it: A review of some aspects of the work of Lawrence Stenhouse. *Journal of Curriculum and Supervision, 4*, 30–42.

Ryan, G. W., & Bernard, H. R. (2000). Data management and analysis methods. In N. K. Denzin & Y. S. Lincoln (Eds.), *Handbook of qualitative research* (2nd ed., pp. 769–802). Thousand Oaks, CA: Sage.

Schön, D. A. (1987). *Educating the reflective practitioner*. San Francisco: Jossey-Bass.

Schubert, W. H., & Lopez-Schubert, A. (1997). Sources of a theory for action research in the United States. In R. McTaggart (Ed.), *Participatory action research* (pp. 203–222). New York: State University of New York Press.

Seidman, I. (1998). *Interviewing as qualitative research: A guide for researchers in education and the social sciences* (2nd ed.). New York: Teachers College Press.

Shank, G. D. (2002). *Qualitative research: A personal skills approach*. Upper Saddle River, NJ: Merrill Prentice Hall.

Sparks-Langer, G. M., & Colton, A. B. (1991). Synthesis of research on teachers' reflective thinking. *Educational Leadership, 48*, 37–44.

Stenhouse, L. (1981). What counts as research? *British Journals of Educational Studies, 29*, 103–122.

Stevenson, R. B. (1995). Action research and supportive school contexts: Exploring the possibilities for transformation. In S. E. Noffke & R. B. Stevenson (Eds.), *Educational action research: Becoming practically critical* (pp. 197–209). New York: Teachers College Press.

Stinnett, T. A., Oehler-Stinnett, J., & Stout, L. J. (1991). Development of the teacher rating of academic achievement motivation (TRAAM). *School Psychology Review, 20*, 609–622.

Wolcott, H. F. (1994). *Transforming qualitative data: Description, analysis, and interpretation*. Thousand Oaks, CA: Sage.

Zeni, J. (Ed.). (2001). *Ethical issues in practitioner research*. New York: Teachers College Press.

INDEX